D1338287

JAM TOMORROW

JAM TOMORROW

MEMORIES OF EVERYDAY LIFE IN POSTWAR BRITAIN

TOM QUINN

Jam Tomorrow has been produced by
David & Charles in association with
The Reader's Digest Association Limited.

David & Charles is an F+W Media, Inc. Company
4700 East Galbraith Road
Cincinnati, OH 45236

A catalogue record for this book is available from the British Library.

ISBN: 978-0-276-44504-0

Printed in China by RR Donnelley
For David & Charles Ltd
Brunel House, Newton Abbot,
Devon, TQ12 4PU

For David & Charles:
Editorial and Design Director: Alison Myer
Commissioning Editor: Neil Baber
Editorial Manager: Emily Pitcher
Editor: Verity Muir
Art Editor: Prudence Rogers
Designer: Joanna Ley
Project Editor: James Loader
Production: Ali Smith

CONTENTS

INTRODUCTION

When World War II finally ended a subtle change came over Britain; a change that was all the more profound for hardly, at first, being noticed. Young people who had served in the forces had seen the world and realised that the old certainties of prewar Britain had no divine sanction. The world could change without the permission of those who ran the country, an older generation trapped in a world view that was deeply conservative and unchanged in many essentials since Victorian times.

The desire for change among younger people stemmed from a feeling that somehow the old way of doing things had led to catastrophe – the catastrophe of war, followed by years of rationing and belt-tightening.

In many ways the old order represented a seriousness about life that was now discredited. People were still polite and deferential to authority, the church and social superiors, but were beginning to think that deference was not all it was cut out to be.

The influence of America, first glimpsed through the attitudes and values of GIs stationed here, was profound. Americans seemed to the hidebound British to have a thrilling grip on life and a huge appetite for fun, which was extraordinarily infectious. Although older people often found the Americans and their influence brash, there was no denying its energy. To young people, the new American music and the dances that accompanied it were intoxicating. The foxtrot gave way to the jive; Rock and Roll was here to stay and it inspired and led a series of changes in fashion that created the youth culture we still have today.

American youth culture was essentially rebellious and its heroes – epitomised by James Dean – could now be seen on the big screen as cinema audiences soared during a decade of escapism and fantasy. Through the big screen it was possible to escape the drab reality of rationing and shortages, utility clothes and utility furniture. In the cinema the sun always shone and life was beautiful.

The chance to realise that sunny ambition was offered in this new postwar world through the growth in leisure and gambling – bingo became a craze because it offered overnight the chance to escape into a world once inhabited only by the traditional rich.

For those who didn't win, hard work might achieve the same ends – labour-saving devices such as fridges and washing machines became a real possibility and holidays, particularly in the new and wildly popular Butlin's holiday camps, ushered in a brave new world of pleasure that cocked a snook at that old world where ordinary people were told simply to work hard and obey the rules.

The new world also saw technology not as a threat but as part of the dream. New space-age materials including plastics, nylon and terylene made clothing and furniture cheap and cheerful.

As the 1950s neared the 1960s the British people decided that the old slogan 'Jam Tomorrow' – a slogan that had dominated life for too long – should become 'Jam Today'. This book is an account of how the British learned to live again.

Dance hall craze
Dances such as the Lindy Hop swept across the nation's ballrooms in the early 1950s. 'No Jitterbugging' appeared in the windows of the more traditional dance halls.

A different world

BELIEFS AND ATTITUDES IN POSTWAR BRITAIN

Challenging the foundations
The postwar explosion of leisure activity and consumerism – particularly among the young – challenged the Christian institutions that had been the backbone of Britain for so long. Church service attendance figures slowly declined, and in some parishes women outnumbered men by three to one.

For some, the postwar era was an age of deference and respect; respect for authority, the church and for one's elders and betters. For others it was an age of forelock tugging, snobbery and class division. No doubt the truth lay somewhere between those extremes, but above all this world of rationing and shortages was a world of change. Like it or not, the old certainties were vanishing – and fast. The pace of social change was accelerating as it continues to accelerate today, and the sense of loss among the older generation was matched only by the excitement of a younger generation impatient for the brave new world that beckoned.

Money maker
The finance centre in the Square Mile of London was deemed a prestigious and safe industry in which to work. Tradional garb of bowler hat and umbrella was obligatory. Despite only around a third of the working population having their own bank accounts as late as 1950, the sector was dominated by the "Big Five" banks of Barclays. Lloyds, Midland, National Provincial and Westminster.

Money

Money has changed beyond all recognition since the 1950s. Apart from the difficulties of calculating sheer loss of value, we have to look back through the vast change that came about in 1971 with the introduction of decimal coinage, and return to a time when credit was not easily available, and when the jobs that people held still reflected the influence of a rigid class system.

Tom Phillips remembers working in the City during the late 1940s and 1950s.

> "It was absolutely nothing like today – people who worked in the City then all considered themselves gentlemen, a word that has lost all the old connotations it once had. They got in because they'd been to the right school and university and spoke properly and they earned double or triple the average salary, not ten or twenty times average salaries as they do now. It's very difficult to get an idea of values today because the amounts people were paid in those days seem so tiny! An agricultural worker in the mid 1950s might earn £7 a week for a 50-hour week but he'd usually have a rent-free cottage. In the city we probably earned three or four times as much as that or more – perhaps as much as £1,500 a year if memory serves. But my aunt bought a house in 1957 for £4,500, which seemed a huge amount even though we were well off. Today a house that cost roughly three times your annual salary would be [considered] very cheap!
>
> On the other hand, in the late 1940s and early 1950s you could survive in what was called genteel poverty on £300 a year, but you'd have to scrimp and save to an appalling level. It was still quite common then for middle-class people with small private incomes to spend their lives in small hotels where they paid for bed and board, but it was a awful existence trying to keep up appearances on tiny sums of money. I had an elderly aunt who'd never married who did this. It must have been miserable, particularly as in those days people still felt pitied if they lived like this and were unmarried. They'd been left on the shelf, they thought."

Petty cash
(Left–right) 1940 Mint Bank of England one pound note with signature of K.O. Peppiatt, Chief Cashier; a 1945 King George VI three-penny coin; a 1949 King George VI pre-decimal "quarter-penny" farthing.

Tom Phillips's memories of money and its relative value are matched on the domestic front by Sheila Kehoe's recollections of shopping in West London.

> "After the war and until the early 1950s ten shillings would buy you meat for Sunday and vegetables, butter and bread for the week, but meat was on the ration so we didn't get much. Prices went up very slowly. We were definitely very hard up compared to today but we would calculate that the Sunday joint would do for Monday and maybe Tuesday as well if we just had a small slice each!"

LOOSE CHANGE

Sheila Kehoe regrets the replacement of the old coins, with their evocative names – shillings, florins, farthings, guineas and crowns, and the quirky abbreviation d for pence, coming directly from the Roman *denarius* – by the unromantic new pence, with the banal official pronunciation "pee".

> "I used to give my son sixpence a week pocket money in 1955, which was considered quite generous I think. He could buy lots of sweets with that and I can remember that you could get four Black Jack chews or little sweets called Fruit Salads for a penny – that was because the shopkeepers still took farthings. They were tiny bronze coins with a wren on them. Lovely little things. You won't believe this but the farthing

On your bike
Cycling was a fundamental means of transport in the ten years after World War II, second only to the bus. The average commute to work in postwar Britain was five miles and, with a fraction of the vehicles on the roads that we see today, cyclists were the main traffic, as seen here in Oxford, 1950. Government recommendations for the appropriate cycling clothing were displayed in the Army and Navy Co-Operative Society store.

was still in use till 1960! I miss the old coinage. It was so much more interesting – you'd handle coins a hundred years old every day. And a half crown was a magnificent thing, a really big solid coin that still had some real silver in it. And what about the Joey – the wonderful old threepenny bit? It was always the children's favourite. Pound notes were really big back then too – I mean large in size – and it was rare even to *see* a five-pound note – like seeing a 50 today. There was a joke that did the rounds of a small shopkeeper being so unfamiliar with large notes that once when he was offered a five-pound note he said to the customer, 'I'm sorry, we don't take cheques!'"

Out in the countryside of Norfolk Will Constance remembers that the agricultural labourer had a far harder time making ends meet than the factory or office worker. The farm-hand was always the worst paid and usually worked the longest hours of any British worker, a situation that probably remains unchanged.

"I bought a top-of-the-range racing bike with drop handlebars and six gears for £30. It was a beauty ..."

"The old boys I knew worked six days a week for about £6 in 1953 – but that was up from about £4 in 1946 – and might have to feed five or six children on that. It was also 50 or more hours a week. A pint of mild, which we drank a lot round here, cost about a shilling then. Imagine the conditions he had to work in for that money – out in all weathers; too hot in summer and half frozen in winter!"

For most farm workers the cost of travel was not a problem since they usually lived on the farms where they worked. In the town, buses and trams were the usual way to get about and bicycles were hugely popular. Once you'd paid for the bike it quickly repaid the cost in saved fares. John Quinn in Manchester remembers the cost of what was still in those pre-car-owning days one of the most popular ways of getting about.

"I bought a top-of-the-range racing bike with drop handlebars and six gears for £30. It was a beauty, but that was a lot of money then – equivalent to about a month's wages or more. I used it for holidays and for getting to work, seeing friends, going to the shops – everything really."

John Quinn also recalls the social divide between those paid weekly wages and those who lived on investments or monthly salaries.

"No one has wages now – we all get salaries. Wages were paid each week to those with manual jobs because it was a cash economy back then. Very few people, except the rich – the upper-middle classes and aristocracy – had bank accounts because you had to pay for them and you needed a minimum amount in the bank to make it worthwhile. Getting a salary was a real sign of status when most people were paid cash at the end of each week. And thousands of people still had the idea that the height of respectability was not to work at all but to live on your investments, however tiny they might be."

ON TICK

Money, as John Quinn would be the first to point out, had a lot to do with social class. For those without bank accounts loans were not easily obtainable – Barclaycard, the first all-purpose credit card, was not launched in Europe until 1966 – and credit that was available before then was regarded with suspicion.

"The big thing about money then was that buying on tick or hire-purchase – the 1940s and 1950s equivalent to buying with your credit card – was definitely frowned upon. We all used to dread having to tell people we'd bought something on tick. There was a social stigma to it and it was difficult to get anyway when there were no credit cards and very few had bank accounts. You'd have a bit of card or paper

Price increases
Rising standards of living and increased consumerism brought a steady growth in demand for new material possessions. Spying an opportunity, manufacturers and outlets started advertising hire-purchase opportunities for items that people couldn't afford to pay for in full at the outset. This credit agreement sated the nation's frivolous purchasing desires, while also recognising that having a disposable income was rare.

like a small rent book and have to go into the shop each week to pay it off bit by bit and each line in your little book would be filled in and signed by the shopkeeper. If he knew you well he might just remember and trust you to pay him what was owed on payday, which was Friday."

Paying for food and drink on tick more or less vanished with the arrival of easy-to-obtain bank credit. But another major part of the cash economy back in the 1950s was paying rent for where you lived. The idea that ordinary people might buy their homes had gained momentum with the growth in building societies but most people still rented, as John Quinn recalls.

"Rents were tricky. I think that by the mid 1950s you might think of good wages as anything from £8 to £10 a week, but you might have to pay £3 or £4 a week to rent a two-bed flat if you had kids and you might spend £3 or £4 on food if you had a family. It was also easy to move from one rented flat to another as there were so many; because people had no money they rented out rooms and whole floors of their houses.

Food was far more expensive in real terms than it is now, when people complain if they spend more than ten per cent of their money on food. Clothing was pricey too because there wasn't much ready-to-wear stuff in the shops. People had their clothes made. Burtons had started to make off-the-peg suits but they cost 50 shillings each, which was expensive. Millions of men only had the one suit as a result and there were no leisure clothes at that time, which is why you see so many really elderly men today still wearing a jacket and tie every day – they feel naked without a get-up that they wore seven days a week throughout their lives."

Bucking the trend
While congregation numbers for urban parish churches were steadily falling, rural parishes – such as this one in Lovington, Somerset – generally managed to maintain their attendance at services. Overall, however, the picture was bleak as people's faith was challenged by hard times, memories of the war and the emergence of alternative entertainment and social acceptances.

Religion and churchgoing

The total number of Anglican churchgoers at the end of World War II and well into the 1950s was at least double the size of congregations in the 1990s, by which time church attendance was estimated to have dropped to around one million mostly elderly communicants.

Clearly the change in social attitudes, the determination to throw off the shackles of duty and convention which came with the 1960s, had much to do with this decline, although attendances had already begun to slip after the war as the church gradually lost its influence in urban and rural communities.

However, church-going continued to be seen as an unquestioned sign of respectability in the two decades following the war, as Pam Tarlton recalls.

"My father was the local solicitor in our village and he grew up simply assuming that everyone would attend church – well, everyone who had a position to uphold.

Continuing traditions
Despite dwindling congregations and changes in atttitudes, the Church of England was still a powerful and influential part of the establishment. Here Cathedral clergy, resplendent in their vestments, pass in front of Salisbury Cathedral following Matins in 1949.

"... with bell ringing, church fêtes and jumble sales the local church helped us through some difficult years ..."

That's a phrase you don't hear today but back then it was still very important. Being seen to be respectable was vital because people were obsessed with keeping up standards. I don't think anyone bothered to ask themselves why they were trying to keep up, but it was unquestioned and going to church was part of it. For the local solicitor not to have gone to church might have meant fewer clients and gossip, net curtains being pulled back, loss of caste, that kind of thing. We knew of people in the village and the outlying hamlets who never went to church but we thought of them as generally beyond the pale. They always had lots of dirty children, dogs roaming around, scrap metal in the yard and so on. We didn't want people to think we were like them. You also have to remember that vicars and others in positions of authority in the church back in the period after the war weren't as friendly and welcoming as they tend to be now. They liked to flex their muscles a bit more then and were very quick to judge and to criticise. I think that didn't help because they were always seen as reactionary in this way so when the social barriers fell down in the 1960s and people didn't go to church many vicars thought they could go round and give them a good telling off. That just alienated people further."

Leading the congregation
In remote rural areas the church retained its traditional, focal role for much longer than in urban areas. The church would provide villagers with a sense of community, as well as offering other social and cultural benefits. A good vicar was often key to attracting large congregations, such as at the village of Parracombe, Somerset (below).

A TASTE FOR FREEDOM

The war had given, for the first time, the experience of foreign travel to young working-class men. They saw at first hand ways of life that they had never experienced before, which worked a profound and rapid change in their attitudes. In many respects they were less prepared to accept authority and the constraints that it imposed, as John Quinn recalls.

"Young men coming back after the war hated the idea of falling in with all the old routines. They'd seen too much of life in different countries and weren't prepared to put up with being bossed around any more either by church or, if they could avoid it, by the state. It was really the end of all notion of forelock tugging in front of what would once have been called your betters. Young men and women could have their own identity and forget all about duty and the church. It was freedom really. In Manchester as in other cities I think church attendances declined far more quickly than they did in rural areas because everything moved quicker in the town.

Even in the 1950s some churchmen saw their ministry as including the poor and the unwashed but most far preferred to mix with the well off, the genteel. It was only much later when churches could no longer pressurise people into going that they took on a role they still have now, like a branch of the social services. They do good deeds, help poor people a bit and

visit the sick and elderly. Some did that sort of thing in the 1940s and 1950s but more do it now. I do remember going a few times to services in a big old red-brick church in Salford I think and attendances were still big with everyone in their Sunday best. But that church was demolished in the 1970s. That sums it all up really."

Rural parishes retained the strong church-going tradition for much longer. Jim Swire has warm memories of the church where his family worshipped in Sussex.

"I remember enjoying church. Me and my brothers could sing at the tops of our voices – it was the only chance we got to sing and we loved it – and the vicar was a very friendly soul. I remember he went on his bicycle to visit an elderly relative of ours every day for two weeks, brought her fruit and even read to her – but he wouldn't read *Sherlock Holmes*, which she loved. He said it might over-excite her, which made us laugh! But what with bell ringing, church fêtes and jumble sales I'd say the local church helped us through some difficult years."

Surveys

By the late 1940s we were all still using products that had been around since the Great War – Worcestershire Sauce, Marmite, Lux Soap Flakes, Lyons Tea – but the world was beginning to change and market research was to become the new big thing as brands began to compete. Before the war there had been a few surveys, but by 1947 they were becoming far more widespread.

It all started with Mass Observation, a social research organisation created in 1937 by the anthropologist Tom Harrisson, the poet

Public opinion
Mass Observation was the government's pioneering way of keeping in touch with the mood of the nation. Started just before the beginning of World War II, it was generally seen as an intrusion of privacy and often met with resistance. The subjects of observation projects make interesting reading, however, from attitudes to juvenile delinquency to the Labour election campaign and even weeping habits at the cinema.

Vote Labour
Clement Attlee led the Labour Party to its largest victory at the polls on July 29, 1945. During his six years in office he carried through a vigorous programme of reform, which was to include the establishing of the Bank of England and the National Health Service.

Charles Madge and the documentary filmmaker Humphrey Jennings. Harrisson's intention was to create an "anthropology of ourselves", and Mass Observation aimed to record everyday life in Britain through a panel of 500 volunteer observers and writers who kept diaries of their own lives or replied to questionnaires. Mass Observation also employed people to record conversation and behaviour in a variety of public situations – at meetings, religious occasions, sporting and leisure activities, in the street and at work.

The unfamiliar researchers were received with consternation and sometimes suspicion. Rose Plummer a domestic servant from London, remembers being questioned in great depth in 1950.

"A woman came to the door and told me she was from Mass Observation, which I'd never heard of – people were much more cagey about anything that looked like nosiness in those days so I was a bit cold with her at first but she was very nice so after a while I let her in, particularly when she said she wouldn't use my name. I rather liked talking about myself but looking back I think I spent the whole hour she was there moaning about the ration and the price of food and coal! We also had an outside loo and no bath and I asked her what she was going to do about it – she must have thought I was mad!"

"... there were very few brands, so there was no point asking us which we liked best!"

The consumer reseach that we take for granted now was a novelty in those days. Lisa Edwards recalls her surprise when spoken to.

"You have to remember that back in the 1940s and early 1950s we bought the same old things from the same old shops all the time – new lines and new products never really appeared. Things we remembered from before the war – meat and eggs and fish – were still hard to get because they were on the ration and there were very few brands, so there was no point asking us which we liked best! Asking consumers questions didn't start till the late 1950s, by which time there were more companies making soap powders, butter, different kinds of breakfast cereal, and so on. But apart from tins of Heinz beans and different spreads there still wasn't that much to choose between. I do remember Lyons had a survey to see who liked which of its teas best – that must have been in the early 1950s, because I remember thinking how unusual it was."

Politics and elections

After the shock of Winston Churchill losing the 1945 General Election, Britain looked forward to a new beginning with homes and jobs for all, better food and better wages. The new Labour Government led by Clement Attlee was hard pushed to meet these optimistic expectations, but Britain was a far more politically aware country then than it became in the disillusioned 1960s and 1970s. British people displayed an intense interest in political matters and, within communities and even families, there could be extreme polarisation of views. Steven Day remembers endless political debates just after the war.

"We took politics really seriously back then. You have to remember that back in the 1920s and 1930s capitalism was blamed for the Wall Street Crash and the Depression and mass unemployment. Then came fascism and we all split off into

Shock victory
The outcome of the 1945 general election was a shock for the Conservative government. The country was eager for change and the Labour Party, led by Clement Attlee – seen waving to the crowds at Transport House in Westminster (left) after the victory – was voted into Government.

Wage packet
The coal industry was nationalised in 1947 and revolutionised the rights of employees. The newly formed National Coal Board offered paid holidays, sick pay and rest homes for miners to recover after accidents at work. Some 700,000 people were employed in the industry in 1950, but rates of pay were contentious even then.

extremes – I remember how horrified I was when my brother Joe told me he was joining the fascists. I was an ardent socialist as were all my friends. But we weren't socialists the way people were in the 1960s and 1970s – we were much more extreme. We believed that private ownership of the mines, the railways and docks and of production generally was too important to stay in the hands of capitalists because they were in it for private profit not for the good of the nation as a whole, and that couldn't continue. Wall Street and the Depression had been caused we thought by capitalist greed. We didn't realise that Government control of everything would turn out to be cumbersome and inefficient. We thought it would operate for the good of all."

Some members of the upper-middle classes and aristocracy embraced the idea of a vaguely socialist Utopia, which partly explains why the infamous Establishment trio Guy Burgess, Donald Maclean and Kim Philby – all three Cambridge-educated, communists and from privileged backgrounds – could work for decades as spies for Soviet Russia. Moreover, well-known Establishment figures such as Bertrand Russell, George Bernard Shaw and others made socialism the political choice for intellectual Britain. Amy Capper in Newcastle was not entirely convinced.

"Well, we were Labour supporters but in our everyday lives we were very conservative and all that political discussion was a bit above our heads. My parents voted Labour because their parents had been miners in the days when

Going to the polls
Despite polling nearly 14 million votes – which was then the record number of votes recorded by any British political Party in any election – the Labour party lost power to the Conservatives. Schools, churches and pubs were converted into polling stations and the election on 23 February 1950 achieved an 84% turnout.

Conservative campaign
Most observers believed that the Conservatives would win the 1945 election, despite the publication of opinion polls showing Labour six points ahead. Along with the campaign poster above, the Conservatives appealed to the nation under the slogan "Vote National – Help him Finish the Job", and duly found themselves out of step with the public's mood.

miners were paid a pittance for doing one of the most dangerous jobs in the world."

Outside the intelligentsia, however, there were many upper-middle class people who were not attracted by socialism, and at election time wealthy landowners could still exert a covert influence over their employees and tenants. Jim Swire remembers the village school on polling day.

"It was all so quiet and well behaved: the policeman standing there by the entrance and the returning officer who was the local landowner dressed in tweeds and looking very stern. Even in rural – some would say feudal! – districts like ours people thought about voting Labour, but many of the farm workers felt slightly intimidated by the officials and the older ones were terrified that their bosses would find out that they'd voted for the other side, meaning Labour! Landowners, the aristocracy, the upper classes and even the middle classes in those days routinely used socialist as a term of abuse. It was on a par with being called a bugger!"

Amongst women, the tendency to vote according to background or social position was even stronger. Pam Tarlton remembers a rather less politically aware environment.

"Well-brought-up girls were not supposed to be interested in politics – and we weren't. It was considered rather sordid if you can believe that now, like playing with the local children from the council estate! But we never thought about voting for anything other than the Conservatives. Politics had nothing to do with it. It was a class thing. Working-class people voted

Labour; we voted Tory because it helped define us as superior. What nonsense it now all seems!"

The role of women

From the early part of the 20th century when a few brave women decided to live unconventional lives by becoming painters or writers – women such as the artist Vanessa Bell and her sister Virginia Woolf, around whom the Bloomsbury Group of writers, artists and intellectuals was formed – conventional views of women's roles were under attack.

Despite the opinion that middle-class women would be coarsened and corrupted by work it became essential during the Great War that they work. In machine shops it was quickly discovered, to the embarrassment of the authorities, that it took on average three weeks fewer to train a woman machinist than a man.

After 1918 there were attempts to get women back into the home and away from work but it was clear that having tasted freedom they were not going to go quietly back to the kitchen. Secretarial work gradually became acceptable, at least until marriage, and by the 1940s and 1950s there were women doctors and even a few women MPs. But the formalities were extraordinary by today's standards, as Ruth Wadham recalls:

"When a woman applied for a secretarial job – or any job for that matter – she had to dress smartly for the interview, and being smart in those days meant wearing white gloves and a hat. No girl would dream of turning up for an interview without them – you wouldn't be offered the job. The point of the gloves was to show you were a cut above the rest – genteel in other words."

CLASS

Class distinction continued to operate strongly amongst women in the workplace, as Amy Capper in Newcastle remembers.

"Well-brought-up girls were not supposed to be interested in politics – and we weren't."

Typing pool
Developments in society's expectations and technology meant that women could work in roles and sectors that had previously been closed to them. Older, traditional industries were in decline, while white collar work was on the increase. The future belonged to managers, technicians and, in turn, secretaries, such as these seen here at Unilever in 1955.

"The divide between working-class girls and middle-class girls was unbridgeable. Posh girls dressed differently and spoke differently and went to different places to eat and socialise. Girls had grown up with their mothers not letting them play with the rough and poor kids down the road and so they had that built into them.

It makes me laugh when people talk about the changing role of women because mostly it applies to posh women. Before 1918 the key way a woman could prove she was posh was not to work. Working-class women had always worked – in factories as well as at home. So the changing role of women in the 1940s and 1950s had more to do with the changing role of middle-class women."

Another traditional source of employment for working-class women was domestic service. In the 20th century the life of a servant was tough, with many women exploited and under-regarded, as Rose Plummer recalls.

"I had a job for a short while in a laundry and then in domestic service, where you were treated as if you didn't exist – it was long hard work for little pay and I remember how sad I felt when I heard my dad say once that my mum, who'd also worked in domestic service, was so clever that she could have been a secretary if her family had had a bit more money. He meant she had the brains but not the money or social graces – she had a cockney accent and had only been to the local board school, so it was impossible. But later I realised how sad it was that the height of ambition for him was secretarial work."

Immigration

There had been immigrants in Britain – particularly in London – since late medieval times, but their numbers remained vanishingly small in relation to the size of the country until the 19th century, when improved communications, particularly steamships and railways, made travel much easier.

In the 19th century London's East End, which had been a haven for Protestant Huguenots from France and the Low Countries for 300 years, became a mecca for Jews fleeing economic hardship and religious persecution all over Eastern Europe and Russia, while the Irish came in their tens of

Overcrowding
The postwar period saw a significant housing shortage where people – young and old – were forced together to live in over-crowded homes or in temporary accommodation. The country's new immigrants were particularly vulnerable to exploitation. With many landlords operating a colour bar, they were often forced to accept high rents for crumbling rooms.

Accommodation wanted
Several hundred West Indians were sent to Liverpool (pictured right) to boost production during World War II, many of whom settled after the war. A study, carried out by Anthony Richmond, determined that by 1946 they were subject to considerable prejudice in the workplace by skilled tradesmen.

thousands to Liverpool and other major cities in search of work. But more widespread and far more noticeable immigration came after World War II when, in the mid 1950s, wave after wave of Caribbean immigrants arrived in the UK, encouraged by the government to make up for labour shortages, particularly in transport.

John Rogan remembers growing up in Central London at that time, and the changing ethnic and cultural mix of the community.

> "We lived in Lambeth, where everyone round about including my family was of Irish descent. My parents had experienced discrimination – outsiders are always disliked by the indigenous population. It may have been a myth but it was generally believed that landlords would put up signs saying 'No children, no dogs and no Irish'. When black people started to come things got much easier for the Irish because they weren't so noticeable. But there was a lot of discrimination – most of it in the form of jokes and for years people thought it was OK to make racist remarks as long as they were funny. If someone was offended we'd just say, 'I was only joking,' as if that made it OK, but when I was at school for years we all said, 'Oh he's a bit Jewish,' meaning someone was tight-fisted, and I remember being amazed when I learned that being Jewish actually referred to a religion! I thought it was just a phrase that meant being a tightwad!"

The number of immigrants in need of housing gave great scope for exploitation, and some unscrupulous property owners made huge profits from the situation. Bobby Sharpe remembers West Indians in Ladbroke Grove, where the notorious slum landlord Peter Rachman was to operate in the early 1960s.

> "The period before Rachman wasn't much better, because landlords could do what they liked in the 1940s and early 1950s.

There were no rules or controls on them. They could charge anything and up your rent by any amount and if you couldn't pay they'd just chuck you out. Ladbroke Grove was an incredibly run-down area after the war – smoke-blackened houses that hadn't been repaired for years, many very badly dilapidated because people had no money for repairs on houses that never went up in value. They were a liability but of course when the immigrants, particularly West Indians, began to arrive the landlords really had a field day. They split big houses into 20 or 30 rooms and charged what they liked, but the West Indian arrivals always seemed quite cheerful because they'd come from far worse poverty. It could be quite comic because they'd be living in a squalid room but would spend huge amounts on giant, immaculately polished cars!"

"They split big houses into 20 or 30 rooms and charged what they liked ..."

The arrival of immigrants also created tension in the workplace, as competition for jobs increased, and the good-humoured tolerance of British workers hardened into racism.

In Liverpool James Lanigan remembers the dockers from the Caribbean.

"At first they were so exotic-looking that we really liked them – they were treated like lucky mascots, but as the numbers grew people began to resent their presence. It got worse whenever people were laid off because black people were seen as taking white people's jobs. But I admired their courage because they had to put up with a lot of abuse and what would now be called casual racism. It was just automatic. In the army it was even worse – I remember after the war doing my National Service and hearing a Caribbean bloke being called the sort of names that would now land you in prison!"

Sex, marriage and courtship

Philip Larkin's famous lines sum up the world of sex – or the lack of it – before the 1960s:

Sexual intercourse began
In nineteen sixty-three
(Which was rather late for me)–
Between the end of the Chatterley ban
And the Beatles' first LP

In the 1940s and 1950s sex was something largely unmentioned and unmentionable; it seemed something that only married couple did officially and then only because it was the only way to have babies. So far as advertising and the media were concerned it might as well not have existed. Attitudes amongst the

Breaking the rules
Attitudes towards relationships during the 1950s were in a state of transition. The shift from courting to dating transferred the power in the relationship dynamic – men paid for the dates, they were the ones in control. Books told girls never to invite a man to her home, or elsewhere, as this would be breaking "the rules".

working classes were, however, more realistic. Rose Plummer recalls:

"I remember reading that the aristocracy and the working classes always took a much more relaxed view of sex than the middle classes, who were obsessed with being respectable and doing the right thing. I'm not sure that's really true but I know my grandmother had an illegitimate child and the family just accepted it and got on with it, and we were definitely working class! She wasn't thrown out like you read in books. There wasn't that much of a sense of shame. A middle-class family in the 1940s and 1950s at that time might well have just thrown the girl out on the street. In the 1930s and even 1940s, too, girls who got pregnant outside marriage were sometimes put in mental hospitals and didn't get out till the 1970s. Officially sex outside marriage was still seen in some quarters as evidence of instability or madness, incredible though that seems now."

People held more tolerant views towards the sexual shenanigans of the wealthy, as Tom Phillips recalls:

"The aristocracy always had sex outside marriage so long as it was discreet. Who could have told Edward VII it was wrong to have a string of mistresses? But the hypocrisy of it was breathtaking and turned many against the Royal Family. The war changed a lot of our attitudes – it was said that on VE Day couples among the crowds celebrating in London were so ecstatic that they had sex in shop doorways.

Also society had been so disrupted with men away for long periods that both men and women had experienced a sort of sexual freedom that made them reluctant to go back to accepting the old rather repressive Victorian view of sex. I know my parents were horrified at what they saw as the new attitude to sex."

But marriage – and monogamy – still remained the expected destiny for most people, particularly women, as Libby McIntyre's experience demonstrates.

"... society had been so disrupted with men away for long periods that both men and women had experienced a sort of sexual freedom ..."

Declining morals

Sexual content appeared in movies and magazines with greater frequency during the 1950s as an emerging youth culture experienced a new liberalism. A Mass Observation survey of some 2,000 people in 1949 revealed that 44% of those surveyed felt that "standards of sex morality today" were declining, while 17% felt that they were improving. The remaining 39% were undecided.

"In Scotland I think we were always a bit late to catch up when things changed, but like the rest of the country we didn't know anyone who just lived together – I mean outside marriage. Getting married was almost like getting a job – you just had to do it. It was much harder, unless you had money, to just go off and rent somewhere and work on your own if you were a woman. No one would rent you a room – they might think you were a prostitute! Today girls often rent flats on their own all the time and no one would dream of thinking they were on the game, but it was very different back then."

Police, crime and prison

World War II changed the general outlook and attitudes of the British forever. But in one or two respects it was to take another 20 years and more for deeply held views – about homosexuality for example – to change. There was little attempt to understand or rectify the causes of antisocial behaviour, and attitudes to crime and punishment among the law-abiding classes were almost Victorian in their rigidity.

Pam Tarlton recalls the general view of the middle and upper-middle classes.

Miscarriage of justice
Teenager Derek Bentley was executed for his part in the murder of PC Sidney Miles after a bungled break-in at a warehouse in Croydon, Surrey. On January 28, 1953 a large crowd gathered outside Wandsworth Jail, shouting and pointing to the police to take down the noticeboard which announced his execution. The public felt that a great miscarriage of justice was taking place, and that Bentley's involvement and mental disabilities coupled with inconsistencies in the police's account of events made the punishment unjust. Bentley's conviction was quashed in 1991.

"We were absolutely strict in our attitudes in respect of crime. I'm rather embarrassed to admit that we thought the courts were far too soft even then – when we read that so-and-so had robbed a bank or a shop we really felt that the only answer was to lock them up for good. There was a view back then that criminals were born not made – now that view has completely changed. Back then we thought that someone who committed a crime would only do it again if he was let out of prison – the favourite phrase was that it was bred in them. Everyone thought of prison as a punishment not as a means to rehabilitate criminals. The funny thing is that now we think of prison as about rehabilitation first

The legal year
A ceremony to celebrate the start of the legal year has taken place at Westminster Abbey since the Middle Ages. Sir Hartley Shawcross, the English jurist, leads the King's Counsel in the procession from Westminster Abbey (left), marking the opening of the legal year of 1946. The ceremony has been cancelled twice in its history, once when the Abbey was damaged by German bombs in 1940, and then again in 1953 to make way for the Coronation.

and punishment second, but all the evidence suggests that it is absolutely useless as a way to rehabilitate people."

DISCRIMINATION

However, working-class people tended to be critical of the law and its enforcers, often suspecting that someone who came from a privileged background would receive more lenient treatment from the courts. Printer John Rogan, who grew up on a council estate in Central London, cites the notorious case of Derek Bentley, a working-class youth who was executed in 1953 for his involvement in the fatal shooting of a policeman, to justify a widely held view that the legal system was biased in favour of the Establishment.

"We always thought that respect for the law was for the toffs because the law protected the haves from the have-nots. You saw it all the time – a posh bloke up for some offence would be let off quite lightly where an ordinary man up for the same offence would get a much more severe sentence. The reason was that the posh bloke had probably been to school with the judge! We always thought – and I still think it now – that if you'd been to a

"Everyone thought of prison as a punishment not as a means to rehabilitate criminals."

"... if you sat on a park bench for too long they'd move you on and if you so much as gave them a sour look they'd arrest you ..."

Bobby on the beat
Styles of policing gradually changed after World War II. In 1948 Aberdeen adopted the so-called "team policing" method, which was soon rolled out to Liverpool and beyond. The team comprised four constables and one sergeant, along with a car and two-way radio, who patrolled ten traditional beats. The days were numbered for the lone bobby on the beat.

posh boarding school and you broke the law the penalty should be more severe, not less, because you'd messed up after being given every advantage. A lot of my views I got from my dad, who became a communist.

The Home Secretary who refused to pardon Derek Bentley for shooting a policeman in 1953 was a toff and Bentley was just an ordinary kid from South London. The Home Secretary refused to accept that Bentley had a mental age of about 14 but if Bentley had been to Eton you can bet that he'd have got life in prison and been out in ten years."

Many working-class people did not see themselves as allies of the police, who could in turn be high-handed in their treatment of the poor. Rose Plummer remembers attitudes to the police in Islington, North London.

"We were bloomin' terrified of them – they were real figures of authority back then. If you stood for too long in one place on the street or sat on a park bench for too long they'd move you on and if you so much as gave them a sour look they'd arrest you.

I once saw two men arrested outside a pub for fighting and one broke away from the young red-faced policeman who was trying to arrest them. He started running and the policeman blew his whistle – no radio in those days – but no one helped him catch the bloke who'd run away. We always sided with the underdog and even a bloke who'd been in a fight was the underdog if the alternative was handing him over to the Old Bill."

Authority and the Establishment

Attitudes to the Establishment and authority generally after the war and in the 1950s were complex. However, it is certainly true that deference to the well born was far more evident than it is now and it was almost unheard of for the monarch or any member of the Royal Family to be criticised. Tom Shackle remembers how, even in everyday life, the habit of judging others according to perceived status was deeply ingrained.

> "We used to say that people looked up and kicked down – it is very hard now to put yourself into that old way of thinking because it has completely vanished. People took pride in showing others just how deferential they were to those above them. People imitated their betters, to use the phrase we used then. A good example is Margaret Thatcher. To get on she had elocution lessons because if you had a regional accent back then you were marked down in a peculiar way. She knew she could not become a barrister with a Lincolnshire accent because we all deferred to what was called Received Pronunciation. You wouldn't be admitted to chambers (essential for barrister trainees) and you'd be hard pressed to become an MP or anything else important unless you sounded right. If you wanted to be part of the Establishment you had to sound right. Can you imagine a person today having elocution lessons to try to sound posh?"

ROYALISM

The attitude to the Royal Family was protective and at times almost reverential. Behaviour on the part of Royals that today would be censured, ridiculed or even punished hardly raised an eyebrow. Pam Tarlton, who grew up in rural Gloucestershire, gives examples of this.

> "I can remember a story about a man who had criticised Princess Margaret in a newspaper article. A few days later after his article appeared he was physically attacked by several respectable men in bowler hats as he left his office in Fleet Street. They punched him till he fell down. Now those men probably knew that the stories about Princess Margaret's affairs and so on were true but she was above criticism as far as they were concerned simply because she was a member of the Royal Family.
>
> It was the same with the abdication of Edward VIII before the war. The public were hugely sympathetic to Edward and were quite happy with the idea of him marrying an American divorcée but if there had been a man living at the end of the street who got divorced the gossip and ostracism would have made his life a misery. If I think about it now I realise how silly our attitudes were – the upper classes should have behaved better than the rest of us as they'd had every advantage but we gave them every sympathy when they failed, almost as if having a privileged life made it harder to do the right thing!"

"People took pride in showing others just how deferential they were to those above them."

This disillusionment with the wealthy and the influential went along with a growing perception that power was now within the reach of ordinary people. Rose Plummer, who takes a dim view of the Establishment, articulates a view that was becoming increasingly common.

Respect
Postwar Britain was a society with very stringent morals, and ideas on right and wrong were clearly defined. Respect for the police was high: a survey by anthropologist Geoffrey Gorer in 1950/51 revealed that, of the 11,000 people canvassed, just 5% felt any hostility towards the force.

POMP AND CIRCUMSTANCE

The Coronation, 1953

By any standards, the Coronation on June 2, 1953 was an extraordinary and successful event. It was the BBC's biggest-ever outside broadcast; three million people lined the streets of London to catch a glimpse of the royal procession. Street parties were held in towns and villages all over Britain, and the dancing carried on well into the night. The people truly believed that their country was turning a corner, and was now going to prosper under its new queen.

A day to remember
Over 20 million people gathered around television sets to watch the BBC coverage of the Coronation in hazy black and white, while dedicated scrapbooks and notebooks were produced for the loyal nation to document the occasion.

Collectibles
Many schoolchildren were given specially made mugs to celebrate the occasion, while a limited number also went on general sale along with toffee tins, plates and other memorabilia.

A lick of paint
Coronation day was a welcome opportunity to spruce up the war-weary façades of some of the nation's homes. Streets were cleaned, windows were washed, stone was painted and street parties were planned months in advance.

English weather
It seemed impossible that more time, effort and money could have been expended by residents on the decoration of their streets. Those who had been unable to watch the ceremony and procession on television were able to go and watch it in colour at their local cinema.

Colour co-ordination
Red, white and blue flowers were planted in gardens and windowboxes to maintain the theme of the day, while little girls wore coloured ribbons in their hair to match. Bunting hung from every available railing, and some people even slept on the streets to secure their prized place on the procession route.

CAUTION
CHILDREN
PLAY HERE

Making your own fun

CHILDHOOD

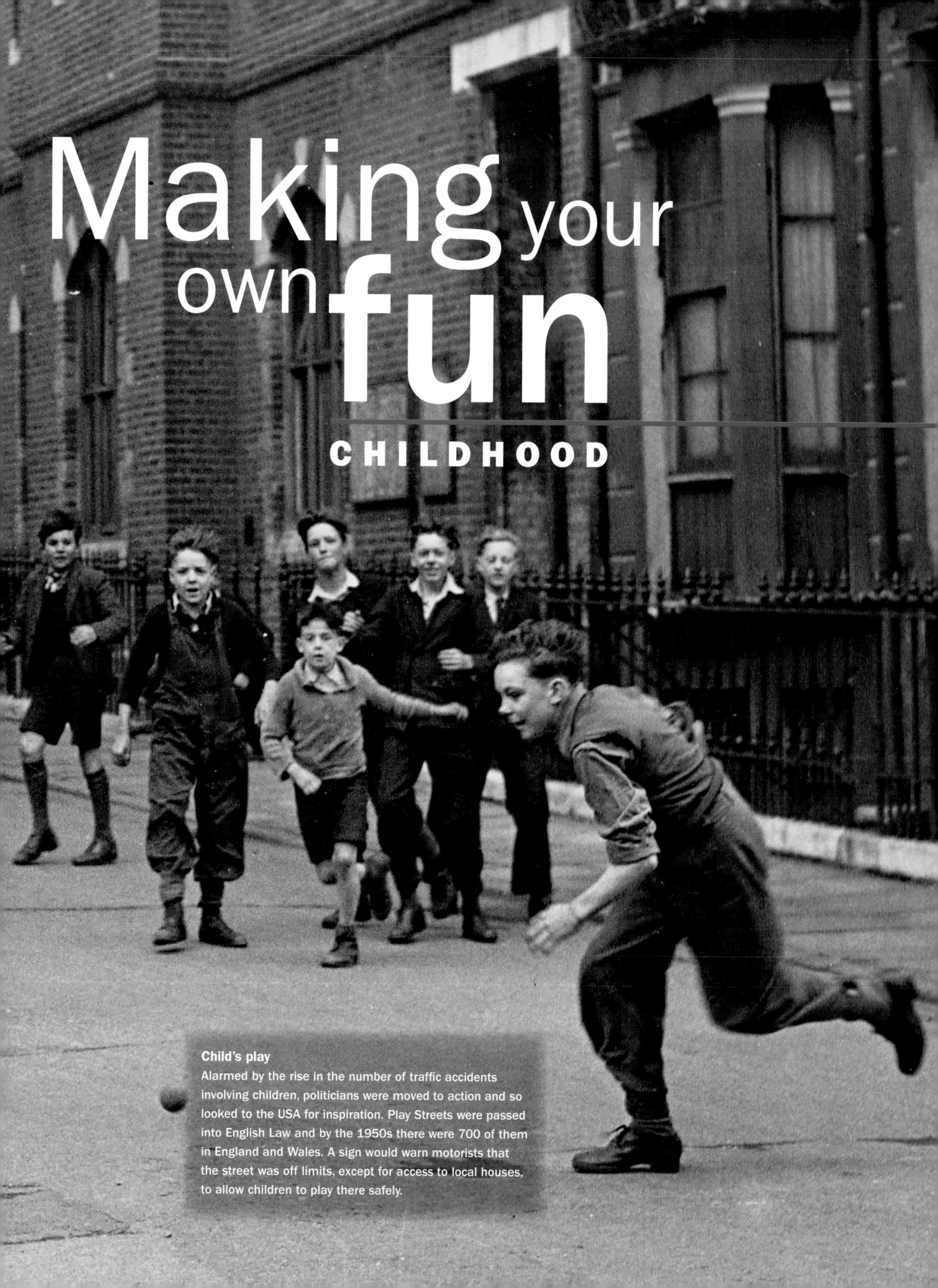

Child's play

Alarmed by the rise in the number of traffic accidents involving children, politicians were moved to action and so looked to the USA for inspiration. Play Streets were passed into English Law and by the 1950s there were 700 of them in England and Wales. A sign would warn motorists that the street was off limits, except for access to local houses, to allow children to play there safely.

For most children the postwar life was a world of hand-me-downs, Sunday school, street games and strict discipline at school. There were no trainers or tee-shirts, no computers and hardly any TVs. Children dressed, as they had always dressed, like miniature adults: in little woollen suits with short trousers and almost always with shirt and tie. Poorer children wore a patched and frequently mended version of this attire. At the other end of the social scale the children of the rich still wore boaters and top hats and spoke in accents unintelligible. But with few cars this was still an innocent world where children could play safely in the street or roam the fields all summer long.

School of hard knocks

The experience of being a child in the 1940s and 1950s was probably closer in many ways to the experience of growing up in 1900 than to the world we know today. Children were subject to physical discipline at home and at school; there were few elaborate Christmas or birthday presents, no computer games or electronic toys and no DVDs. It was an era of short trousers and chilblains, playing outside, Horlicks and hot water bottles.

And if life was unchanging it was at least partly because people tended to do things without thinking about them much. In schools, for example, children took strict discipline and Spartan conditions for granted, as John Rogan recalls well.

"Learning your times table was absolutely compulsory and they were rigid about spelling ..."

"I went to a great junior school and a terrible secondary school, but neither was chosen for me. They were just the schools where all the local kids went. The junior school was only an ordinary state school but it was run like a public school, because I think most of the teachers had been to public schools. Mr Busby took us for sport and he would get in early and stay late so we could practise. Lessons were always very quiet – you would be hit really hard with a leather slipper in front of the whole class if you said a word out of turn. Learning your times table was absolutely compulsory and they were rigid about spelling – you just had to learn it. Other things I remember are iodine on grazed

Education for all
The 1944 Education Act organised schools into three progressive stages – primary, secondary, and further education. Often described as 'secondary education for all', the Act's greatest achievement was to raise the school leaving age, which was initially at 14 to 15, in 1947.

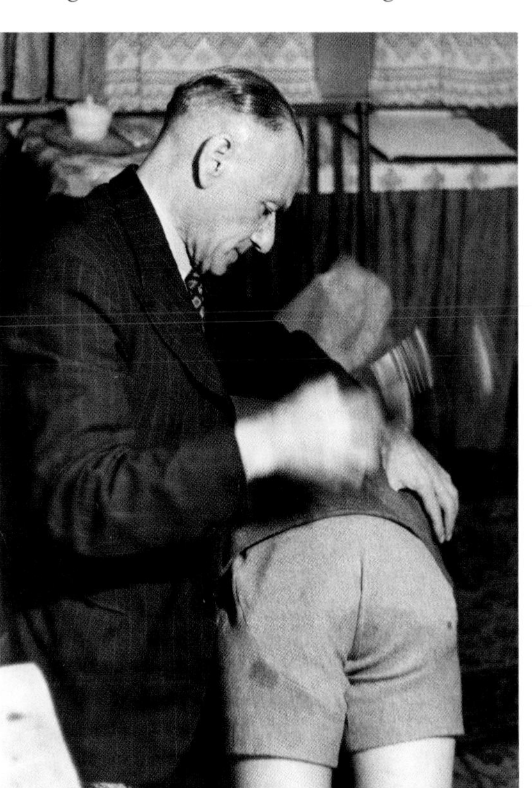

Corporal punishment
Tradition was still the backbone of school life and discipline. Although the cane was used less indiscriminately and frequently than earlier in the century, school children between the ages of eight and 11 could still be punished with one stroke of the cane for offences including inattention, bad work and "inbred tiredness". The highest number of strokes of the cane (four) was generally reserved for playing truant, but a child could get two strokes for "inertia", "not trying", "idiotic behaviour" or "stealing and lying".

Free milk
Following the 1945 General Election, Prime Minister Clement Attlee appointed Ellen Wilkinson as Minister of Education – the first woman in British history to hold the post. Wilkinson had long been a campaigner against poverty and in 1946 persuaded Parliament to pass the School Milk Act. The act ordered the issue of one-third of a pint of milk free to all pupils under the age of eighteen.

knees – the school had a nurse who put it on every time you fell over and it stung like hell. I remember too being dropped off while it was still dark at 8.30 by my dad. He had a little seat on the back of his bicycle that I sat in – not strapped in or anything. I just hung on. I also remember the smell of the plastic cups we had orange juice in at 11 each morning with one rich tea biscuit. We had free milk too in half-pint bottles – I was milk monitor and drank all the extras when the other kids didn't want theirs. For a while I was also the ink monitor – we used desks that had ink wells in them and every morning a boy would go round with a big bottle of ink filling the ink wells. Incredibly Victorian.

My secondary school, which I only went to because my brother was already there, was on the other side of the high street and much rougher. Some kids didn't have a bath for weeks on end – a mate of mine who I used to bunk off with lived in a terrible poverty-stricken council flat. He hardly ever saw his parents and at age 11 was fending for himself. We heard about one boy who used to be sewn into his clothes at the beginning of winter – with brown paper layers underneath – and not let out till spring!"

THE TOFFS

Pam Tarlton remembers a very different sort of life at Cheltenham Ladies' College.

"There was an obsession with being ladylike. We really did walk round with piles of books on our heads to improve deportment and we learned to write elegant letters, to speak beautifully, to appreciate music and so on. Some girls, but very few, went on to university. I would have gone but my parents felt they couldn't afford it. I think they rather bankrupted themselves paying for my schooling and then I had to get a job. No grants in those days remember. But my days at school were not entirely happy – I was a day girl so always felt rather out of it and the boarders sometimes made my life a misery."

Even when they were out of school, there were attempts to curtail children's freedom. At the

weekends, attendance at Sunday school was for many children part of an unchanging routine, as Mark Greenway recalls.

"My brother and I went to Sunday school because that's what all our friends did. Just like all the mothers did their washing on Monday – they all did it on that day just because they didn't want to be different. Now that's all been reversed. Instead of trying to be the same we all try to be different – well teenagers do anyway.

We didn't really enjoy Sunday school but we had to go, and I now realise that my parents – who weren't religious at all – probably saw Sunday school as a free baby sitter! The rest of the week they never had any time to themselves so they must have really looked forward to time on their own on Sunday.

Our Sunday school was held in what used to be the village hall. It was freezing in winter. They'd tell us Bible stories, some of which were quite interesting, but they did go on a bit about sin and being good and they were so serious. Having fun and mucking about seemed like bad things to

"We really did walk round with piles of books on our heads to improve our deportment ..."

Privileges of education
Mass Observation surveys discovered that out of those who had attended private schools such as Cheltenham Ladies' College shown above, not one mentioned the class of degree they had, or the number of examinations they had passed: of the most importance was the kind of school they went to.

Off to Sunday school
Strong attendance across the spectrum of social classes was experienced by Sunday schools, but the biggest effect was on the working classes. In addition to the religious education, they received literacy support, storytelling and performance activity, as well as day excursions that might otherwise be out of reach in their everyday schooling.

Freedom to roam
A sanguine approach to children's safety ensured that they had a freedom to play and explore that would be the envy of children today. After a cursory warning not to take sweets from strange men they would be gone for hours.

our Sunday school teacher but then she was in her 60s in the 1950s so she was effectively a Victorian, with all the most repressed Victorian attitudes. We were made to sing Onward Christian Soldiers and To Be a Pilgrim to a slightly out-of-tune piano and we might then make little gifts for orphans, though I have no idea if our little cut-out pictures and potato prints ever left the building. But they liked to instil the idea that we should do things for others and not for ourselves, which looking back seems a rather noble aim. I have friends whose kids go to Sunday school now and the religious element is almost nonexistent and fun is emphasised. Such a change from my day."

Discipline and freedom

Back in the 1940s and 1950s it was rare for children to have parents who didn't slap them now and then, and in school corporal punishment was accepted practice, with teachers quick to discipline children who misbehaved, as Kevin O'Brien remembers.

"I remember bunking off when I was at junior school, but it wasn't done with any real intent. I was with a couple of friends waiting one morning in the playground for school to start when I suggested that the three of us go back to my house and play in the garden. I don't think we thought we were doing anything naughty really – we'd have been about seven at the time. Anyway my mother spotted us straight away when we started shouting in the backyard and marched us back to school. The teacher lined the three of us up in front of her and my mother and smacked the backs of our legs really hard just behind the knee. I do think it was rather humiliating and it certainly hurt! I don't think you'd get away with that now."

But while children were subjected to strict control in the classroom and home, once they were out in the open, away from school and parents, they had more liberty than today's younger generation. Growing up in the Sussex countryside, Jim Swire recalls a freedom to roam that has now all but vanished.

"My dad was a tough old boy. He used the strap on all of us, but it was just part of life and we accepted it. I don't think it was a good thing really because some abused it and really hurt their children, as they do now. There was still a view that if you spared the rod you'd spoil the child and you'd almost have to kill your nipper to be in real trouble with the police.

Even if we had to put up with that – and an occasional slap from Mum – we did have something wonderful that kids don't have now. We were always free in the summer holidays to roam wherever we liked. We used to go miles across the South Downs, hunting rabbits, bird-nesting, climbing trees and playing in the farmers' barns. We'd stay out all day with just a slice or two of bread and butter wrapped up in paper. My mother never worried about us being hit by a car or kidnapped – such things were unheard of back then in our part of the world."

City children could enjoy similar happy days, as Ian Smart remembers from his childhood in London's East End in the late 1940s and early 1950s.

"We had a lot of freedom – all day we'd play in the streets in summer and winter and to be honest my mum didn't mind much if we missed school. Never made a fuss. She thought book learning was a bit of a waste of time and wanted us to be finished with it and out there earning a living as soon as possible. We used to wander up the local markets and meet our mates. Or go down to the river and mess about, and as long as we were back by tea time we never got in trouble. All that stuff you hear about kids being beaten is rubbish too – my dad never touched us. He used to play with us like a kid himself when he had a bit of time and he hated seeing kids hit. Mind you, if he had hit us I think my mum would have hit him!"

Little adults

Clothes rationing was introduced in 1941 to conserve material needed for military purposes such as uniforms and parachutes, and lasted until 1949. Throughout this period parents were encouraged to "make do and mend" (indeed, they had little choice) – to repair clothes all the time and, when there was more than one child in the house, to pass garments down the family as older children outgrew them.

Street games
Children who grew up in urban areas would enjoy as much outdoor playtime as those in rural areas, albeit with different games. Generally, once a child had reached school age they would be allowed out to play football or street tennis with the other boys from the neighbourhood. Cars were few and far between, and safety was of little concern. Today, playing football in the street is against the law.

In those days, children's clothes did not markedly differ from adults' clothes – except of course in terms of their size – until well into the 1960s. Today jeans and T-shirts and a host of other garments mark children and teenagers out as different; they provide a specific identity that was completely lacking half a century ago, as John Rogan recalls.

"At my school most of the kids had their school uniform and very little else. If you met them on a Saturday they'd be wearing a different jumper maybe but with an old pair of school trousers. And loads of kids still turned up with patches all over their trousers. My mum used to put patches on and I remember being really embarrassed that people would notice. We always had darned socks and the elbows on our jumpers were always patched too. My mother would have thought the world had gone mad if someone had suggested she throw out a jumper, socks or trousers just because they had holes. But at the local secondary modern there were some really poor kids – they'd have bits of newspaper in their shoes to cover up the holes. Even in Central London, two minutes from Parliament Square where we were, people were very poor and it showed in the kids' clothes. I don't remember anyone having jeans or anything kids have today. The worst thing was swimming trunks – they were wool, if you can believe that, and as

"We always had darned socks and the elbows on our jumpers were always patched too."

Points system
Children's clothing and footwear had lower points in the rationing system to make allowances for quick growth and wear and tear. Even so, items that weren't worn out would be recycled among family members or patched up, and some would go to the clothing exchange set up by the Women's Volunteer Service.

Threadbare clothes
During the first year of peace the clothes ration reached its lowest ever level. As stocks became exhausted, clothes became increasingly threadbare. In September 1948 footwear, children's clothes and some miscellaneous items were derationed until the whole ration was finally abolished in 1949.

soon as you went in the water they started to get pulled down by their own weight as they absorbed water. They sagged and felt like they were being dragged down to your ankles – it's amazing any of us learned to swim when we spent all our time hanging on to our swimming drawers!"

David Westall has similar memories of such austere times.

"We had a best suit for going to church and our school clothes and a few hand-me-downs – everyone except the very rich had hand-me-downs because no one threw anything away. I had my brother's jumpers and trousers and then my younger brother had them as they got more and more patched. As long as you weren't the odd one out you were O.K. so far as clothes were concerned. We used to see the posh kids going to school in stiff collars and very smartly ironed shorts but we never played with them so it was a different world and we never thought about it.

I remember we had relatives who lived outside Windsor and we saw the Eton school boys in the High Street regularly. I couldn't believe it – stiff white collars, top hats and tail coats. And they definitely looked down on everyone – you'd see them in the shops talking to 60-year-old shopkeepers as if they were servants."

RESPECTABLE CLOTHING

Middle-class children did not have to endure the sartorial privations of their poorer contemporaries, but there was nothing about their clothing that resembled the individuality and verve seen in teenage outfits today. Pam Tarlton, growing up in Gloucestershire, remembers the oppressive respectability of the clothes she was made to wear.

"My main memory of clothes is of how much underwear we had to put on! Several sets of knickers – sort of under-

Down with drabness
In 1947 under the headline "Down with Drabness!" mothers of girls were urged to make an effort stating that "it cannot be too strongly emphasised that efforts made by the mother to dress a small girl prettily and suitably are of inestimable value in later life".

Paper round
Being a paper boy was a rite of passage for most young boys past the age of ten. Delivering papers was a way of making pocket money to spend on comics and sweets, or the latest highly prized trainspotting book. It was not an easy job, however – very early starts were necessary to ensure that each household had its paper in time for breakfast reading, and the boys' often threadbare trousers or shorts would do little to keep off the cold winter mornings.

knickers to start with, then heavy woollen things. We also had party frocks and day dresses all made for us by a local dressmaker who had patterns she claimed were the latest fashion from London, but I suspect they dated back to the 1930s or earlier. Despite the war and the fact that hemlines had risen there was a terror still that girls would be seen in any way as sexually attractive, so clothes were boring and outdated, and in country districts like ours this was even worse because we were always a decade or two behind the big cities in terms of fashion.

What also seems really funny now is that there was an obsession with being ladylike – we really were told things such as: 'If you dress and behave like that no decent man will want you,' as if the sole purpose of a girl's life was to grow up, be beautifully dressed and behave in a feminine way just to get a man, have babies, and start the whole thing off again!"

"Can you imagine the stupidity of it – wearing shorts when it's four degrees below freezing?"

Earning a few bob

One of the few employments permitted to children under 16 who are still at school, the newspaper round was and probably still is the quintessential first job. But after the war, when virtually every house was heated by open fires, getting up at 6am to traipse the streets with a heavy bag was not for the fainthearted, as David Westall remembers.

"When people think of the newspaper boy they think of a cheery whistling little chap with a thick muffler and a cheeky air. When I started my paper round in 1948 it wasn't a bit like that, probably because I started in the middle of winter. My memory is that it was terribly cold and of course like most boys at that time I only had shorts to wear. Can you imagine the stupidity of it – wearing shorts when it's four degrees below freezing? It was so silly and unthinking that it's hard to believe it really happened. My top half was warm enough because I went out with two pullovers, a scarf and my school cap. But my legs were blue when I got back.

There were several papers that have gone now – the *Sunday Pictorial* I think and the *Record*. But the Sunday papers weren't as stupid as they later became. Huge plastic bags full of supplements and advertisements and other rubbish. Paper shortages and cost meant that the newspaper proprietors just published the news and we poor paper boys weren't crippled with the weight of our bags. They were heavy I remember because as the bags we carried got older the straps became thinner and really cut into you. I didn't have a bike either so it was a long slow walk for me.

Newspapers were an essential item in most households and the saving in weight to the paper boy compared to today's journals was made up for by the volumes.

As well as there being more newspapers in those days – I mean more titles – I think circulations were higher. People couldn't bear to be without a paper because without TV it was their main way of getting the news. I can't really remember but I think I got about ten shillings a week! There were quite a few little old ladies living on their own in awful dirty freezing houses who could hardly afford heating but they'd never miss their paper. And of course the newspapers could be recycled. Everyone used them to light their fires and many cut them up to hang in the loo!

"... newspapers could be recycled. Everyone used them to light their fires and many cut them up to hang in the loo!"

The best bit of my paper round was when I got home and my mum always had a mug of very hot sweet tea for me or sometimes Bovril. Funny time to have Bovril I know but nothing since has ever tasted as good. She was very good in other ways too – she worked full time in a factory but was my alarm clock. She was the one who woke me at six!

I did it every day – seven days a week for more than two years and it was great to be able to buy things with my own money. I remember I bought a gyroscope – a wonderful thing that I still have today. I also bought American comics that were

The meaning of the word
The slapstick and juvenile humour of the *Beano* and the *Dandy* set the definition of 'comic' in the postwar period. At their height they were selling two million copies a week. Before the 1950s adventure in comics was generally confined to boys' "story papers", which were the illustrated text narratives such as *Rover* and *Wizard* that had emerged in the interwar years.

just coming over as well as the *Eagle* and second-hand copies of the Biggles books. Wonderful stuff."

Deep in London's Metroland Mark Greenway recalls summer mornings on his paper round.

"I didn't mind getting up at all. I always volunteered for the biggest round. I cycled miles but found a way to strap my newspaper bag on the pannier at the back so I didn't have the thing dragging round my neck – my dad rigged up a long piece of elastic with a hook on the end. I used to spy out places to fish and sneak into the grounds of old houses out towards Pinner where there were still odd farms and old houses. I loved it – so much so in fact that I sometimes went off into a dream and took too long over the deliveries. The newspaper shop owner used to give me a terrific telling off!

In winter it wasn't so much fun but I got paid well and saved up for all sorts of marvellous things. I was the only boy in my school who had a telescope."

Pocket money and treats

With sweets rationed throughout the war and afterwards, treats for many children were something they could only dream about. It wasn't until 1953 that sugar became freely available again and sweets were suddenly available if you had the money to buy them – though such was the rush that many shops sold out almost immediately.

The nation's teeth might have benefited from the lack of sticky treats but that cut no ice with millions of youngsters, as Rose Plummer recalls.

"We could never get sweets for the kids during the war but we'd give them a

Sweets off the ration
Food minister Gwilym Lloyd-George made de-rationing a priority for his Department. As well as sweets, he took eggs, cream, butter, cheese, margarine and cooking fats off the ration books. Sugar was de-rationed in September 1953, mainly as a result of pressure from sweet manufacturers, and was celebrated in a similar way by children across the country, as seen below.

spoon of honey now and then if we could get it and after the war it wasn't much better. But what you don't have you don't miss – it was the same with bananas. No child born in the 1940s in England had ever seen one, let alone eaten one, so they could only imagine what they tasted like. When sweets came back on the ration in 1953 there was a bit of a stampede. People got so excited about it – adults more than children, because they remembered what it was like to be able to buy a packet of sweets before the war. But sweets were the main reason kids started to demand pocket money – at last they had something to spend it on. I gave mine four or six pence each, which was enough for a couple of bags of sweets or a comic or two. Oddly in those days we must have known they were terrible for kids' teeth but no one seemed to mind. Maybe because most adults lost their teeth early and expected their kids to lose theirs early too!"

"All the sweets were in huge identical-sized glass jars lined up on wooden shelves ..."

The sweet shop of the 1950s offered a very different buying experience to the banks of branded bars and packets that modern children are faced with.

"I remember our local sweet shop – it was run by a very elderly lady who always seemed to be in a bad mood and hardly spoke to you when you went in. All the sweets were in huge identical-sized glass jars lined up on old wooden shelves behind her. We'd usually buy a two ounces-worth, which was quite a lot. She'd weigh them in an old-fashioned scale where she'd put a two-ounce weight on one side and add sweets to the paper bag resting on the other side until it balanced out. I think it cost about three pence for two ounces of sherbet lemons. These were rock-hard boiled sweets that you sucked until you reached the sherbet in the middle. Delicious, but heaven knows what they did to our teeth!

Other treats the kids looked forward to each week were comics – they loved *Eagle*, *Hotspur* and the *Beano* – the *Beano* was the one comic my children preferred to sweets!"

Games and street games

After the war and well into the 1950s most parents took a relaxed attitude to their children playing in the roads around where they lived. There was as yet little fear of abduction by strangers, and there were so few cars about that most kids, even in city centres, were able to play in the street quite safely.

They played football, cricket and some rather more unusual games, as Kevin O'Brien recalls from his early days in Liverpool.

"We used to play a game called Knock Down Ginger. I've no idea how it got that name but you'd knock on someone's door

Feeding the eyes
The advent of television marketing saw the rise in popularity of branded sweets, such as Trebor, Mars and the legendary Spangles. Prewar favourites, such as toffees, aniseed balls and barley sugars were still popular, however, and would still be served from the iconic tall glass jars (above).

and then run away and hide. It sounds so stupid but at the time we thought it was hilarious. Best of all I loved playing football – except we played with a small hard rubber ball or a tennis ball because no one could afford a real leather football. They cost a fortune and cheap plastic and rubber hadn't come in yet. Once you could play well with a tiny ball it was easy playing with a full-size ball though I didn't have one till I left school and got a job.

What I most remember about those times is that we had a lot of fun – you could play in the street all day as there were so few cars in our part of the world. A lot more down south in London probably, but no one we knew could afford a car."

Ian Smart recalls street games in East London.

"We used to play flick-ups with flattened milk bottle tops (nearest to the wall was the winner), or cricket using a plank and a wicket chalked on a wall, and best of all we used to tie ropes to the top of a lamppost and have huge amounts of fun turning it into our own merry-go-round – you grabbed a rope, ran and jumped and swung round the lamppost. My dad bolted a swivel to the top of one lamppost so when we swung we kept going round and round without the rope getting shorter with every turn.

We also collected cigarette cards and flicked them up again the wall – nearest the wall won the cards thrown in that round."

National vitality
In the aftermath of the World War II experiments in free play sprang up across Britain. Play provision was at the centre of planning for new towns, on the bombsites, and in the streets and school playgrounds. The image of children at play became a symbol of a new world in the making. Even public health campaigns to combat tuberculosis and rickets in Britain's airless slums used the image of children at play as a symbol of national vitality.

GO-KARTING

John Rogan remembers a rather more dangerous street game.

> "Every kid back then wanted to make a go-kart. The Thames used to be full of rubbish so in the holidays we'd go down at low tide and search the banks for old wheels at Lambeth and Vauxhall. The best sort were the great big wheels you got on the back of old-fashioned prams. Once you had those you got a builder's plank about five feet long and bolted it to the wheel's axle. You then got a small set of wheels for the front – usually from a child's pushchair – and bolted the other end of the plank to that with a central bolt so the wheels would turn but you could also steer. Two bits of rope were used to steer. Me and my mates had more fun with that old go-kart than I've ever had in my life with anything else. I still miss it today!"

"We used to tie ropes to the top of the wall and have huge amounts of fun turning it into our merry-go-round ..."

Protective middle-class parents, however, usually denied their children such freedom. Tom Phillips has very different memories.

> "Good God, we were never allowed to play in the street. My mother would have thought that dreadfully common but we looked with envy at the kids who were allowed out. We learned to play cricket and football only at school. At home we played snakes and ladders, Ludo and later on Monopoly. The street, I'm sorry to say, was for the rough boys."

Parties and celebrations

Huge numbers of street parties were organised to celebrate the end of the war. Apart from the sheer relief that the world – or at least Europe – was at peace, there was a need among ordinary people simply to enjoy themselves, as Rose Plummer recalls:

> "Lots of roads round us were closed for celebrations after we heard the news that the war was over – it was amazing how people came together and even very small kids who couldn't have understood what was going on were really electrified by the atmosphere. It's the atmosphere that I really remember because the food at the street parties was nothing to write home about because food and drink were in such short supply. But on the other hand we were really good at making the best of things. I remember giant piles of potatoes, egg and ham pies that were made mostly of bacon fat that had been grated to make it nicer. Custard puddings too that I'm pretty sure had been sweetened with apple juice. After rationing I remember trying bought custard and thinking how incredibly sweet it was."

In the West Country David Westall recalls how even quieter celebrations within the family would take on a patriotic aspect.

"My parents still drank to the King and Queen! They also celebrated their wedding anniversary in gin, and our birthdays. We were allowed to have six friends to the house for tea – bread and butter, home-made cakes and apple pie – I've never had apple pie as good since, and the recipe died with my mother."

The limited resources available meant that thrift and ingenuity went hand-in-hand to produce a feast, as Mark Greenway's abiding memory of birthday celebrations shows:

"We always had bread and butter pudding – thick and brown and greasy with lots of dried fruit; it weighed a ton! My mum used to make it out of old bits of stale white bread and looking back I think it was a miracle how she did it. The problem was that she worried so much that we ate too much on our birthdays that next day we'd have to have cod liver oil. Why she thought that was the right thing to have after eating a lot has always baffled me. But cod liver oil was seen as being good for everything back then."

Large employers would throw Christmas parties for their workers and other local children. London train driver Reg Coote remembers how he would get together with other friends in the railwaymen's union to organise parties for children at Christmas.

"We used to organise dinner dances and a big kids' party every Christmas because a lot of these kids were from very poor homes and they didn't get birthday parties at home because there was no money. A lot of kids turned up in rags.

The children's party was held in a big listed building in Vauxhall in Central London – the Brunswick Building, which is still there. I can remember carting hundreds of party hats and jellies around the streets of South London in a mate's old car and being terrified we might squash everything before we got there!"

Teenage kicks

Despite being on the winning side in World War II Britain had to reconcile itself to a dramatic loss of influence on the world stage as the end of hostilities coincided with the final collapse of most of the old Empire. What's more, Britain was virtually bankrupt. Morale was low despite the initial euphoria that

Partytime
From VE Day parties went on throughout the summer of 1945. For many children who'd learnt to go without it was probably the first real party they had ever experienced. VE night was also the first time children had been able to light bonfires since 1939, because of air raid precautions.

Christmas crackers
With rationing still rife, Christmas crackers were an expensive luxury that few could readily afford. They were sparingly decorated, with little description and only a few illustrations and would cost around 8s 6d. However, a box of crackers could guarantee "a snap, two novelties and a motto".

"We loved all the new films coming from America because they had new music, which was so exciting."

Dare to be fashionable
The epitome of Rock and Roll and fashion clothing, the teddy boy subculture was so called as a result of the Edwardian-inspired clothing that they favoured. Teddy boys (above) represented a generation and a youth culture with a disposable income that was the first to be heavily influenced by music (right). It encouraged individual, less formal fashion, rather than the same jacket and tie combination that people had been wearing for years.

greeted VE Day. The Establishment was seen by many as having failed. With the country down in the dumps young people began to reject the values of their parents' generation and they looked to the new superpower, the United States, as Amy Capper recalls.

"Even in Newcastle upon Tyne back then we were fascinated by all things American. During the war young boys admired the GIs we saw all over the place and because they came from a country where soap and stockings weren't rationed the teenage girls couldn't get enough of them. We loved all the new films coming from America because they had new music, which was so exciting. We loved rock and roll I think at least partly because our parents hated it."

American films and music introduced British teenagers to a new type of screen anti-hero – tortured, volatile yet sensitive. It was the era of rebellious young stars like Marlon Brando and James Dean, and many young people found them irresistibly attractive. David Westall recalls the appeal of the new youth culture.

"I can remember seeing James Dean in *Rebel Without a Cause* in the mid 1950s and it was a revelation because it was the first time a teenage hero who was surly and troubled had been seen in a film. Everyone identified with him and all the girls were in love with him. I can remember how we all had quiffed haircuts and leather jackets within a few years and we all copied that ultra-cool surly look. This was a bit before Mods and Rockers, which didn't really get going till the end of the 1950s and early 1960s, by which time I had a job and had sort of grown out of it."

FORMICA, GLASS AND CHROME

Young women also succumbed to the dangerous charm of American pop idols. Lisa Edwards recalls her teenage years.

"It's the milk bars where we all used to hang out that I remember – there's still a classic 1950s one in Islington near the Green and it hasn't changed a bit. They were all chrome and glass and Formica. We used to just meet our friends there and

Female 'teds'
The teddy girls were the first British female youth tribe. They dressed in fastidious oufits taken from the fashion houses of the time, which had launched haute-couture clothing lines recalling the Edwardian era.

Milk bars
The 1950s milk bar was seen as a foreign invasion, a mixture of American kitsch and continental pretence. The Festival of Britain encouraged the building of milk bars for their teenage clientele. The Moka on Frith Street, London's first milk bar, was opened by Gina Lollobrigida in 1953 and within months it had inspired a space-age recess on every British high street.

talk, which was something new. We loved Jerry Lee Lewis, Bill Hayley and of course Elvis Presley. You can't imagine the excitement there was when *Rock Around the Clock* came out. It was like nothing else we'd ever heard. The big band sound seemed like old people's music after that.

I remember too the first time I had a ride on the back of an old motorbike behind my then boyfriend. It was the most exciting thing that had ever happened to me. My parents hated it all."

Gwen Morgan recalls the clothes worn by these new rebellious youngsters.

"Well, there were those who liked what we called the Marlon Brando look – greased-back hair and leather clothes. Then there were the preppie types: very neat and tidy with smart jackets, but both styles came from America. Girls wore full or circular skirts pushed out with net petticoats or they wore neat pleated skirts, and everyone wanted them made in Terylene, the first manmade fibre. Now people only want natural fibres!

We girls also wore scoop-neck shirts or tight polo necks with knotted scarves

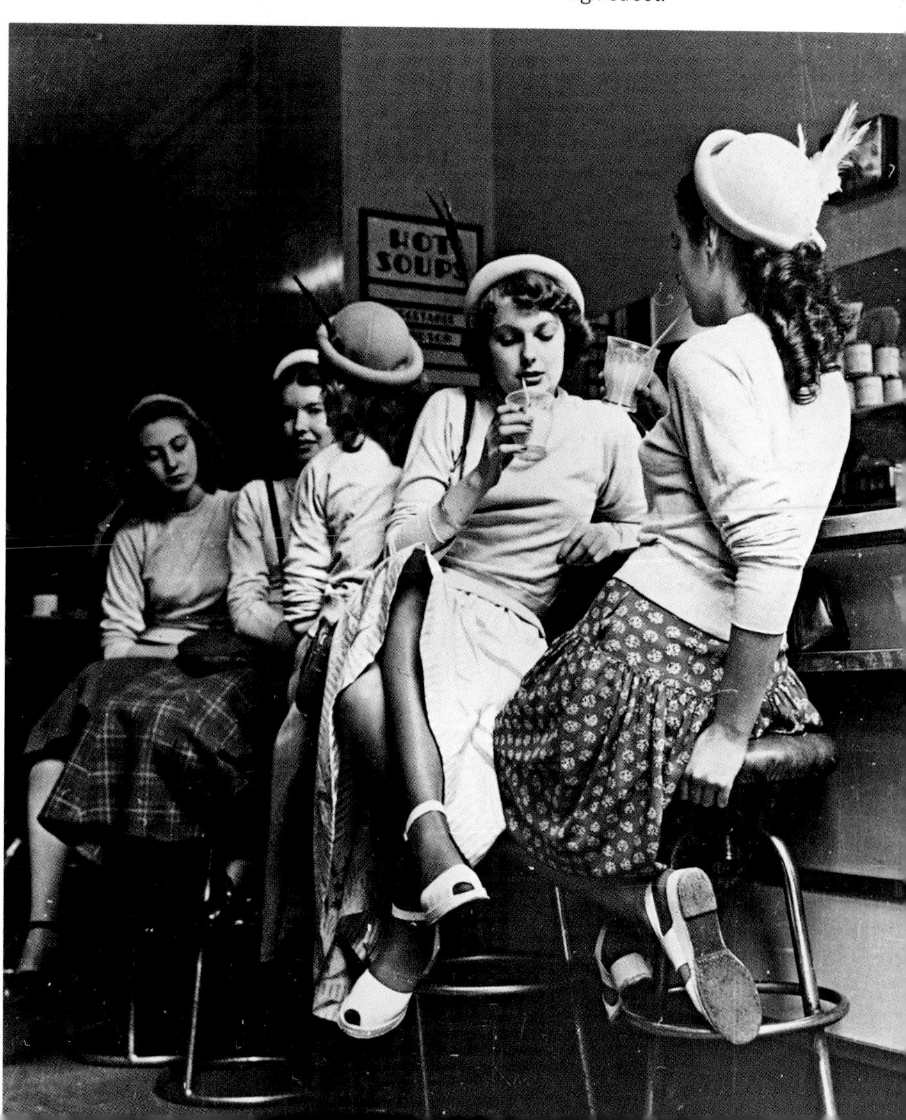

Undergraduates
Numbers at universities increased from 50,000 at the end of World War II to 80,000 at the start of the 1950s. Greater financial provision was made for students from poor, working class backgrounds, making higher education a possibility for more of the population. However, the syllabuses remained largely unchanged despite the increase, and funding for the institutions was poor and sporadic.

round our necks. We loved it because it was our look and defined us as young – just like youngsters wearing jeans and hoodies now!"

University and apprenticeships

Less than one per cent of teenagers went to university in the period after the end of the war and well into the 1950s. This was partly because there were so few universities anyway and partly because there was as yet no grant system. Oxford, Cambridge, London and a few major cities including Newcastle and Reading had universities (the so-called redbrick universities), but without financial help few young people could afford those extra years beyond the age of 18. An additional factor was that the most famous universities had a deeply unquestioned tradition of accepting boys from certain kinds of school regardless of their ability. For girls the situation was even more restrictive, as Pam Tarlton recalls.

"I desperately wanted to go to university and I was certainly bright enough. My A levels were excellent and I'd been to what was then the best-known girls' public school in the country – Cheltenham Ladies' College. When I started to look around I was horrified to discover that women had only been admitted to Cambridge University in 1947. Before that they could only attend lectures after asking permission and they could not take degrees. It made my blood boil. What on earth was the point, I thought, of having a women's college – Newnham was founded in 1880 – if women were not allowed to take degrees? Mind you, it made it easier to bear when I was told by my father that I would have to get a job instead. I ended up working for MI5, which was great fun!"

While an Oxbridge education may have been denied to all but the children of the

"I was ten minutes late for work, lost half an hour's pay and was fined 10 shillings."

Establishment, the redbrick universities offered their own brand of privilege to those with sufficient financial resources.

John Quinn remembers Manchester University in the postwar years.

"I was one of those reasonably bright grammar school boys who were good at science and got in that way. There was never a hint that we should apply to Oxford or Cambridge because the perception then was that your chances of getting in had much more to do with background than ability. I can remember that was still true in the 1970s when Prince Charles went to Cambridge with very average A level grades and I don't think anyone would pretend that his position in society had nothing to do with it!

Manchester was really fun though – we smoked pipes and wore tweed jackets with patches on the elbows and thought that we were very superior!"

However, for the vast bulk of people the only alternative to university for the reasonably bright was an apprenticeship, and among the biggest employers of apprentices from one end of the country to the other were the railways. Richard Hardy began his career after the war.

"I went straight into a job as an apprentice at Doncaster, making motion pins and bolts on a lathe. I did my practical work, on the lathe, during the day – and they were very long days I can tell you for all apprentices – and I was expected to do my theory at home at night. You were only paid when you came to work – no salaries, and being late was a serious matter. During my apprenticeship I was late once. I was going to work on my bike at 3am one moonlit Sunday morning when a policeman stopped me for not having a light – I was 10 minutes late for work, lost half an hour's pay and was fined 10 shillings. That's how strict it was and it was the same whichever trade you were apprenticed to."

Vocational careers
Apprenticeships were generally relied upon to ensure that the country's workforce was skilled and trained. However, three quarters of young people entering the workforce in 1950 were doing so in unskilled industries. Education provision had to adapt to match the changing face of the economy and the country's industry, and so it was the universities that were turned to in order to provide the skills and training required.

TOY REVOLUTION

The changing world of childhood

In country districts and indeed in many towns and cities children traditionally made do with hand-me-down toys that were often home made. But as the austerity years came to an end, toy manufacturers saw the potential of a new and growing prosperity. Wooden dolls and wooden trains gave way to Barbies and Hornby electric train sets; Airfix launched the first of its glue-together models. The toy market was born and it has been growing ever since.

Wooden toys
Toymaking during the war had ground almost to a standstill as factories and materials were turned to the war effort. Production resumed with fervour in the late forties, and the technological advances made during the war were put to use. Despite their durability, the days were numbered for wooden and homemade contraptions.

Miniature houses
Germany was traditionally the main producer of dolls houses and miniature furniture, but export restrictions over both world wars opened the market for other manufacturers. Wartime production advances led to postwar mass manufacture of cheap, sheet metal houses that were simply painted and furnished, enabling more children to own their own miniature house.

I want one of those
From small-scale comb production to injection moulded toy kits, Airfix were the pioneers of plastic model making. A commission to create a Ferguson tractor kit as a promotional item in 1948 paved the way for the Spitfire, the first of many model aircraft in 1953.

Educational toys
Before restrictions on raw materials were lifted, toy production tended to just be printed board games, such as ludo, snakes and ladders or Magic Robot. Board games were quick to make and cheap to buy.

Novelty characters
Doll manufacturers started using celluloid in the 1860s, but by the 1950s vinyl became more popular. It was a safer material, which didn't melt or fade in sunlight. Demand for novelty dolls increased during this period due to the rise of television, cartoon and film characters.

Britain Can Make It
The Victoria and Albert Museum staged the 'Britain Can Make It' exhibition in September 1946, which included toys. The export market for children's toys played a vital role in rebuilding Britain's economy in the postwar years.

Overworked and underpaid

THE WORLD OF WORK

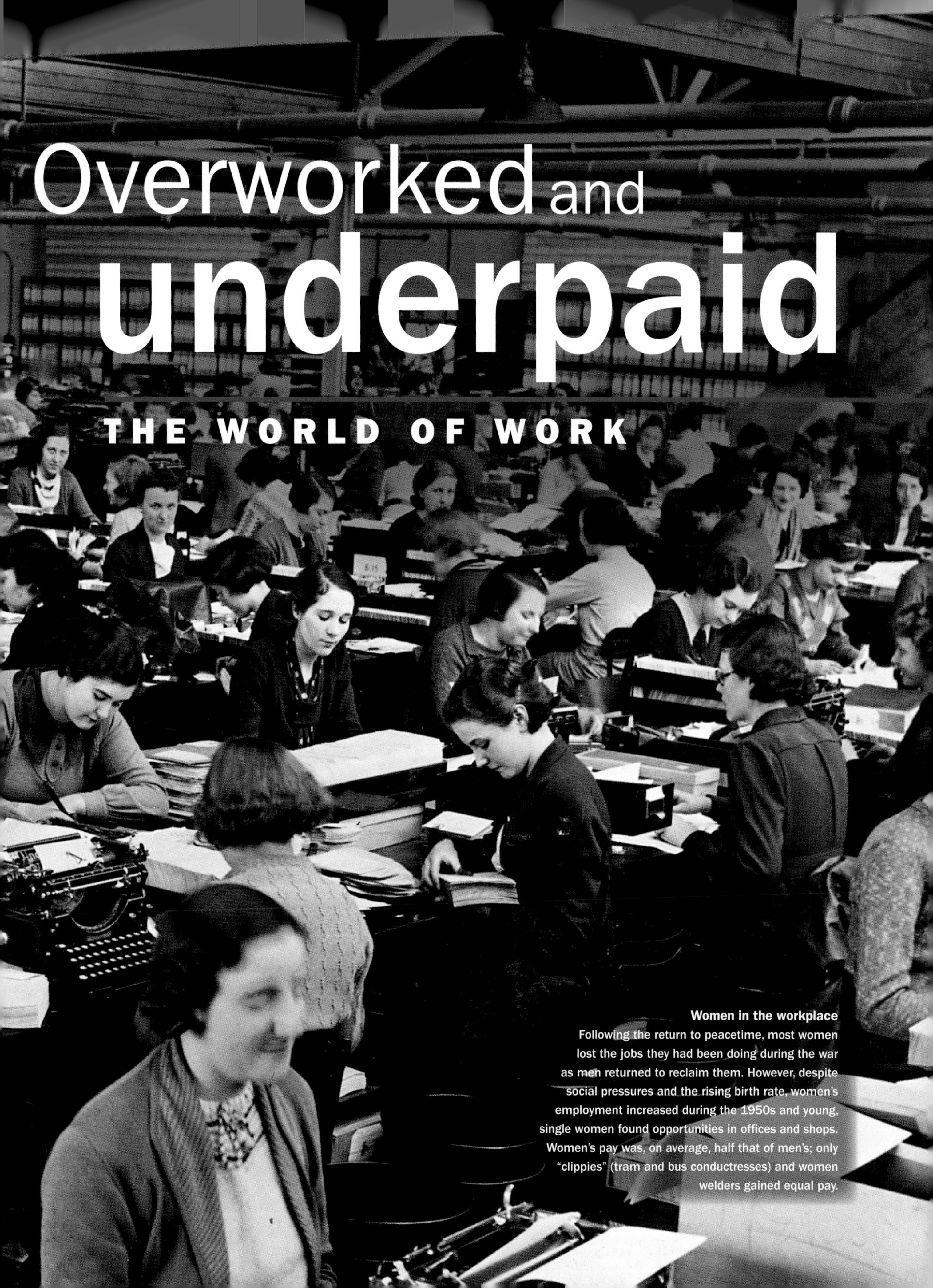

Women in the workplace
Following the return to peacetime, most women lost the jobs they had been doing during the war as men returned to reclaim them. However, despite social pressures and the rising birth rate, women's employment increased during the 1950s and young, single women found opportunities in offices and shops. Women's pay was, on average, half that of men's; only "clippies" (tram and bus conductresses) and women welders gained equal pay.

Work was never the same again after the war. Sons still followed their fathers into traditional trades but less often than in earlier times, and the trades themselves – from wheelwright to panel beater – were already under threat from mass production. Regional accents began to be heard in the Stock Exchange and even at the BBC. There was a mass exodus from domestic service. Trade unions became more powerful as factory production rose; the rich found themselves heavily taxed and politically marginalised. It was the beginning of the age of the common man.

Industry and factory work

For a decade and more after World War II ended Britain struggled financially. Life was tough for British workers: conditions in the workplace were often poor, wages were low and working hours long by the standards of more recent times, as Nick Richards recalls.

"I worked in a factory in West London making bread and cakes. I used to cycle three miles to work leaving home at 6am and working till 6pm. Employers were crafty in those days. They set basic hours at around 40 a week but you couldn't live on the money you earned in 40 hours so we all did lots of overtime. You did earn more for each extra hour – the famous time-and-a-half or double time – but it meant long days. And of course everyone, or almost everyone, worked on Saturday mornings as standard. I can remember the relief when the bell went at 1pm on Saturday because I had the prospect of a bit of free time and a sleep-in on Sunday. But even with lots of overtime, Saturday working and long hours I never earned enough to buy my own house or even a car. Factory work was very badly paid unless you had a strong union. Without a union you were treated very badly because employers had all the power.

Anyone who thinks unions are a bad thing should go back to the 1940s and 1950s when an employer could fire you just if he fancied it and could pay rates as low as he liked. Like a lot of the worst Victorian mine and factory owners the man who owned the factory I worked in was very religious. It always struck me as odd that he could squeeze his employees as hard as possible and then go off to church on Sundays with a clear conscience.

There was no health and safety either – even a bread factory was very dirty, very dusty and very noisy, with wires hanging from the ceiling and mice everywhere, but the bread was at least made fresh every day and people would queue each day outside to buy it, although of course we also delivered across London. I knew men who worked with me who remembered when the deliveries were by horse and cart. We supplied Lyons' Tea Shops with bread and cakes too, and the ABC, both of which have gone now. I remember being amazed when I discovered that ABC meant Aerated Bread Company!"

Transport was one of the biggest employers, and central to all transport after the war and until well into the 1960s were the railways. Dick Potts remembers working as an engine cleaner in Birmingham.

Snack food
By the time that biscuits came off ration points the cost between quality and cheap manufacture had narrowed owing to the introduction of automatic machinery, as seen in the Glengarry Bakery, Glasgow, 1955 (left). The changes in consumer habits by the 1950s meant that more snacks were being consumed between meals.

Jobs for all
Boom times for British industry ensured that the 20.3 million people in employment were likely to stay that way. For example, Kilmarnock in Scotland was home to over five different industries, including a whisky distillery, as well as heavier industry, (as shown above) in 1955. Unemployment rates were so low that Britain was enjoying an unexpected but welcome affluence, and seemed in good stead to withstand any future economic slumps.

"When we cleaned the biggest fireboxes on the old steam locos – and that was most of our job because there were a lot of locos – we used to have to climb inside them! They might be 10 feet long on a really big engine. Working inside was more thorough and when you're young you don't worry so much about the safety angle. We'd be in there bent double and raking the filthy ash down into the ashpan and brushing off all the barnacles. You were continually breathing clouds of dirt. The dust and heat were incredible and you were always told when you climbed out of a firebox that you should stay still for a few minutes while you cooled down, otherwise you'd faint!

We heard stories – and I'm pretty sure they were accurate – of men going into the firebox while the fire was still burning. I wonder what the health and safety people would have to say about that today!"

"You were continually breathing clouds of dirt. The dust and heat were incredible ..."

THE PRICE OF EQUALITY

Factory work could be equally gruelling. Rose Plummer recalls making components for telephones in a London factory:

"We used to make all the old mechanical bits and pieces that modern phones just don't need. I only worked there for a while because I hated it. All day we did the same repetitive task – putting little brass rings on the ends of ceramic widgets. To this day I still don't know exactly what they did in phones – some sort of conductor I think! We started at 8am and finished at 5pm so it was a long day, and all that for just a few pounds. A lot of men did the same work and were paid half as much again as we were. We didn't complain because everyone in those days – women and men – just accepted that women were less able and therefore deserved less pay just because they were women. If you could have shown that we did as much work and the quality was better they'd have still paid us less. One thing it was better than was domestic service, because at least they treated you as if you existed!"

Office life

It's only comparatively recently that offices began to be designed specifically for the purpose. Journalists and civil servants, local government workers, doctors and accountants – all who were at work in the 1940s and 1950s remember offices heated by coal fires and fitted out with the sort of furniture that might equally be found at home.

White-collar work was seen as decidedly superior to blue-collar work; one used brawn, the other brain. Near the top of the office-work social ladder, working for MI5, Pam Tarlton recalls the sort of job a well-brought-up girl could expect.

"I can't tell you too much because I signed the Official Secrets Act, but I worked at Blenheim Palace during and after the war in a set of temporary huts put up in the courtyard at the front of the palace. It was all about taking dictation and endless typing but there was a great sense of camaraderie among the girls. We had to be very smart each day – white gloves, suits and white shirts, but the huts we worked in were freezing because they were only heated by old and very inefficient oil stoves.

We were called girls by all the men and no one thought of objecting, although I know that's frowned on now. The idea

The role of women

The range of jobs available to women may have been expanded during the first half of the century, but the work they actually did was still largely gender-determined. Teachers, nurses, secretaries, waitresses, shop assistants, barmaids and textile-factory hands were typical female members of the work force as their aspirations and awareness of inequality grew.

No place for a woman
After the war women were encouraged to get back to secretarial work or running the home. Despite staffing the toolroom during the contingency of war their presence was no longer acceptable, and management would ensure that women were wholly excluded from the traditionally male-dominated industries such as banking and engineering.

that we might ever have been promoted beyond the typing pool would have seemed less likely than a Martian arriving. We knew it was impossible and the men would have thought we were mad even to suggest it. The unspoken assumption was that we would work for a bit and then leave to get married. Girls back then were thought to be inherently giggly and silly and lightweight. But I knew the real truth when I realised that most of the bigwigs in their pinstripe suits didn't have the brains to learn how to use a Remington typewriter, let alone the Pitman shorthand we had to use. Most of the girls were brilliant at it and it was difficult to learn. The idea that these overweight old colonels could learn it was laughable."

HOT OFF THE PRESS

Patrick Hamilton recalls the very male atmosphere of a London newspaper office.

"We worked in an upstairs room in an 18th century house just off Fleet Street. I was a sub-editor. The house was pretty unchanged from when it was used by a family – all the fireplaces were still there and we used them in winter. I can remember coal being carried up the stairs. I had a big old black Imperial typewriter made in the 1930s; there were hunting prints on the wall, old rugs on the floor. We all had Parker fountain pens and no one had heard of biros! The floors creaked, plaster was crumbling off the walls and there were mahogany seats in the loos! It looked like a gentleman's club and the pace of work was similarly old-fashioned. We arrived at 10am and usually finished about 4pm, but standards were high. We were never, for example, allowed to leave split infinitives in articles and I see these all the time even in *The Times* these days."

"We had to be very smart each day – white gloves, suits and white shirts ..."

Trades and crafts

In town and country many ancient trades – from clockmaker to coppicer – were carried on through the late 1940s and 1950s, but they were already in decline as plastics and other cheap materials made their more expensive products uneconomic. By the mid 1960s most of the old trades had gone. John Brooker made and repaired fans, as he explains:

> "The fan disappeared because women started to smoke. I know that sounds rather surprising, but I'm sure it's true. Right up to the 1920s every woman had a fan – from printed paper fans for the less well off to incredibly expensive ivory and mother-of-pearl fans for the rich. Once the flapper girls came in fans must have seemed a very old-fashioned encumbrance when you could be rather racy and have a cigarette in your hand instead. But I was still making and repairing fans in London after the war and into the 1950s. The French firm Duvellerois was I believe the last to go. They had a shop in Regent Street until about 1963. I used to make fans in a tiny workshop with an open fire and most of the work came from elderly women who would have grown up in the early 1900s and they were so used to having a fan that they never quite lost the habit, which just about kept me in business."

Kathleen Clifford worked in another dying but nonetheless fascinating trade: legal wig making. For decades she made wigs for the ancient London firm of Ede and Ravenscroft in a tradition that went back centuries:

Gentlemen of the press
Fleet Street, the traditional home of the British newspaper industry, was a largely male-dominated environment and journalism was pursued with a paper and pen (as shown left at the *News of the World* in 1953).

"I started as a girl of 15 and never worked anywhere else. We were one of the last legal wig makers left in the world. There were four of us making something like one thousand barristers' wigs a year, about 120 bench wigs (a judge's working wig) and about 100 full-bottomed wigs (worn at ceremonial occasions and only by judges).

The wigs were all made on wooden head-shaped blocks – many were more than a century old. Outworkers wove the horsehair to begin with and we stitched it on to a silk netting base. It had to be neat with tight curls and with no gaps – not an easy thing when you're working with horsehair, which was curled using old-fashioned curling tongs, which were left on a fire to heat up. Our employers seemed very grand but they were nice enough to us, but it all sounds very Dickensian now!"

Dying trades
Before the war many rural blacksmiths, saddlers and rope-makers had been in the comfortable employ of large country estates, such as this saddler in Wiltshire (below). The drop in social prominence of the estates caused a great many to lose their jobs, as did advances in technology that rendered these skilled craftsmen and their products obsolete.

CONVENTIONAL CRAFTSMEN

Out in the countryside other crafts and trades survived until well into the 1950s. On many farms horses were still commonly used as working animals, although in decreasing numbers, and making the harnesses and tackle for them was the job of skilled specialists. Terry Davis, for example, made horse collars.

"I was trained as a saddler, but got more interested in collars and heavy working horses generally. After my apprenticeship I worked with an old man who'd made collars when working horses could be found on every farm in the country, so I had insider help as it were.

The point is that a horse collar is like a handmade pair of shoes. You can't rush it and each collar is made exactly to the measurements of a particular horse. No collar will fit two different horses,

Clock making
Many clock factories ceased production during the war years as manufacturing materials were limited and skilled craftsmen away fighting. The return to manufacturing marked a dramatic shift in the processes and materials used to make clocks. Wood, significantly cheaper than brass and more readily available, was now widely used to make the movements. Brass, when it was used, was used sparingly.

although a well-made collar will outlive the horse, its owner and probably me too.

But like all individual craftsmen I did the whole job – I bought the leather in, cut it to size, stuffed the straw in, added the attachments and so on. The same was true for village clockmakers, blacksmiths and furniture makers.

When I was young every third village might have a collar maker or saddler, but even by the 1950s it was a dying trade as farms moved to tractors. It was a lovely life though – you needed only a small workshop with your tools and materials and you knew all your customers personally."

"When I was young every third village might have a collar maker or saddler, but even by the 1950s it was a dying trade ..."

On the land

On farms across Britain there was a feeling after the war that agriculture had kept the country going at a time of greatest need. But farms were changing and the pace of change continued through the 1950s and 1960s. Mechanisation and increased use of chemicals soon doubled and then tripled agricultural output.

Reg Dobson recalls working on his parents' Shropshire farm at a time when much of the old agricultural world still remained.

"All I remember is long hours and hard work, freezing weather, filthy mud everywhere. I was expected to work seven days a week from six in the morning till six at night. There were 125 cows to milk by hand every day. We were slaves and it was still an agricultural world that looked like something from the 18th century.

For example, an old man called Punch used to carry off the pails of milk as they were filled. He wore a great wooden yoke, like you'd put on a pair of oxen, and on each side would be suspended the pail.

My happiest memories of all are of ploughing and harvesting – you could talk to the horses as you paced the fields. Far more lonely with a tractor and other modern equipment with its noise and fumes, but that was already coming in even as I learned to drive the horses and carts. And harvest time was like a celebration for us – weather was great, we'd have as much cider as we liked and we'd wait with our guns for the harvest of rabbits that would bolt as the standing corn was gradually cut down."

"... harvest time was like a celebration for us – weather was great, we'd have as much cider as we liked ..."

Blundell Rowley Williams's family had owned land in North Wales for centuries. Their concerns were that their way of life was already fading into history as farming became a far more industrial process.

"Back in the 1950s we could afford to run the farm – employing lots of local people – and simply run things at a distance because, like most gentleman farmers, we had money in the bank and no mortgage. We hunted several days a week in season while the farm looked after itself.

We all rode – it was unthinkable then for a boy or indeed a girl of our social class not to learn to ride because hunting was our social life, largely. All our friends and neighbours hunted. Hunting lay at the

Harvest time
Although the Agriculture Act of 1947 gave farm labourers improved security of tenure and a wages board, the workers of all ages were poorly paid (two-thirds of average manufacturing wages) for punishingly long hours. Some ricks were riddled with vermin and many of the threshing men wore bicycle clips to stop rats and mice from running up their trouser legs. Despite this, most have fond memories of the harvest time in the final glory years before intensive farming took over.

Land girls
The Women's Land Army (WLA) was formed during World War II for women to take up job vacancies when men were away fighting. In 1945 servicemen began to return to Britain but the WLA was still hard at work, ensuring that there was enough food for the country. Their efforts were required for several years once the war had ended, with the women teaching men how to operate the machinery that had been introduced in the years that they had been away.

heart of all our social activities because we had hunt balls and so on. Things had to change after the war and I will admit that we were excited by the arrival of tractors and other mechanical aids in the mid and late 1950s, but pretty soon we missed the horses."

DIG THIS

A major change to the rural landscape came during World War II, with the arrival of the Women's Land Army. These women, drawn from all walks of life, were recruited to fill the jobs of male farmhands who were fighting abroad. Many of them – the Land Girls, as they were called – had no previous experience of agricultural work, which was often gruelling and monotonous, but many enjoyed it, if for no other reason than the camaraderie involved. Sue Moffat, who volunteered to work as a landgirl in Hertfordshire, came to love the new experience.

"Well, girls had never really been allowed to do land work before the war – it was considered too tough and the men would have hated it anyway. But we were just as good if not better. I worked on two farms, endured long days, mucking out pigs, feeding the sheep and helping with lambing and at the harvest. It wasn't difficult to learn but by golly it was hard – 12-hour days were common and you worked seven days a week sometimes. As soon as the war was over of course we all went back to civvy street. I really

"I worked on two farms, endured long days, mucking out pigs, feeding the sheep and helping with lambing ... It wasn't difficult to learn but by golly it was hard ..."

missed it – some of my friends for life were made on those farms. And the freedom of wearing trousers after boring skirts I can't tell you. We used to wear jodhpurs and sometimes overalls. I think the jodhpurs were easier for the men to accept because girls had sometimes worn them for hunting. They were far more shocked by overalls!"

Service of the nation

National Service, in which young men were conscripted to serve in the armed forces for a couple of years, was introduced after the end of World War II and remained in force until 1963, the last men being recruited in 1960. For many of these men it was a defining period: rich and poor alike were taken out of their everyday lives and saw something of the world, an experience that helped change what had been a deeply conservative society.

Paul Cowie remembers being called up in 1952.

"You received a letter through the post, a travel warrant to whichever camp you were being sent to and that was it. If you failed to report for training a few weeks later they'd send the police for you. You could find yourself in the army, navy or air force. I got the navy. You did have some choices though – if you signed up for three years you got a bit more money. If you did the basic two you got paid less. After training, which seemed to me to be all about marching on parade and peeling potatoes, you could be sent anywhere in the world where the British still had territory or interests. Don't let people tell you that the Empire had disappeared by the end of the 1940s. It hadn't. I was sent to Egypt and Malta. It was great making friends and travelling, particularly for someone like me who would never otherwise probably have seen anything of the world, but at the time I couldn't wait for it to end!"

David Rose's military service in the Imperial Airways Marine Service turned out to be the beginnings of a career in the rapidly expanding postwar industry of commercial aviation. He recalls his own experience of it.

"The flying boat service was vital to keep goods, passengers and important letters moving. I jumped at the chance to join the old Imperial Airways Marine Section during the war. The Marine Section was needed to operate the launches used to take departing passengers out to the flying boats and bring the arrivals in. You have to remember that the flying boats were the Jumbo Jets and Airbuses of their day, but they took off and landed about three-quarters of a mile out to sea! At Southampton where I was based the planes took off out in the harbour.

To a large extent only military people and other government officials could afford to fly then but their journeys were important. And it was the same until well into the 1950s – anyone going out to an important government post went via Imperial Airways. All the flying boats were C class in the 1940s when I started work: there were Caledonians, Carpathians and so on.

Flying was expensive but if you needed to fly it was really your only choice – Heathrow and other airports just hadn't been developed yet."

National service lineup
Between 1945 and 1963 2.5 million young men were obligated to do their time in National Service, with 6,000 being called up every fortnight. These teenagers (below) were conscripted for national service at the Royal West Kent Depot for their inoculations in 1954. Initially public opinion was behind the idea of peacetime conscription, and it was clear in the immediate postwar political landscape that Britain had considerable responsibilities but only a limited number of men still in service.

BACK TO SCHOOL

But if air transportation was something new, many professions seemed, after the war, to have changed little in the past hundred years. Teaching, for example, was still based on principles laid down in the 19th century. Margaret Rose qualified as a teacher just after the war and taught for many years in her local junior school.

"The biggest difference back then was that if a child was naughty it was routinely smacked. I know that seems dreadful to many people now but back then no one even questioned it. We used to be kind to the children too, it wasn't all cruelty – we were allowed to hug them if they were upset. Again that's something that was later outlawed, which seems absurd to me.

Schools were very formally run in the 1950s. The headmaster called us by our surnames and attendance at daily assembly

Radical selection
If pupils passed the 11-plus exam they would go to grammar school from which, if they did well, they could expect to go on to a well-paid career. For pupils who failed the 11-plus the good technical colleges and secondary modern schools offered plenty of opportunities, but they were more likely to find themselves in menial and manual jobs.

Physical education
Elementary school physical education in the 1950s advocated the aims of complete education through programmes that emphasised mastery of skills in games, sports, dance and similar activities.

was compulsory. There were no foreign children at all and there was a culture in which boys were expected to be tough and girls were expected to be ladylike.

I later worked in a London school where we had a very nice woman teacher from the Caribbean. It's awful to think of it now but she had a cup kept separately for her tea. Again it was the sort of thing that went unquestioned at the time. The other thing that was sad was that there was no attempt to protect children who were poor – I mean those entitled to free lunches were always made to feel different. At lunchtime they had to file out separately – I'm so glad that sort of thing has been abolished.

On the positive side, that time brings back memories of great politeness and friendship, well-behaved and well-dressed children, inkwells and cold classrooms, the smell of coke – the boilers were fuelled using coke – and a determination that the children would learn at least to read and write well and to do their multiplication tables. We thought the time tables so important, and I still think they are."

Retail

In the late 1940s and early 1950s supermarkets were still something rumoured to exist in the United States. For most of Britain shopping involved a trek from one small specialist shop to another, and with fridges almost unknown we had to shop several times a week for food. Most shops were still family owned and run, although thousands employed extra help. Burton's, for example, had grown from its modest beginnings in 1903 to be the largest multiple tailor in the world by 1952, the year of the death of its founder, Sir Montague Burton.

Eric Gray remembers his experience as a Burton's employee.

"I worked in Burton's back in the 1950s when suits were just starting to be available off the peg. We sold what was called the 50 shilling suit, which is what most people ordered. It was available in a limited range of dark colours and in three weights – heavy for winter, medium and light for summer. My boss who managed the shop had various ways of dealing with customers – he would be incredibly nice and deferential if the person seemed to be

Tailor-made
The public of the late 1940s became resentful and impatient when rationing was not relaxed on clothes – garments were still being made, but were then exported in an effort to rebuild the British textile and wool economy. However, the wealthy still had their uniforms tailored at the best tailors rather than wear standard issue, and *Tailleur Luxe* trade magazine aimed to give general tailors an idea about good fashion lines of the day.

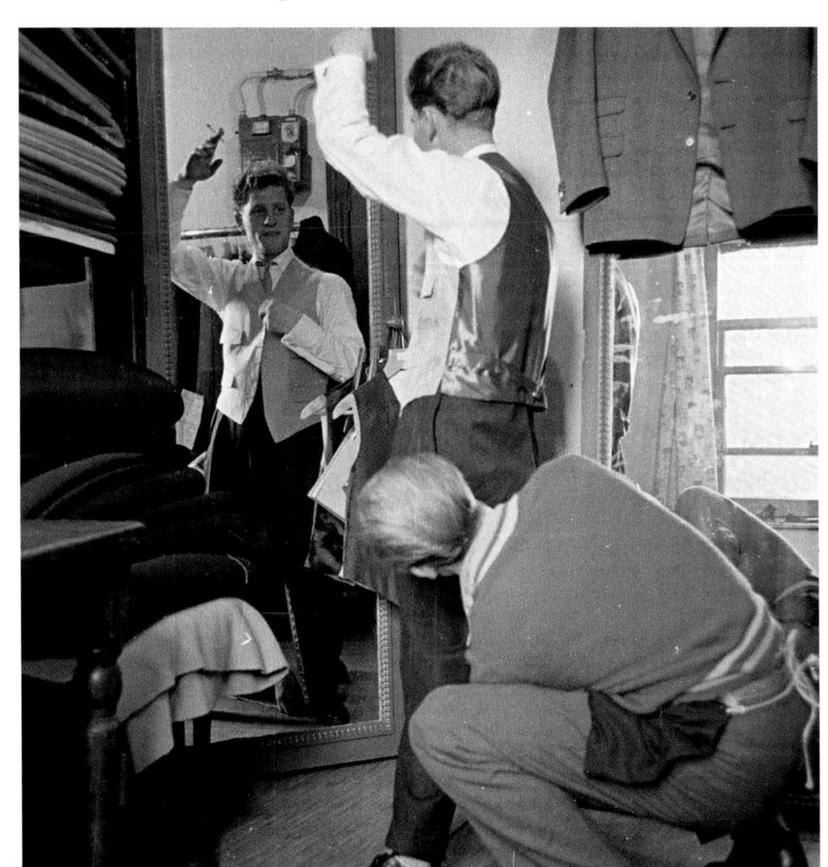

well off and ordered a better-quality suit or several suits; he'd be a bit stiff but polite to the ordinary customer or someone he didn't know, but he could be almost dismissive if he thought it was some poor working man who could only afford one suit. Hard to imagine now, but most people still had their suits made then. The shop workers like me had to be very deferential by today's standards and customers were occasionally rude in a way that is unimaginable today. Shop workers were looked down on by some customers."

THE BIRTH OF THE DEPARTMENT STORE

Whiteley's in Bayswater, west London, was the city's first department store. The original store traded for 118 years, before being closed for refurbishment in 1981. Dorothy Jarvis recalls working there.

"I worked in Whiteley's in west London after the war and it was huge fun – the pay was terrible but the other girls were such a laugh and we were able to dress very smartly every day, which we loved. The store had one of those wonderful paying systems involving hydraulic tubes. You took the customer to a little booth, wrote out a bill, put the bill and the customer's money in a short aluminium container, screwed a top on it and then put it in an overhead tube. A vacuum system then sucked it through half a mile of tubing to the financial office where the bill was logged in, a receipt filled and the customer's change and receipt placed in a return canister. It was incredibly inefficient but I think many shops used it because they didn't trust people on the shop floor with money.

"At one clothing shop that I worked in the owner used to insist on offering tea to every customer."

The design and layout of the shop would seem very old-fashioned now but we thought we had the most glamorous job in the world.

After I married and had children I went back to shop work for a while but it was never the same. At one clothing shop that I worked in the owner used to insist on offering tea to every customer. If you were that nice to them, he used to say, they could never leave the shop without buying something!

My last job back then was in Greggs, which sold eggs and butter and bacon and cheese. It was a beautiful shop – white tiles everywhere and personal service for everyone. You could buy a single slice of ham and no one would bat an eyelid."

Clothing was a big item of expenditure after the war so it's not surprising that there were still huge numbers of small tailors and clothing shops catering for a world that still lacked the sort of cheap high street clothing outlets we take for granted today. Ben Farby recalls what he called the rag trade in East London.

"I came to Britain as a refugee after the war and like many Jews I knew about the rag trade – the clothing industry. I worked in small shops in what was still largely a Jewish East End. Most of our customers were Jewish and we would gossip about the old days and the words you'd hear often came from Central Europe a century earlier. Clothes were *schmutter*, from an old Yiddish word. But all over the East End clothing was the big retail thing – from Petticoat Market to Cohen's Gentleman's Outfitters. In all the shops people would make time to talk. There was no hurry over a fitting, no pressure. That whole world of politeness and buying clothes only when you really needed them has vanished forever."

Self-service
Postwar austerity influenced both consumer tastes and company profits. When Marks and Spencer trialled a self-service format at its store in Wood Green, north London, in 1948, its style and layout was unmistakeably based on an American model, but nevertheless was a great success.

POWER OF THE PEOPLE
Working in the factories

The last great movement of working people from the countryside to the towns took place in the 1950s as higher wages and car ownership made commuting viable. The rich found that they could no longer rely on a supply of cheap labour as factories offered better wages and far better conditions. Work for women expanded hugely and the new factory workers found that they not only helped to make consumer goods, but they also had the money to buy them.

Chocolate factory
Chocolate was regarded as essential nourishment for troops throughout the war, and production was placed under the supervision of the government. New technology postwar improved production speeds in order to meet the insatiable demand for chocolate.

Trade unions

The Communist party, or Reds, which came to the fore in the 1930s, had little success in conventional politics. In the late forties it recruited support through the workplace, infiltrating trade unions and promoting industrial action.

Women in the workforce

The percentage of women in the workforce dropped during the postwar years. This was due to several factors, such as the decline in various female-dominated industries (textiles, for instance) and the baby boom. Many of those still in work turned to secretarial and administrative roles in the growing service sector, leaving manual work free for men.

Disposable income

As employment rates increased, so too did the amount of disposable income. This, along with the rise in available consumer goods and the development of must-have fashion, led to more advertising being aimed at women.

Bank holiday bottleneck

Gridlock on the nation's roads on Bank holidays is not a new phenomenon, but without motorways the postwar boom in car ownership put a particular strain on the country's struggling road network. The quintessential run out to the seaside was further hampered in August 1956 by adverse weather across the South East, which saw heavy rain and hail add to the misery of the journey home, as seen here in Brighton.

Mobilise the nation

GETTING AROUND

For those happy few who could afford a car the postwar roads gave a sense of undiminished freedom; parking was virtually unrestricted in every city and town and freight still went mostly by rail. But even as that car-owning social revolution gathered pace most people still travelled by bus, or train; by bicycle or on foot. In rural districts and even here and there in odd forgotten corners of our major cities horse transport survived for milk deliveries and among the few remaining rag-and-bone men.

Travel promotion
The 1948 nationalisation of the rail network saw the creation of British Transport Films, whose role was to promote the railways as the best means of reaching destinations around the country. This scene from the 1950 film *Party Travel* advocates the railways as the ideal way to travel as a group or family.

Trains

With motorways still a decade and more away, most freight was still carried around Britain in the years after the end of the war using what was, in essence, a Victorian railway system. It might have been old but it was built to last and ensured that the relatively small number of cars on the roads enjoyed a freedom from traffic jams that is unheard of today.

However, as far as passenger transport was concerned, the railways had, by the end of the war, deteriorated markedly in terms of comfort and cleanliness, and this decline continued into the 1950s, as Tom Shackle recalls:

> "The trains were dreary, badly maintained and positively shabby in the years after the war because they had reached their peak of profitability years before, and the owners and shareholders didn't want to spend money cleaning the railways up if it meant lower dividends for them. When British Railways came into existence

things weren't much better. Vested interests among ministers who were often shareholders in the railways ensured that rail owners and shareholders were paid far too much in compensation for a system they had allowed to decay.

I can remember travelling from London to Oxford and though the locomotives pulling our train still had a certain magic the carriages had lumpy dirty seats dating back to the 1930s, the walls and floors of the carriage were grubby and the food at stations was either nonexistent or terrible. You had more space in those days between seats, which was a good thing, and I always rather enjoyed carriages where you sat opposite your fellow passengers with a corridor down one side – the unfairly reviled slam-door carriages. Those old carriages were comfortable and sociable compared to the sardine tins they call carriages now!"

Mark Brown recalls similar levels of service on Birmingham trains.

"My main memory is that the trains were always filled with cigarette smoke. I was a doctor and even I smoked. We really didn't mind the smell but if we went back now we would be appalled, I think. There was a sense of overall dreariness too because the trains were soot-blackened – but then so were most of the houses in Birmingham. They always seemed particularly bad around Birmingham New Street Station. Going by train out towards Wolverhampton and smaller places like Claverley was better as you gradually escaped the grime, but services were often poor because freight had priority after the war, because the country had to be got back on its feet."

THE BIRTH OF BRITISH RAIL

The different regional companies that had been responsible for rail transport in Britain were amalgamated into one organisation, British Railways, in 1948. This brought about huge administrative changes, but Bill Sidwell, who worked on the railways, was little affected at the time. He recalls the moment of nationalisation.

"I was at Gloucester in 1948 when nationalisation came and I can honestly say it made absolutely no difference to me, but on the dot – at midnight on the day it happened – all the trains in the area blew their whistles. I remember my phone ringing at around this time. The caller said that a train had been derailed in the Great Western Region. We were the London and Midland but we had a crane that would be suitable for this particular derailment. When the person on the other end of the line said he wanted the crane he said he wanted it for the British Railways Board – it sounded so strange because it was the first time I'd heard the name."

Rod Lock has similar memories from his time working as a station master in Norfolk, but he also recollects how little things had changed.

"... freight had priority after the war, because the country had to be got back on its feet."

Changing the paintwork
Prior to nationalisation the country's railways had been run by the "Big Four" regional companies – London, Midland and Scottish (LMS), London and North Eastern Railway (LNER), Great Western Railway (GWR) and Southern Railway (SR). All the iconic liveries on freight and passenger trains and locomotives had to be changed to match the new company, (left).

It's quicker by rail
The mood surrounding the railway network post nationalisation was very negative. Standards were down, performance was poor and steam engines and branch lines were proving themselves to be uneconomical. Amidst this climate and crippling underinvestment, tireless advertising campaigns and slogans were launched in a bid to challenge the public's opinion, and convince people that the best and most relaxing way to travel was by rail.

Class travel
Travelling by rail was not a regular occurrence for the working classes, and was generally saved for long distances or holidays. Regular rail travel and commuting was generally the preserve of the middle classes, as with these children returning to boarding school (right). Trainspotting, however, knew no such social boundaries. Train services at weekends and during the holidays would often be full of boys going in search of that elusive engine number.

"The war was a big disruption to the railways, but by the late 1940s and 1950s it was pretty much as it had been in the 1930s. We had our regular passengers but it was never busy and we knew everyone. The trains might have been shabbier but they were still usually on time!

East Winch was a quiet station so far as passengers were concerned, but like every other station in the land it was run according to a long established set of rules, a set of rules that applied in principle whatever the size of the station. It was all about meticulous records and that was true for the mineworkers, dockers, Civil Service and any big organisation you can think of.

"It cost one old penny for a bus ride to Notting Hill Gate from Ladbroke Grove, a journey of about one mile."

I always remember the massive books of commercial instructions we kept in the little stationmaster's office. For example, the coaching arrangements book was like a bible and it provided guidance on just about everything you can imagine. I don't remember referring to it that often, but we always knew that when you did need it, whatever query you had, you would find the answer in there. And that was true even though much of the information it contained dated back half a century or more.

Every week amendments would arrive and I had to paste them into the book. Most of my work was to do with freight and the book listed a number for every possible cargo, from diamonds to coal, and if a new cargo came along it had to be allocated a new classification. The basic rule was the higher the number the more valuable the cargo. Not much in the way of diamonds passed through East Winch, but if they had we knew what to do with them! All government jobs were run like this, whether it was the Civil Service or local government, steel, gas or electricity. We thought meticulous record-keeping was the key to efficiency."

On the buses

Before Mrs Thatcher decided that everyone in Britain should have a car and removed the duty local authorities had to provide buses, the rural bus network was one of the glories of the British countryside. The abolition of this service hastened the departure of the rural population for the nearest town and left many elderly and infirm people stranded in remote villages.

With regard to public transport in towns, the bus had largely taken over from the tram and then as now was a cheap and easy way to get about, as Sheila Kehoe, from London, recalls.

"It cost one old penny for a bus ride to Notting Hill Gate from Ladbroke Grove in west London in the late 1950s, I seem to recall. A journey of about one mile. In those days the Routemaster – the famous red London bus everyone loves today – was a recent arrival and seemed very modern. There was an older bus, probably an earlier version of the Routemaster, that was far more common. Today it would look like a real dinosaur – it had a sort of prominent snub nose that was rounded off more in the later version. But I remember the smell of diesel as the bus laboured slowly up Camden Hill, and it really did labour. Those old engines were reliable but crude. We always tried to sit in the two rows of sideways-facing seats close to the entrance to the bus and downstairs. They were right next to where the conductor stood in his little cubby-hole. As they were

Give way to buses
The bus was the most popular form of transport from 1940 to 1960. Services in London were provided by the London Passenger Transport Board (LPTB), and covered the heart of the city as well as Greater London. The bus network in Greater London was complemented by trams and, later, trolleybus services (buses powered by overhead wires). Together with a British manufacturer, the LPTB designed the RT-Type AEC Regent bus (above), which had an open rear platform and was made with light materials to boost fuel economy. It was this bus that paved the way for the famous Routemaster that still runs today.

closest to the entrance to the bus they were open to the air – it meant you were kept refreshed in summer and you weren't choked with cigarette smoke.

I remember once an elderly woman sat next to me. She wore glasses with blue lenses, and many elderly people did then. She told me she was going to a talk at the National Gallery and that she was 98 years old. I remember being incredibly impressed!"

London and other cities have retained their bus services though prices have increased enormously. In the countryside things were very different. Sheila Kehoe again:

"One of the things we've completely lost are Green Line buses. Back in the 1940s and 1950s as you got out into London's suburbs you'd see lots of bus stops with the familiar London Transport sign but it would be green. This was where the country buses stopped. These single-decker dark green buses brought the countryside much closer for Londoners and it was very sad when they disappeared. Mind you, most of the countryside around London has been spoiled anyway with shopping malls, ring-roads and such like. I can recall getting a Green Line bus out to Cranford near Heathrow Airport and to Yewsley – both seemed timeless and deeply rural but would be unrecognisable now. Conductors – and all buses back then had conductors – had a sort of aluminium machine they carried round their necks like a camera. When you asked for a ticket they adjusted a few buttons to get the right fare and then cranked a handle, which printed your ticket."

"These single-decker dark green buses brought the countryside much closer for Londoners ..."

Getting around
Coach services around London began in 1930 and ran from the capital to towns within a 30-mile radius. Fuel and rubber shortages prevented operation during the war, but services were restored and expanded in 1946. A coach station was built at Poland Street in the heart of the west end to ease the congestion caused by lines of competing coaches waiting around the city. Green Line (pictured below showcasing a brand-new coach) recorded 30 million passengers in 1952.

Dwindling numbers
From the initial influx of the 1930s and 1940s, passenger numbers on the nation's buses started to fall as the motor car rose in prominence and availability, and the choice of leisure activities on offer grew. Birmingham's bus fleet (pictured left) peaked at 1,800 vehicles, but shortages in staff availability meant that not all of its routes could be operated reliably.

CROSS COUNTRY

At this time, when few people owned cars, buses were a vital link between the town and the countryside. Out in deepest Norfolk, Will Constance recalls catching the bus into town during the 1950s.

> "We called it the charabanc then and boy, did it change our lives! In Scole where I lived we'd always moved about by foot or wagon back in the 1920s and even 1930s, and so our expectations were that we would never really go anywhere much. But when the buses started, in the late 1930s I think it was, everything changed – gradually at first but then faster. By the 1950s we had several buses a day, solid old things. Very functional and not much in the way of comfort – too hot in summer and bloody freezing in winter. But they meant my wife could take the children into the town, which was a real treat for them. We'd go in for dances and then catch the last bus home, singing at the top of our voices but never really rowdy. Getting rid of rural buses was the worst thing we ever did because it killed many rural areas."

City trams

Trams hung on in a few cities until the early 1950s, but they were already seen as dinosaurs; less flexible than the new motorbuses, their passing was lamented by few at the time, which is ironic given that they would be ideal in our congested city centres today, and have indeed proved popular in the few areas where they have been re-introduced.

John Quinn has fond memories of Manchester's trams:

> "They were the lifeblood of the city – brightly painted and very efficient because of course they didn't get stuck in the traffic; not that there was much traffic back then. I wasn't at all surprised when a few years ago they decided to bring them back. The rattle of the wheels on the sunken rails was the sound of my

"... our expectations were that we would never really go anywhere much. But when the buses started everything changed ..."

childhood and youth – it was a very distinct sound that modern trams don't have. A sort of unique metallic rattle and clang. The seats on the trams weren't that comfortable and the tram lines were very tricky for cyclists – if your front wheel got stuck in the groove cut for the tram lines you invariably fell off and many of the tramlines were set in old cobbled streets, so it was a very hard fall."

The decline of the tram
With towns and cities expanding as new housing schemes were implemented, the knell started to sound for the tram. With expensive tracks to lay, an increase in car numbers bringing new regulations regarding road width, and a complete lack of flexibility when compared to the bus, the tram was no longer a competitive option.

Riding on the trams was an exciting experience for young people coming into town from the villages. Jim Swire in Sussex recalls going into Brighton to ride the trams.

"Well, it was a bit of fun for us. We'd sit on the top deck and there was no roof so on a summer's day it was as good as a holiday – and cheap too! The seats had backs that could be switched to face either way so when the tram got to the end of the line the conductor went through throwing the seat backs into the opposite position so they were facing the right way for the return journey. The conductor came to you to sell a ticket and he had them ready printed and on a sort of board – he'd just pull off the appropriate ticket and hand it to you.

Trams had advertisements on their sides just like buses. There were plenty of cars in Brighton back then, getting in the tram's way sometimes, but we noticed that even in the 1950s you would still occasionally see deliveries being made by horse and cart."

Brighton roads had lots of cyclists then because people generally couldn't afford cars and cycling wasn't so dangerous as a result.

"The clanging bell of the tram was so evocative – I remember how it took me back when I heard a very similar bell clanging on trams in Holland."

London trams provided similar scope for larking about, as Rose Plummer remembers:

"I remember the Bird's Custard advertisements, the Hovis and Capstan Cigarette ads and the fact that up towards the City you'd occasionally still see men in top hats getting on. We used to hang on to the platform instead of sitting down, which really annoyed the conductor, and to show off the boys would jump off while the tram was still going. Most people welcomed the arrival of buses because we thought they'd be quicker and you tended to accept what you were given – in those days if it was new it was good. But I missed the steady rattle of the old trams and was sad to see them go. They disappeared in 1952 I think but other

Swan song
Birmingham was the fourth-largest tram network in the country, after London, Glasgow and Manchester. At its peak the city had 843 trams running an average of 80 miles a day. Manchester was the first of the cities to surrender to the bus in 1949, with Birmingham following suit in 1953. Glasgow's last tram was a decade later.

WESLEYAN GENERAL
2
tinned Meat
NO ENTRY
THE 616 END

places had them much longer – Glasgow I think till the early 1960s.

One place you can still see about a hundred yards of tram track is at the top of Southampton Row, where a railed-off area in the middle of the road had a slope down into what looks like an underground car park. There's still a bit of tram track on that slope."

Pedal power

When cycling as a practical daily activity got going at the end of the 19th century it attracted the well-to-do because early bicycles were expensive. The poor still walked, but by the 1930s cheaper mass-produced bicycles made cycling available to huge numbers from all social classes. After the war bicycle use increased as you moved down the social scale. At factory closing time right across the country a sea of bicycles would flow out of the factory gates, as Eric Gray remembers:

"I used to cycle about four miles to work on an old three-gear bike I'd inherited from my dad. People who cycled to work – and most of my friends did – rarely worried about what sort of bike they rode. I can't remember a fuss about styles of handlebars or number of gears. A bike was just a bike. It was just a means to an end. Most of us had three-wheel hub gears made by Sturmey-Archer – the derailleur

London A–Z
Since 1851 it has been obligatory for taxi drivers in London to pass the "Knowledge". This involves recall of 25,000 streets within a six-mile radius of Charing Cross station, as well as the locations of other important buildings. Here hopeful cabbies set out on their bicycles from Kennington taxi school in 1947 to familiarise themselves with the city.

gear, which gave you five gears, was hardly seen except among professional or top amateur cyclists. Most bikes were made by BSA in Birmingham. No foreign bikes and certainly no Japanese. We used to read about the old Milk Race – the round-Britain cycling race that tried to rival the Tour de France – but we didn't relate it to our cycling.

I knew men who cycled ten, even 15, miles to work but there were few cars so no one ever thought about the safety angle. No one ever wore helmets. In winter it was terrible – imagine, you had to get on your bike before dawn when there would regularly be three or four degrees of frost and you had to wear your work clothes,

which were not that warm. It was an overcoat at best and a hat; none of the specialist outdoor clothes people have now. I regularly slipped on the ice and went home black and blue. It's a wonder more of us weren't killed."

Cycling proficiency
Bicycles were popular with almost every child as they were cheap to buy and granted unlimited freedom. The first Cycling Proficiency Test was held in 1947 and, for the first time in 21 years, road fatalities dropped. The Government later expanded its cycle training into the National Child Cycling Proficiency Scheme, which was taken by more than 100,000 children.

CYCLE CLUBS

In some areas bicycles were much more than a simple way to get to work. David Westall remembers the craze for cycling clubs:

"Yes, there were loads of them. Down here in the West Country every village seemed to have one. They'd meet every week and have committees and organise tours for members. It was fun because you were with like-minded people, mostly young, and we all fantasised about getting the latest equipment, but a top hand-made bike back then could cost more than a month's wages, so it was always just a fantasy for us.

Mind you, a lot of kids made their own bikes up out of various bits. A friend of mine had a bike he'd made from a frame he found in the Thames. He added drop handlebars from his dad's old bike, the panniers he made himself. Other bits were gradually acquired from cycle shops using his spare cash. We went to the Lake District several times, staying in youth hostels. It was the sense of freedom we loved. We all read *Cycling Weekly*. It's still going and it always had these marvellous illustrations by a man called Frank Patterson – he did drawings of cyclists in Scotland and Wales and they really inspired us to go. Back then there were no foreign holidays and we had so little money that going by bike was the cheapest option. We thought nothing of cycling to Peterborough and back for the day or to Ely and back, but the Great North Road was a small road back then, not the A1M as it later became. We once even cycled to Manchester for the weekend!

After motorways came in the fun went out of it unless you planned your route very carefully. We all bought leather Brooks saddles, which were very expensive, but lasted a lifetime. The idea was that the saddle gradually took the shape of your bottom and once it was worn in like this you always switched it on to the new bike – if you ever got a new bike!"

Easier to walk

Tom Jales lived in Old Street in the City of London after the war and each morning at 4.30 he set off to walk to work at King's Cross Station.

"Most working men walked to work in the 1940s as they'd always walked. Even if you could afford the bus or a bike it was always cheaper to walk and people really did have to watch every penny then.

We lived in an old house off Old Street just outside Moorgate, which is all offices now. I don't recognise any of it and I knew every stone and brick back then because I'd walked it all my early life. Going up towards the Angel even at 4.30am you'd see loads of other men – not the toffs or

"Going up towards the Angel even at 4.30am you'd see loads of other ordinary working men."

On foot

For a decade and more after the war ended nearly 30 per cent of the workforce still got to shop, factory or office by bicycle or on foot, compared to around 16 per cent by car. Good weather, as here on London Bridge c. 1950, always encouraged more people to walk. The average distance travelled to work was four miles, which was a huge increase on the average distance travelled to work at the end of the 19th century, when it was just two miles.

the bowler-hatted office types – but ordinary working men. There were loads of buses, but I saved sixpence a week by walking. Then down Pentonville Road for the last mile to the station. I was glad they kept the Grand Midland Hotel because it was the sight that dominated the view for the half hour it took to walk down to my work."

Norfolk station master Rod Lock recalls how people were perfectly happy to walk to catch a train until the buses came.

"I suppose the real trouble with hundreds of small country stations like ours was that they had been built some way out of the village, perhaps as much as a mile or a mile and a half. In the early days of course no one thought anything of it. The train was the only means of rapid movement and people didn't mind the walk because they had no choice. But once the buses started going right into the village the railways lost passengers – people always go for the softest option and you can't blame them, I suppose."

Dick Potts remembers his father's long journey on foot to work in Birmingham:

"We lived in Small Heath and one of my strongest memories of childhood was my dad getting ready each morning for the long walk to the Tyseley shed.

I must have been about five because although I can't remember much from that time, I can just about recall the trams clanking up and down the road and they'd gone by the time I was six. Each morning my dad used to walk for half an hour along the railway track to get to work at the Tyseley shed. It seems amazing now, but he did that walk every day from 1917 until he retired in 1965 – almost 50 years."

Walking holidays had become a big thing for people from the Midlands and Northern industrial towns since the famous Kinder Scout trespass of 1932, when factory workers from Manchester walked peacefully on to land in the Peak District owned by local aristocrats and kept exclusively for grouse shooting. They were fed up with a world of privilege that gave one man access to tens of thousands of acres and barred everyone else.

John Quinn recollects marvellous days on the moors above his home town:

"Many of us loved to walk on the moors because it was so different from what was still a grimy industrial city – Manchester I mean. The Kinder Scout trespassers were still heroes to the young men of the 1940s and 1950s, and their love of the countryside led to the whole modern movement towards designated walks and more recently the campaign for a general right of access to coastal and other land. With a few exceptions the hugely wealthy landowners still didn't want what they referred to as common people on their land, even though in most cases their ancestors had only got the land by sucking up to some monarch or other. That's how young men on the left thought of it in the 1950s. But by then the National Trust and

Ramblers' Association
When the Ramblers' Association first came into action much of Britain was out of bounds to walkers, but it coaxed and campaigned and achieved a seismic shift in the nation's attitude towards the countryside. The postwar establishment of ten national parks and a "definitive map" to keep areas of Britain "special" ensured a public right-of-way network so that, come rain or shine, people could enjoy a hike.

the Ramblers' Associations had made walking the uplands almost respectable and landowners who'd always tried to keep people off had to make an accommodation with the rest of us."

Motorbiking

The war had widened the horizons of the millions of young men who served abroad during the conflict. Back in civvy street they had no desire to fall back into the tired routines of their parents. As clothes and music began to change, to the horror of an older generation, so too did fashions in transport. And the great symbol of youthful transport in the 1950s was the motorbike, as Kevin O'Brien remembers.

"We loved motorbikes. No girl would be interested in you in the slightest just because you had a bicycle and cars were way too expensive, but motorbikes we could just about manage on our wages. You could get one second-hand for maybe £30 and we all learned how to look after them, so there were no maintenance bills.

All along our street on a Sunday morning you'd see teenagers and blokes in their twenties tinkering with their motorbikes and carefully polishing every bit of chrome. Looking back I realise the bikes were a huge status symbol. Having one put you in a special exclusive club where you just felt great about yourself. It's hard to explain now.

But no one ever thought about buying a foreign bike – in fact we probably couldn't have bought one even if we'd known it existed. Everything we bought back then was British made and the British made a lot of motorbikes – there was BSA, Triumph, Norton and Vincent. At the time me and my mates probably rated the Vincent Black Shadow highest, with the Norton a close second. Nortons became real collectors' items later on. We didn't wear crash helmets and our motorbike heroes were James Dean and sometimes Marlon Brando, but I don't remember anything about Hell's Angels and that kind of thing. That came later from the States.

We used to go off for a ride in the countryside and stop at a bikers' café, which was just a greasy spoon café where we'd all agree to meet and chat before going back. Doesn't sound like much but it was our social life and a great way to get a girlfriend! People who rode motorbikes in those days definitely didn't have the slightly menacing air they acquired later. It was all pretty innocent really."

"... it was lovely to whiz along through the narrow lanes in summer with hardly a car to be seen."

Matchless motorcyles
From 1942 the entire output of the Matchless factory was dedicated to producing the G3/L bike for military service (seen below). Postwar G3/Ls were the military version finished in black instead of khaki and, despite its age, it was so well proven and reliable it was able to stay in use by the Ministry of Defence for another 15 years after the end of the war. It was also a popular choice for British trials riders. After the war there were plenty of bikes and spares available to enable champions such as Artie Ratcliffe and Ted Usher to win numerous national events.

Down in Somerset Harry Horn agrees with that assessment.

"I loved my motorbike but only really because it got me to work effortlessly – it was just a tool that made life easier. It had no Hell's Angels connotations then. No one worried about exercise either.

Family transport
The motorcycle and sidecar combination was a familiar sight on Britain's roads until the 1960s. Many young men saved money and bought themselves a motorcycle so, when they married and had children, fitting a sidecar to the much-loved motorcycle was considered a natural progression.

A bicycle was harder work so people aspired to a motorbike. Once you had that you aspired to a car because it was even more comfortable. But don't run away with the idea that motorbikes were used then as they have been used more recently – they were not just used by young people. Older people used them as family vehicles by getting sidecars, which you never see now. I knew lots of people who had a bike and a sidecar for the wife and child.

I was working at Bishops Lydeard, eight miles from Stogumber where I lived in the old station house, but I did the journey pretty quickly on my motorbike and it was lovely to whiz along through the narrow lanes in summer with hardly a car to be seen. I did it for more than 20 years and it made going to work a pleasure."

"... it was just a tool that made life easier."

Cars for everyone

It seems remarkable now but back in 1948 there were at least 32 different motor car manufacturers in the UK, and at the 1948 Earl's Court Motor Show there were dozens of new British-made models.

Mark Brown remembers the excitement of those years.

"The passion for cars was almost all-consuming. A few doctors in rural districts still got around by bicycle; some, amazingly, still used a pony and trap in deepest Shropshire after the war because cars and fuel were so hard to come by. New cars were an impossible dream. I remember the huge queues at Earl's Court. It was the most exciting event of the decade but there was a drawback even if you had lots of money.

BSA Bantam
The BSA Bantam was one of the definitive postwar British bikes. With over 400,000 built over a 23-year production run, it was also the most popular. In the first four years production broke all records. Thousands of people learnt to ride on a Bantam, or had their first pillion experience on one, or rode one delivering telegrams for the GPO.

Earl's Court Motor Show The motor industry's production was compulsorily reserved for export, and the delivery dates for the home market could be anything from 12 months to two years. Such was the hunger for cars that huge crowds inundated the first postwar Motor Show at Earl's Court (shown right). Over the ten days a total of 562,954 people visited, almost double the previous record.

"... people were prepared almost to bankrupt themselves to get hold of a car ..."

Almost all car production after the war could only go for export. That was the law. It was part of the government's desperate attempt to get the country back on its feet.

So we all stood there looking at these beautiful motor cars, knowing that even if we could afford to buy one there was at least a two-year wait in store for us. But even with those difficulties people were prepared almost to bankrupt themselves to get hold of a car – it was the ultimate status symbol and really did give you freedom. You could park pretty much anywhere free of charge for as long as you liked even in Central London – you could park anywhere in fact because there were no yellow lines and no other restrictions.

I managed to buy a second-hand Morris Minor by 1955, but then I was a relatively well-paid doctor."

British rivalry Historically the great rivalry of the British motor car industry was between Austin and Morris. Between 1946 and 1950, however, their combined market share slipped four points to 39.4 per cent, with Ford emerging as a serious challenger. Austin Motor Works in Birmingham (shown right) had been making cars since 1910, but its solid-looking cars couldn't compete with the sleek saloons coming from other manufacturers.

WOMEN DRIVERS

For women the situation was more difficult, since driving was men's work exclusively. Pam Tarlton remembers the excitement of being allowed to get behind the wheel.

"My father taught me because there were no professional driving instructors and you didn't need a licence then anyway. You just got in and were shown what to do and off you went. There were no safety belts, but the oddest thing of all were the funny little trafficators – to indicate left and right. All cars had these, instead of more modern indicator lights, fitted to the corners of the car. The trafficators were tiny illuminated arms and when you indicated left or right they moved out and up from the side of the car to show which way you intended to go.

We used to start the family car using a crank handle inserted through the radiator at the front because batteries back then were not very powerful, and after a couple of turns if the engine didn't fire up the battery would be too weak to do it again. I was one of those girls who was determined to learn how to drive myself – my mother had never learned and was terrified of the whole thing. She used to say cars are only suitable for men. She had a friend who used to drive her husband to the station to get to work but he would turn the car round before leaving her so that she could drive back. Women were so patronised and I was determined not to be. I quickly picked it up and drove for the next 28 years without an accident."

It was the fact that cars represented a new and previously unheard-of freedom that made young women such as Pam Tarlton so determined to learn how to drive. But for others it was the sheer glamour of the new. Robert Sharpe recalls favourite makes from the time:

"Oh, I was a real car enthusiast. I read everything I could get my hands on and drove whenever I could, although it

Moggy
The Morris Minor was considered a very light and responsive car. There was even a saying that if you drove over a penny in a Morris Minor you knew whether you'd gone over "heads" or "tails" side up!

Institute of Advanced Motorists
Despite prejudice against women drivers, the 1957 School of Motoring was run by Denise McCann (pictured below), who also founded the Institute of Advanced Motorists.

was a long time before I owned my own car. I loved the Fords because of their American influence – the Consul and the Zephyr with its fins was also a favourite. But these were expensive and flashy and older people were keener on Ford Prefects, which looked like prewar cars. Vauxhall made the Velox and up in Oxford at Cowley Morris was still making the Cowley and the Morris 6, as well as the new Morris Minor.

I believe I'm right in saying that the Morris Minor quickly became the most popular car in Britain. It was seen as being much easier to drive than other makes – it had very light steering – and that meant anyone who wanted his wife to drive was drawn to it. But there were loads of other cars being made by much smaller companies that sadly have long vanished. A lot were based in Coventry. Singer made lovely cars as well as Humber, Alvis, Riley, Rover and a host of others all now gone."

Air travel

Passenger travel was still in its infancy in the late 1940s and early 1950s before the age of charter flights, high speed jets and low prices, but, incredibly, there had been scheduled passenger flights since just after World War I. These early flights were extraordinarily expensive and this didn't change much by the end of World War II. But there were signs of the huge changes to come in the 1960s.

Hazel Rose was an air stewardess in the days when stewardesses were almost invariably very well-connected girls who'd been to expensive private schools. Working on the new passenger services was seen as an acceptable employment for well-bred girls – but only so long as they did not marry, as Hazel recalls.

"If they found out you were getting married you were usually out on your ear! When I applied to BOAC I really didn't think I'd get in – I had a Yorkshire accent, I hadn't been to an expensive private school and I was too short. For safety

Glamorous travel
The arrival of large capacity jet aircraft in the 1950s saw the flight destination maps and airports expand as passengers were lured by the promise of comfort that earlier propeller planes could not offer. However, the glamour associated with air travel – epitomised by air hostesses who were free to travel to exotic destinations – was the preserve of the well heeled, as ticket prices remained beyond the reach of many for some time to come.

reasons the airlines had a rule that girls who wanted to be stewardesses had to be at least 4ft 4in high and I was at least a couple of inches below that. I got round that problem eventually by getting specially made shoes that looked like the uniform shoes but had a heel. You needed the height just to reach the overhead lockers!

Our six weeks training was at Heathrow, which back then was a few green fields and some Nissen huts! We were taught what to do in a range of emergencies including ditching on water and a range of medical procedures. We were also taught how to use lots of drugs – basic drugs that were kept in a box on every plane for emergencies. Oddly, that box could only ever be opened by the captain.

On the Constellations we had far fewer passengers than they have on modern planes. Sometimes the whole plane was given over to First-Class passengers but by today's standards all the passengers were travelling First Class – there was far more room than today and a much more personal service from the cabin crew, including silver service, beds and even a small library on board. There were separate men's and women's loos and in the women's loo we would put out lots of very expensive cosmetics."

Len Reddington, a wireless operator on bombers during the war who transferred to BOAC when hostilities ended, remembers the operational end of things.

"Wireless operators were the eyes and ears of an aeroplane in the days before voice communication between ground and air was possible.

I was measured up for my uniform at BOAC – a lightweight khaki suit for summer and tropical wear and a double-breasted blue naval officer's uniform for winter. I went to Croydon for training – two months on the special nature of

Boarding passes ready
Civil aviation had been severely restricted during World War II, but when it returned it had larger planes that commanded longer runways, more passengers and, in turn, larger airports. Manchester airport underwent significant expansion in 1949, and it was decided that London's Croydon airport could no longer serve as the capital's main terminus. In 1947 building work began at the Great Western Aerodrome in west London on what was to become Heathrow airport. RAF Northolt (pictured above) served as a civilian airport in the interim.

White elephant
In 1945 Saunders-Roe, a British aero- and machine-engineering firm based at Cowes on the Isle of Wight, won a contract to build three flying boats for the British Overseas Airways Company (BOAC). The Princesses (pictured above) were intended for transatlantic flights, but advances in traditional aircraft technology and airport quality made the cumbersome, fuel-thirsty and rust-prone planes unviable. BOAC cancelled its order and the three planes – only one of which was ever airborne – were mothballed before being dismantled some years later.

civilian passenger flying – and was then sent back to Bristol to fly on Dakotas. Despite all my RAF training I have to say that the standards for civilian flying were actually higher than they were in the RAF. Everything was checked and then double-checked and then checked again!"

FLYING BOATS

Taffy Barrow recalls captaining civilian planes after the war. He flew the now legendary flying boats, large aircraft that could take off from, and land on, water.

"I flew the Durban to Calcutta flying boat route many times and there were no long-haul flights in those days – there were 24 stops on that journey! We had to stop for bad weather because we couldn't fly above it because cabins weren't pressurised. We also had to refuel regularly."

By October 1945 Taffy was captain of a C-Class Empire flying boat. Despite all the flying he did on far more modern planes he still has enormous affection for those postwar days:

"I still think that was one of the nicest of all planes to fly. It really was a lovely old aeroplane and because it had such a short range – three and a half to four hours flying time at most and no navigator – it meant we always stopped somewhere to sleep at night. It was truly leisurely and luxurious by the standards of later passenger flying. It's hard to compare prices but flying in those days was incredibly expensive. High costs were inevitable because maintenance costs were high and there were endless stopovers.

Durban to Calcutta and back took five weeks and the pilot and co-pilot would be at the controls for as much as 220 hours.

Flying on those wonderful old Empires was straightforward, easy and really enjoyable. We talked to the passengers, dined with them in the evenings. It was all so much more leisurely."

Horse-drawn transport

Despite the rise of the motor vehicle and the dwindling popularity of horses, Londoners into the 1950s and beyond insisted on funeral cortèges being drawn by black horses, as Reg Coote remembers:

"When one of the Battersea train drivers died in the 1950s his mates always formed the pallbearers. They carried the coffin out of his house to the horse-drawn hearse – everyone insisted on horses in those days – and the whole street came out to see the coffin away. The chapel would be packed out with his mates too. I remember when old Bill Cook died we followed the black horses for miles."

Horses were also used for milk deliveries in some areas, as Nat Budgen recollects:

"In the north west suburbs of London one old shopkeeper who insisted on using a pony and cart for local deliveries long after the war ended – he had a small field and a stable to keep the pony in and he said it was much cheaper than a van when fuel was so hard to come by. For years after he packed up I used to up in the morning convinced I could hear the clip clop of the horse's hooves on the tarmac."

In rural North Wales Blundell Rowley Williams remembers the pony and trap used on the farm well into the 1950s.

"We couldn't bear to get rid of it because horses and ponies were part of our lives and in summer going anywhere by pony and trap was always far more fun – quieter and open to the air – than a stuffy old car. Mind you, in bad weather we all preferred the car!"

For Joe White, who was farming near Chagford in Devon before and after the war, horses never went away.

"We always kept the fields small and had no mechanisation at all – couldn't be bothered with it. My dad had a good pony to ride into the market at Chagford and we all rode a bit. We used a horse and cart for general work round the farm well into the 1960s – we'd always done it and it was cheap, so why should we change? Of course there were cars but we're in a remote spot here on the edge of Dartmoor and things change slowly. Lots of people round about were too old to bother with newfangled cars and vans and they stuck to the old ways too – you'd see an old biddy now and then slowly going to church or the shops by pony and trap as if cars had never been invented."

Then there were the totters, or rag-and-bone men, as John Rogan recalls:

"They'd go round the streets very slowly with flatbed carts shouting for old scrap metal. The horse would pull slowly along, knowing the way, and people were glad to see it come – the totters would take old prams, old piping, almost anything metal and of course they'd take it for nothing. I heard that when they built the Westway flyover at Shepherd's Bush in the 1960s they had to rebuild stables for the totters who'd always kept their horses round there. I suspect they are long gone now."

Horse power
By the 1920s horse transport was already declining. Carts were still seen in many places, even in Central London, until well into the 1930s, but they were heading rapidly for extinction. However, horses were still being used for some jobs well into the 1950s, as seen below, at Elephant and Castle. Despite the increased productivity that accompanied the switch to electric milk floats, the charm of horse and cart was hard to abandon for some.

OUR FIRST CAR

Motoring for the masses

Laments for the vanished golden age of the motor car centre on the 1950s when the glory of the open road was still a reality. Motorways and traffic jams were unheard of, parking restrictions unknown, and if cars were slower and less reliable than they were to become yet there was sense of adventure about driving that has been lost. When it took years to save enough to buy a car, car ownership was also a huge status symbol.

Family car
Due to increases in wealth, car production and social pressures, the family car became an aspiration for thousands. Ford, Hillman, Standard, Morris and Vauxhall became household names, and the streets of Britain began to fill with saloon cars.

Motor shows
Many manufacturers would take out advertisements which stated their stand location at a forthcoming motor show to attract as much attention as possible, as seen here at the Ford stand. The Anglia (right) was the first Ford to have a four-speed gearbox and electric windscreen wipers.

Export potential
Many of Britain's leading car makers promoted images of Britain's rich heritage when they were trying to sell their cars to overseas markets. A Vauxhall advertisement from 1959 had a sketch of Buckingham Palace as the backdrop.

National style
The major industrialised countries of the postwar era supported their own independent motor industries. In the period before globalisation, there were distinct national styles in design and each vehicle represented a range of different aesthetic and engineering solutions to the problem of creating a functional family car at reasonable cost.

The art of queuing

SHOPPING AND EATING

Bread line
Queues outside bakeries such as this one in Streatham High Street, London, only became a common sight in the aftermath of World War II. Bread was rationed at the start of 1946, but the meat ration was increased to compensate for it. Churchill described the Food Minister's announcement as "one of the gravest I have ever heard in time of peace".

The freedom to buy whatever food we like is something we simply take for granted today, but back in those dark postwar days the British public groaned under the burden of rationing. Children had rarely – if ever – seen a banana or an orange, families survived on a few ounces of meat a week and at one time even potatoes were rationed. Though we now look back on the late 1940s and 1950s as a period of low-fat healthy eating, it didn't seem like that at the time: people wanted food to be fun, but, with fun always just around the corner, they gritted their teeth and tried their best to enjoy a diet that often seemed to consist entirely of dried eggs and whalemeat!

Potato shortage
Like bread, potatoes had to be rationed in the aftermath of the war. Bad weather caused the crop to fail and forced housewives to join lengthy queues for their weekly allowance (as seen below in Camberwell, London).

Still on the ration

Rationing made shopping, cooking and eating a difficult and time-consuming business during the late 1940s and 1950s. Looking back from the perspective of the 21st century it is easy to exaggerate the difficulties because we now have so many convenience foods – whether frozen or tinned – that were simply not available back then. But people managed because they had no choice and they were resourceful. They learned to make do and mend – even on a few ounces of butter and bacon each week. But there was resentment along with resignation, as Rose Plummer recalls:

> "I remember we had to queue regularly for nearly an hour for a few cakes and a packet of biscuits. We thought victory in the war would mean the end of rationing but it was worse – shortages and rationing didn't become a thing of the past. How wrong we were. If anything, postwar rationing was worse than in the war itself, or at least it felt worse. Clothes were on the ration but you could live with that just about because you didn't need new clothes every week.
>
> We had to make do with a couple of ounces of butter, one egg and a few ounces of bacon each week and there was no olive oil or any other cooking fat apart from lard back then, and precious little lard, so everything tasted dry and unappetising. Beer was rationed too but that was probably a good thing and a lot of wives would have liked to keep it that way!"

Shortages and rationing were made more difficult as a result of the 1945 dock strike, which sorely tested the whole idea of working-

"If anything, postwar rationing was worse than in the war itself, or at least it felt worse."

It's all you're going to get
One person's weekly food allowance typically consisted of 4oz (113g) lard or butter, 12oz (340g) sugar, 4oz (113g) bacon, 2 eggs, 6oz (170g) meat and 2oz (57g) tea. The allowance fluctuated throughout the 14 years of food rationing in Britain, which ended at midnight on July 4, 1954 when restrictions on the sale and purchase of meat and bacon were lifted.

Get your books here
Everyone was given a ration book for food and was obliged to register with a grocery store. Each store was only given enough food for the people on its list, which ensured that everyone got a fair share. This protected the poor from high prices and prevented others from hoarding food.

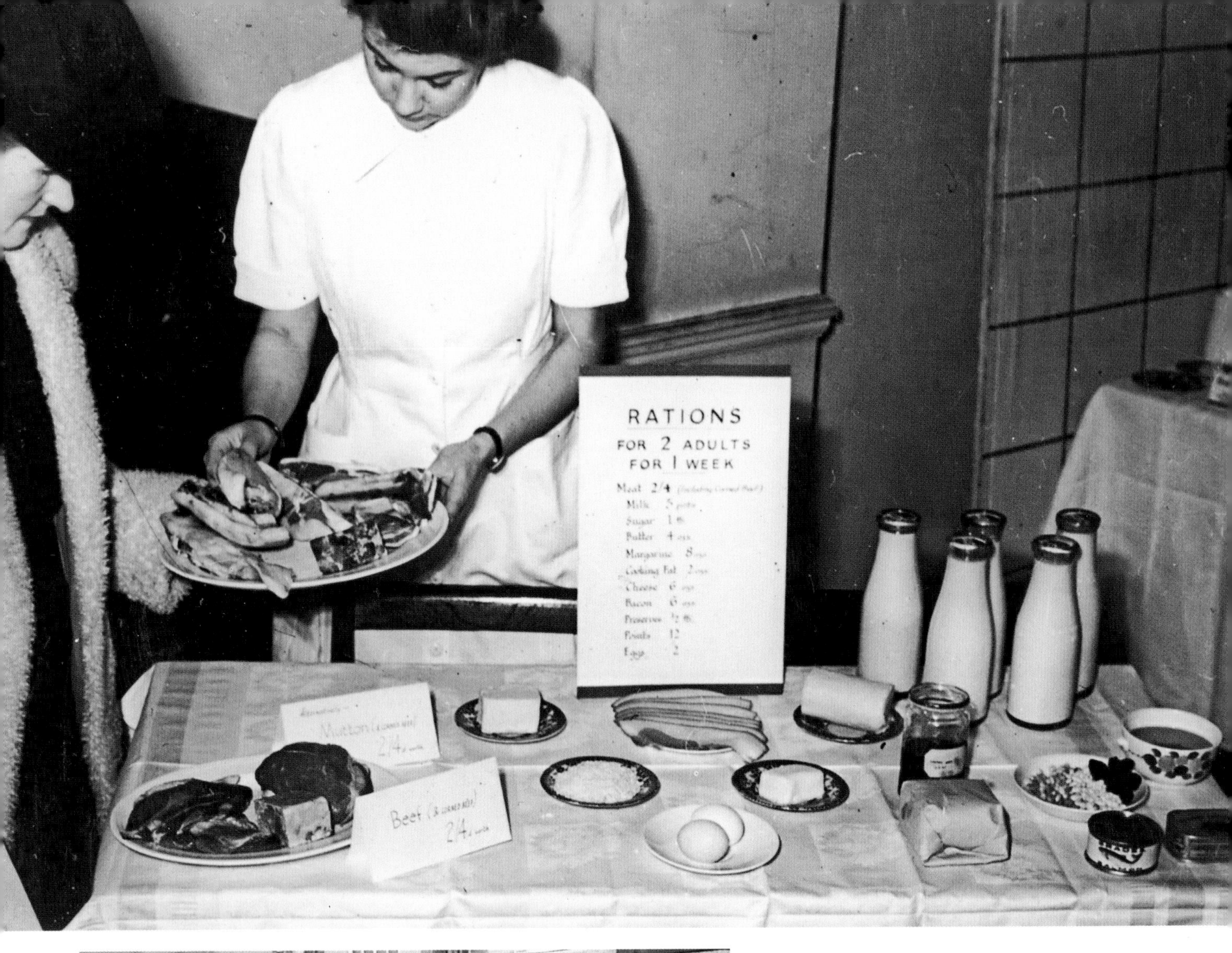

No better off
By 1947 rations were at their lowest. Allowances were 1oz (55g) of bacon per week, 2oz (113g) of butter, 3lbs (85g) of potatoes and 2oz (113g) of cheese.

Saving up
Coupons were issued inside the familiar ration books, and would often be saved up for luxury items, such as lard (for pastry), or sweets.

class solidarity – an idea that had enjoyed a fixed place in the public memory after the Jarrow march and memories of the Depression. The dockers felt badly used, but by going on strike they made life hard for ordinary people and there was huge resentment. Rose Plummer recalls the difficulties faced by housewives.

> "The men sympathised but we were furious because overnight, for example, eggs and bacon that we relied on stopped – you couldn't get them at all and lots of other things that hadn't been hard to get suddenly were. Even bread and potatoes might have all gone by lunchtime from the shops."

Partly as a result of the groundswell of popular anger the dock strike quickly ended, although rationing remained a thorn in the side of almost everyone. But there was a short period during which food availability improved dramatically. This was in the lead-up to the

A reason to smile
An unexpected benefit of rationing was that by the end of the war the people of Britain had never been so healthy. Although there was much less food, it had been less high in fat and sugar, and was shared out fairly across social classes. The preservation and continuation of this fairness and efficiency was one of the key reasons for establishing the Welfare State in 1946.

Queen's Coronation in 1953. The government was determined to make the event popular so it changed the rules temporarily and allowed everyone an extra one pound of sugar and four full ounces of margarine.

However, after the euphoria of that interlude it was back to the usual struggles and difficulties, as Rose explains.

> "Everyone had to be registered with a butcher and a grocer even tso get the tiny amounts of food available on the ration. You had to present your ration book, which was then suitably amended by the shopkeeper to show you'd had your portion for that week."

DESPERATE MEASURES

Inevitably, given the public desperation for sugar, meat and other luxuries, there was a thriving black market, as Lisa Edwards recalls.

"You had to present your ration book which was suitably amended by the shopkeeper."

> Everyone knew the black market was widespread and most people in my experience didn't think it was wrong – the government told us it was wrong, but people I knew thought well-off people were doing very well despite rationing. We used to say that high court judges were probably not eating spam and an ounce of bacon a week. They were getting pork and beef from their estates and because they were important they thought it was justified. So when we got the chance to get something on the side I'm afraid sometimes we took it. To be fair, a lot of people absolutely refused black market stuff because there was a strong feeling of patriotism back then, but I don't think they were the majority. The spivs were blamed but they were only catering for a demand that was always there.
>
> If you knew where to go you could get black market eggs for sixpence each – the farmers made a packet out of black marketeering. A pint of milk would cost a fortune on the black market but people paid. People sold their clothing coupons too, which was illegal, and you'd often see someone in front of you in a queue get a bag of something from

Make do and mend
Clothes rationing began in June 1941 and continued until 1949. Everyone was given a clothing book with coloured coupons to redeem against new garments. When clothes were worn or grown out of people were urged by the government to "Make do and mend", so that clothing factories and workers could focus on making other items, such as parachutes and uniforms or latterly, textiles for export.

Spam
Many tinned foods and puddings were imported from America in the latter years of the war. One of the most successful canned imports was Supply Pressed American Meat – Spam for short – because it looked and tasted like fresh meat, and could be cooked in a variety of ways.

under the counter and no money changing hands. Friends and relatives were always helped out like this and a few people probably slept with people for the chance of some free food – for some it really was that bad.

The worst period of all during rationing was definitely 1947. That was when the butter and meat ration was reduced and potatoes for the very first time were rationed – even in the war they hadn't been."

The British diet

Tinned food was available before and after the war but it was expensive and the British shopper was notoriously conservative – the Brits wanted meat and two veg, not stuff out of a tin. The government of the day – Churchill's wartime government and the Labour government that won a landslide in 1946 – tried to persuade the public that a more varied diet could be both more fun and more nutritious than traditional fare, but Britain was not convinced, as Jim Swire recalls.

"You could get whale meat and seal but I didn't know anyone who tried either, but there were no veggies – I mean vegetarians – back then and we felt terrible because we'd grown up expecting at least a lamb chop or a bit of liver every day or rabbit if we were desperate. In 1946 the amount of bacon and eggs we could have was cut – everyone was furious, though it was a bit better on the farm because of course we kept our own chickens. We heard the Germans were better fed because they needed to be helped as their country was ruined by the war, but it seemed a bit rich that they should be better fed than us!"

Where fresh foods were unavailable, people had to make do with unpalatable dried versions. Rose Plummer recalls the general horror of dried eggs.

"Oh heavens, they were awful – not like eggs at all, but a way for the government to make eggs go farther. They used to issue recipes for using them but the results were always awful.

Things must have improved a bit by 1947 because I remember seeing a banana and there was Bird's Custard, an old favourite, Worcestershire sauce and Lyons Tea. We could get herrings and mackerel very easily but no one seemed to really want them. There really was an obsession with meat. Not like now, when so many people try to eat less meat and more fish and vegetables. We ate a lot more offal then too – liver, heart, pigs' trotters, that kind of thing.

"... we'd grown up expecting at least a lamb chop or a bit of liver ..."

The government tried to tell us that brown bread was better for us but we all hated it – again not like more recent years, when people choose brown bread because it's healthy. Back then we thought it was just the government keeping all the rubbish in the

Help from abroad
In the years during and after the war Canada and Australia produced extra food to be exported to Britain. Meat was a vital and large import; Canadian bacon, Australian poultry and rabbits were sold widely to butchers across the country. In 1949 Australian imports accounted for 3,376,79cwt (112lbs) of meat. Beef was a particularly prized commodity and played a significant role in price wars.

Meat at last
On July 4, 1954 meat finally came off the ration, marking the end of all food rationing. For the first time since 1939, London's Smithfield meat market opened its doors at midnight rather than 6am, and butchers did a roaring trade. Prices soared initially as demand outstripped supply, but it wasn't long before the queues for prized sausages or bacon were a distant memory.

Served hot or cold
Corned beef was relatively easy to obtain compared to other meats in the postwar years. It could be served up in a variety of ways and was used to create salads, sandwiches, hot pasties, and

Cigarettes for all
Craven "A" cigarettes were the most popular cigarettes during World War II. Some adverts claimed that they were made especially to "prevent sore throats".

bread – the bran you know – to bulk it out.

Spam was so bad I can't even begin to tell you, although the kids did seem to like it.

You forget, too, how little the ration was – just a scrap of bacon a week each, two ounces of cheese, half a loaf a day. The only consolation was that we got about a pound of jam a month. Amazingly, cigarettes were not rationed though they were expensive – you could puff your way through 20 Craven "A" for three shillings and four pence. It was better for kids on farms as they had lots of milk and could kill the odd pig – illegally of course, but it went on, and they had apples and plums in the hedgerows.

I seem to remember tinned corned beef coming in eventually and tinned pies. We loved those and people made their own pickled onions – wonderful things when your diet is boring. And by the late 1950s I remember things like Cocoa Puffs and Cocoa Krispies – breakfast cereals we'd never heard of before. What we liked about them was their sweetness. Packed with sugar they were, and we ate them with hot milk, not cold. Everyone back then thought that a cold breakfast was a terrible thing."

"... there's only so many times you can eat Irish stew without wanting to scream!"

COOKING AND RECIPES

Doctors today look back at the 1950s British diet as one of the healthiest on record. Certainly it was low in meat and fat and high in carbohydrates, but for the British people it was dull – hardly anyone who remembers that time has a good thing to say about the food. But, adding insult to injury, the government of the day tried to persuade people that with a bit of imagination they could make dishes fit for a king and all using the most meagre rations, as Libby MaCintyre remembers.

"We did our best to make interesting food from the little we had and I remember my mother – who was from Irish stock – making Irish stew every week, though she would make a joke of it and call it Scottish stew some weeks, Irish stew the next and Welsh stew after that.

All you needed to make it was potatoes, onions, water, salt and pepper and a bit of meat – any kind of meat would do, but the fattier the better. Mutton was best because even a small piece was fatty enough to make the sauce taste rich. We had it with bacon a few times, with beef, rabbit and even a pig's trotter. To be fair it wasn't at all bad and it was just the thing the government was trying to persuade us to have. In Scotland of course onions and potatoes were always in good supply but there's only so many times you can eat Irish stew without wanting to scream!"

By the mid 1950s food was beginning to become a more commercial enterprise – the first advertisements for eggs and Oxo cubes

Warming and flavoursome
Oxo's iconic brand was popular during this era because it did actually contain some meat extracts. Housewives had learned to be creative with what limited meat they had, and Oxo added valuable flavour to some otherwise bland combinations.

Simple kitchens
Cooking utensils were in short supply after patriotic housewives donated their pots and pans to help combat metal shortages during the war. As a result of this and the remnants of bomb damage, kitchens were very basic.

British Lion mark
In 1957 the British Egg Marketing Board started trading to bring stability to the egg market that had just come off rationing, and to give consumers a regular supply of high-quality eggs at reasonable prices. The British Lion mark was introduced and eggs were given its stamp of approval.

appeared, including the famous "Go to work on an egg!" slogan; snap, crackle and pop became a byword for the new cereal; but people still ate largely what was in season, because they ate what was grown in Britain. Imported exotic foodstuffs were unthought of and good old English pies and puddings were made instead, as Amy Capper recalls.

"We loved anything made with suet – particularly dumplings – and bread with lard spread thickly on it and then sprinkled with salt was a real treat. It would probably make me sick now! But it was all about stews with root vegetables because not only was rationing a problem, we also had no money. Houses and streets right through the 1950s looked grubby because no one had the money to paint and repair them. Food, too, was unadorned. I remember a pie we made. The recipe was issued by the government. It was, I think, called Woolton Pie, because it had been invented by the chef at London's Savoy Hotel, who was called Mr Woolton; but it was nothing fancy. It had potatoes, cauliflower, carrots, swede, onions, vegetable extract, oatmeal and

"... what you bought didn't depend on what you wanted, it depended on what they had in stock."

An egg a day
The British Egg Marketing Board used the slogan "Go to work on an egg" to persuade people to have an egg for breakfast. Egg consumption peaked in 1960 at five eggs per person per week.

parsley, with pastry on top. You sliced everything up, seasoned it and bunged it in the oven. Somehow we didn't really think that was being served at the Savoy!"

From one queue to another

In rural districts mobile shops gradually returned to the scene. In the days when people only rarely had cars these shops were very successful. In the towns famous names such as Sainsbury's dominated many high streets, but Sainsbury's was nothing like the Sainsbury's we know today. Rose Plummer remembers the complex business of food shopping.

"Well, at Sainsbury's you had to go from counter to counter to buy your stuff so you might queue three or four times – once at the meat counter, once at the fish counter, next the dairy and so on. But it was an improvement on going from shop to shop. We had heard that in America people went round with a big basket and helped themselves. To be honest I don't think we really believed it because we thought everything would get stolen.

There was also Greggs – a chain of lovely shops, all cold marble and ceramic tiles. They sold meat and bacon, ham and eggs, but still queuing was the big thing. At the end of a long wait in the queue, what you bought didn't depend on what you wanted, it depended on what they had in stock. The assistant would weigh each item – almost all food was still sold loose then – after which it would be wrapped in greaseproof paper. Most of us shopped for fresh food every day because of course no one had fridges."

MOBILE SHOPS

In rural districts smaller shops still dominated the scene but their size belied the wide range of goods they sold, as Robert Westall recalls:

"Down here in Somerset we had to go into the village or into Bradford to shop. I remember one shop sold clothes, matches, groceries, vegetables, ham, eggs, nails, pins, cotton reels, socks and overcoats, kindling and even books. We also had the travelling shop later in the 1950s when petrol and diesel wasn't so hard to get.

Polish shopkeepers
Many Polish immigrants fled to Britain and became shopkeepers (shown above). Despite attempts by the Polish government to lure people back, few returned.

Seasonal taste
Self-service supermarkets were yet to be widespread, so groceries would generally be purchased from local stores. Available produce was usually local and seasonal.

Lion

Villagers would wait for it and have a chat with the shopkeeper, who also drove. The one I remember was a bit like a converted bus but it always had plenty of onions and potatoes, fruit in season, tins of this and that, pickles, jams and marmalades.

Markets started up again after the war and they were very popular – but more for meeting old friends than for buying food. The reason was that you always got the same old food – it was just a chore to get done for a lot of people. No one thought of food as a social thing the way the French and Italians do – it was very practical back then because we had such a limited range of things to eat. People didn't buy recipe books or foreign foods

Limited food
Local markets (above) were at the mercy of seasonal availability for their stock, and poor harvests and harsh winters meant that there was little choice available. The boom in air freight of the late 1950s would change this but, for now, options were scant.

Convenience shopping
Before the advent of the family car shopping trips would generally involve a bus trip and a long walk, so mobile shops such as this one (left), were a lifeline for those living in rural areas. Women took over manning these shops during the war, and the convenience was hard to beat.

The deli counter
The first self-service supermarket opened in Croydon, Surrey in June 1950. Advertising promoted this revolutionary way of shopping, and explained exactly what you needed to do once you had collected your "special wire basket". Delicatessen-style counters were still present for some fresh foods, however, but the pre-packaged revolution was not far away.

Seafood galore
Fish was never rationed, but there were shortages during the Battle of the Atlantic as fishing fleets were kept in their docks. What fish and seafood there was could be preserved in vinegar or in tins, and was ideal for maintaining the country's food supplies. Stocks were buoyed with some oddities, such as whale meat and snoek, neither of which proved particularly popular.

like pasta or risotto rice. That all came much later. They never thought of cooking new things. We were very inward looking when it came to food, I'm afraid to say."

The British may have been parochial in their appetites, but that was to change with the arrival of more exotic food in the shops, as Sheila Kehoe recalls.

"We were astonished when we began to see pineapples and bananas and oranges in the shops again. I think I first saw them in the food hall at Harrods – beautifully presented in a huge decorated display as if they were the finest expensive jewels. Mind you, they were very expensive so I suppose that was fair enough. But in Soho too I remember the small Italian shops began to have real coffee again and in the

Exotic fruits
Between 1951 and 1971 the number of ethnic minorities residing in the UK rose ten fold. One by-product of postwar immigration was that more foreign restaurants were opened and exotic foods were sold alongside the more traditional fare in food markets and arcades, like this one in Newcastle-upon-Tyne (left).

French cafés there was the wonderful smell of croissants and *pain au chocolat*. It was almost as if these shops and cafés were signalling that hard times were coming to an end."

Door-to-door service

Anyone who looks carefully at those old black and white photographs of villages and towns taken at any time from the 1930s to the 1960s will see, here and there along the high street, heavy black bicycles leaning outside butcher, baker, grocer and fishmonger. These were used by the delivery men – for, in the days before supermarkets, getting your food delivered was far more common than one might imagine, as Pam Tarlton explains.

"In my early years, when we lived outside Cheltenham and not even in a village really – in the middle of nowhere in fact – we had most of our groceries delivered. I can remember when the grocer changed from using a specially adapted horse-drawn delivery van to using a motor van. He was so immensely proud of his new vehicle and I think a number of people felt that they should move their custom to him because he would be more efficient. In fact it made little difference because he didn't deliver all that widely and the difference in time between local deliveries on a bicycle and motor van was minimal.

My mother used to leave the order when she went into town by car and then they would deliver later that day. She could easily have brought the shopping back herself but it was almost as if having it delivered conferred status. For deliveries in the village and up to perhaps a mile away they also had a delivery boy who rode a

"She could easily have brought the shopping back herself but having it delivered conferred status."

The new workhorse Commercial vehicles played a key role in bolstering Britain's economy throughout the 1950s. As well as being used for goods delivery and heavy haulage they contributed to the all-important export drive. They were the workhorses for the country's recovery.

Free delivery
Being a grocery delivery boy was hard work. The bicycles, which were laden with neatly packed boxes full of shopping that the delivery boy would load himself, were heavy and unwieldy. They often had to go some distance in all weathers, and were kept busy with regular orders.

bicycle with a big basket on the front. It was one of those specially made delivery bicycles with a big wheel at the back and a smaller one at the front to allow for a much bigger basket in front of the handlebars and just above the wheel. It was all meticulously organised and the shopkeeper was unashamedly a snob – any order for a big house or someone important would get priority treatment."

But what was it like for the delivery boy on that big old-fashioned bicycle? Will Constance worked for a short time as a grocer's boy in Norfolk, and gives some insight into the world of these young workers.

"It all depended on what the owner of the shop was like. I worked for an old boy who said he wanted me always to look busy so I said all right. Then, when I started work he cuffed me hard round the

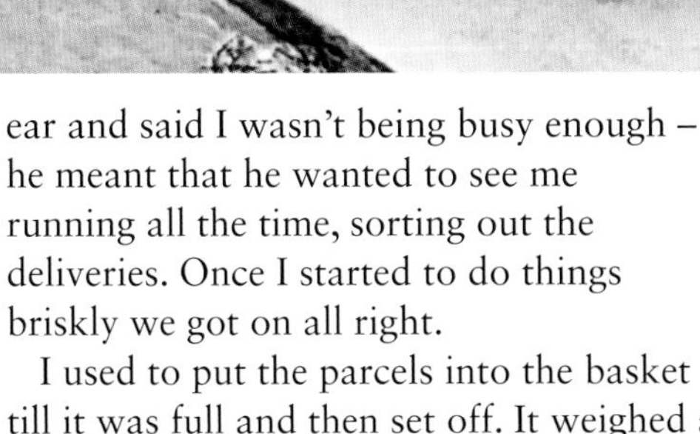

ear and said I wasn't being busy enough – he meant that he wanted to see me running all the time, sorting out the deliveries. Once I started to do things briskly we got on all right.

I used to put the parcels into the basket till it was full and then set off. It weighed a ton! Most of the deliveries were in and around the village but for a young lad it was hard work and such a relief as the basket got emptier. The bike was as heavy as cast iron and top-heavy with all the parcels. If I was delivering cheese on a hot day or other stuff that might go off I'd have less and he'd tell me not to delay. On the hills – not that there are many in Norfolk! – I used to get off and push, but I remember one old lady always gave me a glass of home-made lemonade when I got to her house. Every Wednesday it was and she never forgot for all the months I was there, and I've never forgotten her."

Attracting customers
The growing popularity of large self-service grocers and supermarkets made it hard for small businesses to attract custom. Coupled with increased availability of produce, competition was fierce. Price reductions were the only way to attract custom and shift perishable stock (above).

Family affair
The traditional grocery store (left) was usually family run, and helping out in the shop was a rite of passage for the younger generation. Some of today's familiar supermarket retailers, such as Sainsbury's, started as family-run grocery businesses.

BRAND VALUES

New packaged consumer goods

In the late 1940s the world of advertising had hardly grasped on to the idea of branding and competitive products; the old food and drink brands were tried and tested and relied on their reputation. Birds Custard, Worcestershire Sauce and Oxo cubes among others were part of an unchanging world. But as the 1950s wore on this world began to change; brands began to compete, advertising became aggressive and most remarkable of all – supermarkets arrived.

Advertisements
The 1950s and 1960s revolutionised the kitchen with new labour-saving devices, so when commercial television was introduced in 1955 Oxo was one of the advertisers on its first night. This provided the opportunity to strengthen its relationship with housewives, and continue its status as the ingredient that made cooking so easy.

Instant coffee
Manufactured by multinational companies like Maxwell House, instant coffee occupied a large sector of postwar advertisements, promising to transform women's lives and increase their leisure time by simplifying the coffee-making process.

Supermarkets
The supermarket had a huge impact on shopping, revolutionising the layout of the shop and offering an array of new goods under one roof. In 1950 around 50 supermarkets were in existence; by 1961 there were 572, and by 1969 there were 3,400 across the country.

Soap powder
With only 1 per cent of the British population owning a washing machine in 1952, doing the laundry was a labour-intensive exercise. When Lever Brothers launched Surf, it offered an exciting unique selling proposition – a soap powder that did not need a separate whitening agent.

Help yourself
Following the end of rationing there was a rapid growth in personal consumption in Britain. Both the government and elements of the grocery trade were keen to promote self-service stores, which were more efficient for both customer and retailer as they required less labour.

Make the most of it
Fewer than two million homes had television sets at the start of 1952, and the evening entertainment would consist of the traditional activities of reading, listening to the wireless or playing board games.

Home comforts

DOMESTIC LIFE

Prefabs, jerry-built housing, crumbling eighteenth and nineteenth century terraces, smoke-blackened brick and stone: every image of house and home from the late 1940s and 1950s reveals itself now only through the billowing fog of a million coal fires. But there were hints of a seeming utopia to come: a new world of dazzling plastics and stainless steel that would leave behind forever the gloom of Victorian hand-me-downs.

Prime target
The three main railway stations of what is now Camden was then the boroughs of St Pancras, Holborn and Hampstead – which made the area a prime target for bombing. By September 13, 1944, 744 houses in St Pancras (below) had suffered bomb damage, rendering many homeless. Halifax in Yorkshire "adopted" St Pancras and lorry loads of spare household goods were sent to residents and distributed by the Women's Volunteer Service.

The house is falling down

Those long lines of mock-Tudor jerry-built houses that so rapidly increased the size of our cities in the 1930s only added to a vast stock of often poor-quality housing dating back three and more centuries. World War II had put a stop to almost all new house building and repair, and the poverty of the immediate postwar period made things even worse, as Nancy Behan recalls.

"We lived in a flat in what had been a very grand five-storey family house. On the outside the stucco was peeling, it hadn't been painted for years and the walls were almost black after decades of London smogs. But at the time we never thought anything of it because all the houses were the same – I can't remember a single house in our area being painted in all the years I lived there. Eventually in 1958 we moved

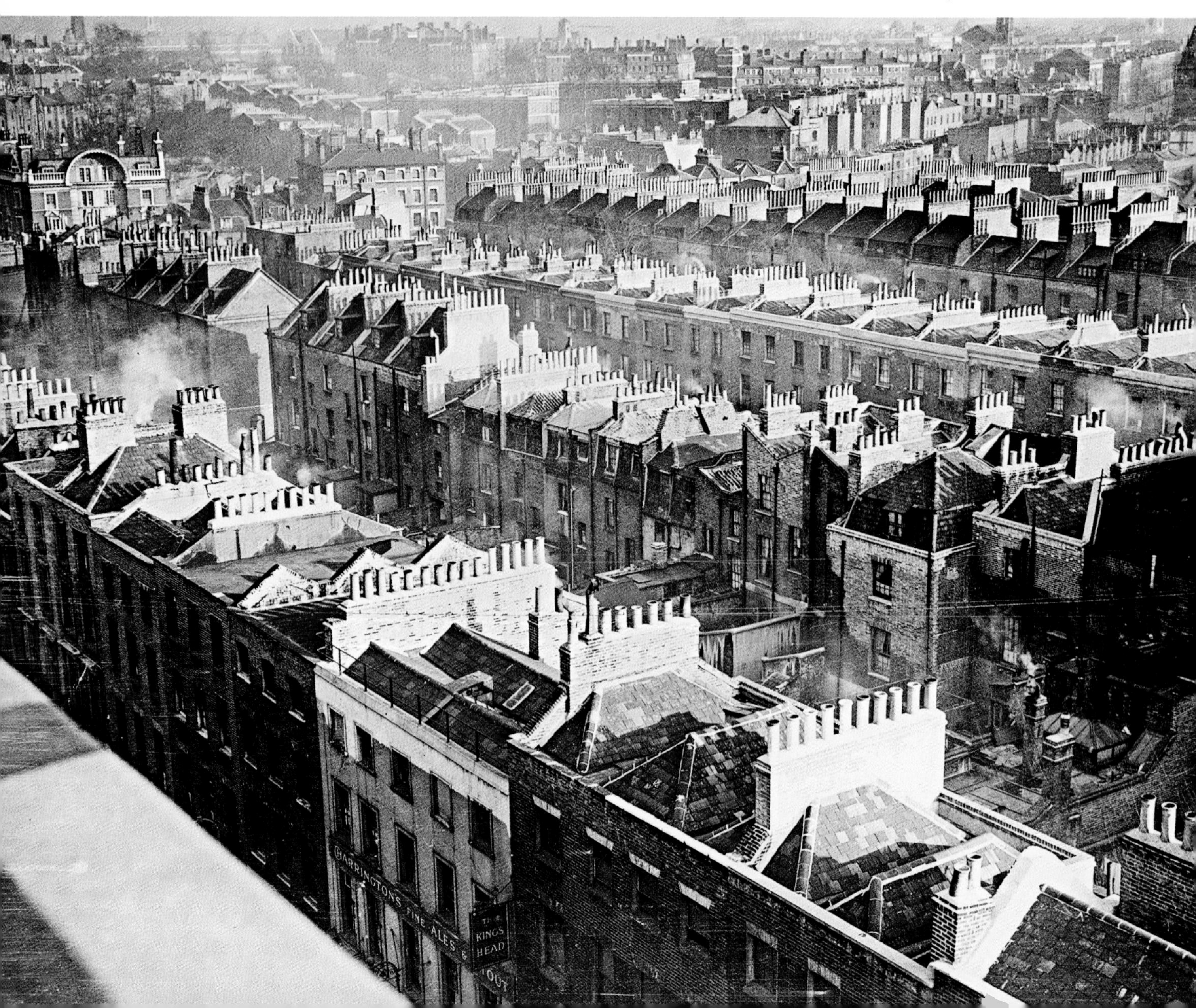

Knock up a prefab
Adequate shelter for the British citizens left homeless by German bombs was a prime issue for the Government. In 1944 Churchill promised a programme of half a million new prefabricated homes, but only 156,623 were built between 1945 and 1949. Each had a similar two-bedroom layout, and were mainly occupied by young couples, such as this (left) in Essex.

to Dorset to the edge of Lulworth Cove, which was a total shock for me. The houses down there were a mix of tiny old tumbledown cottages with holes in the roof and bigger Edwardian villas, but their walls looked so clean after London! Though people had more money in this part of the world and often lived in the whole house – we only had a flat in London – they still didn't spend anything making the outside look smart.

We had a small prefab house on the inland edge of the village. It had been put up as part of a row of concrete prefab bungalows just after the war because of the shortages of housing. It was a funny little place and from the outside it was really obvious it was made of slabs of concrete. It had a corrugated iron roof too I think, but I remember it was very warm after that terribly cold London flat."

New Towns Act
Parliament passed the New Towns Act of 1946 and the Town and Country Planning Act in 1947. Single-family units were constructed and many aluminum, prefabricated houses were constructed, such as this Cheltenham housing estate. It contained 173 aluminium prefab houses which were built and occupied in just over eleven months.

Overcrowding
Homes could not be rebuilt quickly enough to help larger families, and many councils prioritised small-scale building projects. However, this did little to assist larger families, and three families would often have to share a terraced house. A two-bedroom house would typically accommodate three families – one in each bedroom, one in the lounge and another in the kitchen (as shown right).

RISING DAMP

Farmer Richard Body spent his whole life in that ancient remote corner of Kent, Romney Marsh. He recalls houses that had sunk so deep into the marsh that the floors and walls sloped dangerously and the wind blew through cracks beneath the window frames.

"It was particularly bad during the war because a lot of the workmen were away fighting so we were constantly shoring the old house up – no one had a romantic view of these old houses back then. I suppose they'd be listed now but we just thought they were in constant danger of falling down, and on the ground floor it only had rammed earth floors, if you can image that. In the end we got so fed up that we demolished the house in 1960 and built a modern bungalow with cavity-wall insulation, concrete foundations and double glazing. Wasn't as pretty as the old one but no one wanted old things then – reminded us of the grim years after and during the war. We were delighted to escape that old house to our cosy new home that had the advantage of being all on one floor."

Low-income housing could be comfortless and forbidding in more cities than London. In Scotland Libby MacIntyre recalls the tenements of Glasgow.

"We look back on them now and romanticise them a bit but those grim blocks were just that – really grim. I had a

Glasgow slums
The Gorbals tenements in Glasgow (shown right) were built quickly and cheaply in the 1840s, providing housing for Glasgow's industrial workers. They housed about 40,000 people with up to eight family members sharing a single room, 30 residents sharing a toilet and 40 sharing a tap. Postwar housing developments, including high-rise flats designed by Sir Basil Spence, addressed the need to improve environmental and social conditions. Redevelopment of the area began in the late 1950s and the tenements were replaced with a modern tower block complex in the 1960s.

Bath time
In 1951, 38 per cent of households lacked a fixed bath, and seven per cent had to share with other lodgers. Most people took one bath a week and those without a bathroom had to take theirs in a tin bath. During the winter this would be done in front of a fire with each person using the same water over and over, topping it up with extra hot water from the fireside kettle.

few friends who'd grown up there and you had to be tough to survive. The people were crammed in and you had endless stairs to climb to get to the upper floors – terrible for old folks. So they were bad, but they didn't produce the despair and crime that the projects – the housing estates out of town – produced when the tenements were demolished in the 1960s."

Home comforts

There was little progress in interior design for the mass of the British people in the late 1940s and 1950s. People simply had to make do and it was common for beds and mattresses to be inherited (despite the prevalence of bed bugs), curtains and rugs were patched and repaired endlessly, and heating and lighting were to say the least primitive. The new furniture that was available – known as utility furniture – was universally derided as being dull, shabby and badly made. Heating water for a bath was slow and laborious and the majority of Britons bathed at most once a week.

"...the glass of water by my bedside would be frozen over on a winter morning."

John Rogan recalls everyday life in a Central London basement flat.

"I remember most of all the cold – it was always cold from October to March. We had one of those square all-in-one fireplaces with horrible tiles – not the nice cast-iron Victorian fireplaces with inset tiles. The whole of this fireplace was tiled and they were a horrible sort of mottled brown. We sat huddled round this and now and then my brother or my dad would get up and go out through the door into the freezing cellar, which was piled high with coal. They went out with an old zinc bucket, filled it with coal and dashed back in. We bought one ton of coal every autumn and that had to get us through the winter. It always ran out in early March so if it was cold we went round the local park collecting old sticks and old shoes and other rubbish and burned that. Away from the sitting room, where the fire at least heated part of the room, there was no heating at all. I remember the glass of water by my bedside would be frozen over sometimes on a winter morning. And we used to put all our coats on the bed to keep us warm.

No one had heard of anyone having fitted carpets – we all had lino (invariably brown or green) and a few rugs."

By comparison, life in the countryside had its picturesque aspects, but things were still not easy. The old ways were slower to change than in town, as Will Constance recalls.

"We always had big fires at home – one in the kitchen and one in the living room. Neither was ever allowed to go out in winter. They burned day and night. My wife baked once a week on a Friday and washed on a Monday. That was the way all women did it then and if a woman didn't do it like that she was considered beyond the pale. I suppose it was all part of the fact that in every area of life

there was a way to do things and it was strictly adhered to. Any deviation would be frowned upon."

LIFE ON THE FARM

Farmer Reg Dobson, living in a big old house a few miles from Rugby, remembers a life that had changed little in half a century and more.

"Home Farm was 300 or more years old and it had a curious meandering feel to it, with staircases hidden behind doorways and bedrooms tucked away in odd corners here and there, and in under the eaves. It always seemed to be crowded with people in summer. I think all farmhouses were well filled in those days because so many people worked on the land, and the tradition was that workers should live in with the farmer and his family, although by the 1950s this was beginning to change. We never thought of ourselves as well off but we had a nursemaid, a kitchen-maid, my aunt Kate and her son George. But it was a big house to run, what with constant washing and cooking and cleaning and lighting fires, trimming the oil lamps – and trying to stay warm in the terrible winters we had back then."

Like most farms and country houses Home Farm used oil lamps or even candles well into

The country dream
Houses and farmhouses in rural areas may have had the luxury of more living space than their urban counterparts, but these houses carried expensive upkeep costs. They were also under increasing threat from unsympathetic development as the rush to rebuild the nation's homes gathered pace.

Family meal
Gathering for a meal was an important part of the day, and most families would sit down and eat together, whatever their living standard. Meals were generally well balanced, and meat and two veg would be washed down with copious amounts of tea.

the 1950s. City dwellers had electricity made from coal for lighting, but for warmth the vast majority of houses and flats relied on open fires. Outside loos and zinc baths heaved in front of the fire were still the norm, and with so much life taking place in the one heated room it was inevitable that meals should be taken here too.

John Rogan recalls family mealtimes.

"We ate round a table that was in the middle of the sitting room. I'm sure some families chatted away about the day's events but we didn't – my dad didn't get home from work till much later and my mother was so busy that she didn't usually sit to eat with us. We all wanted to eat on our knees by the fire because it was freezing on the other side of the room, but it wasn't allowed. I know some people had televisions by the mid 1950s. We didn't. We had an old upright piano my mum could play a bit and eventually a radio and an old record player. Once we had those we used to listen until it was bedtime."

Sanitation

Before modern indoor sanitation spread widely in the 1960s and 1970s, going to the loo could still be a major expedition for millions of Britons. Huge numbers of houses still had outside lavatories long after the war had ended, and on a freezing winter night spending a penny was something to be avoided at all costs.

Reg Dobson remembers his family's solution to the problem.

Dirty water
To prepare a hot bath, the water had to be heated in a boiler in the scullery, in a series of kettles, or in a back boiler in the fireplace. For families without a bathroom the tin bath would be stored in the yard and then put in front of the living room fire on bath night. Families without a tin bath had a stand-up wash at the kitchen sink.

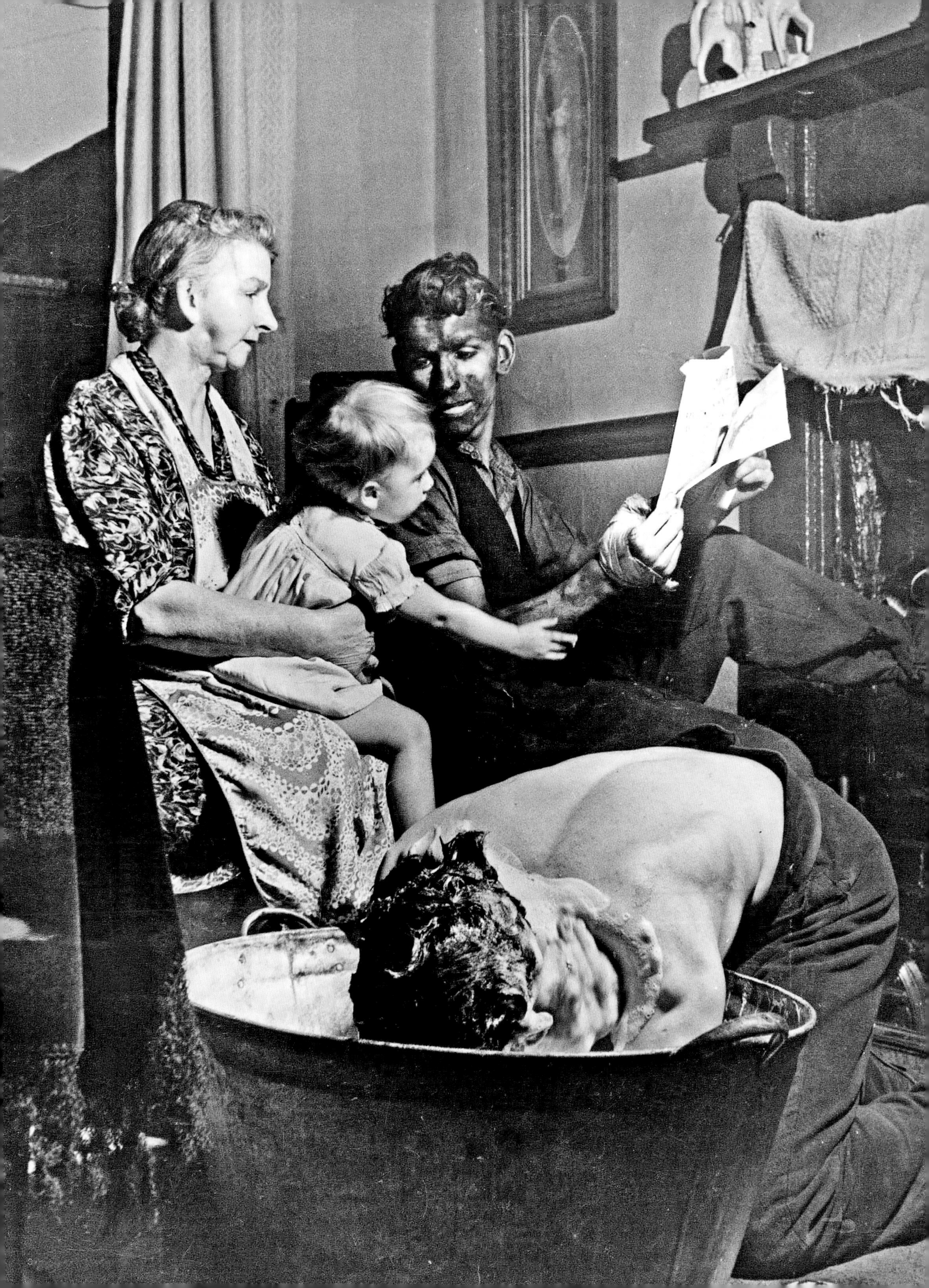

"They just cut newspapers into squares and hung it on a nail."

"We still used chamber pots, though we had a loo in the yard. No one wanted to go out at night or even much in the evening because it was such a nuisance, particularly if it was cold and dark. Loos were awful in other ways too – there were no bleaches or air fresheners that I can recall and I can't remember people buying proper loo paper. They just cut newspaper into squares and hung it on a nail. But we lived near animals and around them so no one was upset by smells or worried too much about what people now call personal hygiene."

Launderettes

In 1949 Britain's first self-service launderette opened for a six month trial. However, the National Survey of Housewives discovered that less than half of those questioned used a launderette, preferring to do their own washing at home by hand.

BATH TIME

The weekly bath was a family affair. Tin or zinc tubs were filled with the precious hot water from the fire, as Reg Dobson recalls.

"I remember my dad only had a bath every couple of weeks or so and my granddad was never known to have a bath. On Saturday nights we children were always bathed in front of a massive log fire in a tin bath in the sitting room. I remember I once refused to get undressed so the nursemaid undressed me, but I was so naughty that when she turned her back I bolted through the back door out into the pitch-dark garden. After a long chase I was caught and carried back to the house

Wash day
Doing the family's washing was a chore that would generally take a day out of the housewife's life to do. Electric washing machines were not commonplace until the 1960s, and the earlier versions were the preserve of the wealthy. Cleaning potions had been made up of all manner of products over the centuries – including some dubious old wive's tale ingredients such as chicken dung and urine – but the 1950s saw the launch of fragrant liquid laundry products, fabric conditioners and all-purpose detergents. The weekly cleaning chores not only began to smell more pleasant, but also became more effective.

where mother gave me (reluctantly) a whack with a stick!"

Personal hygiene had some rather embarrassing aspects, as Lisa Edwards recalls.

"The truth is that people back in the 1940s and 1950s were rather smelly. I suspect that only the very rich could afford to have baths more than once a week or even every day, and only the very rich led the sort of leisured lives that meant they never worked up a sweat.

"... my dad only had a bath every couple of weeks or so and my granddad was never known to have a bath."

Ordinary working people such as my dad came home physically exhausted, were too tired to organise a bath, and put the same clothes on again each day, so inevitably they smelled. Mind you, I grew up thinking that each person had their own smell and it wasn't unpleasant – my grandmother had a certain kind of smell, as did my mother and father. Each was slightly different."

Will Constance remembers the difficulties of keeping clothes clean in the days before washing machines and dry cleaning.

"My wife washed clothes on a Monday but with a big family you couldn't do everything every week, and farm workers knew their clothes would get dirty as soon as they were clean, so they were very rarely washed. You'd just take them off and put them back on in the morning. Often they'd be covered in mud or cow muck but as it was what we all did no one took any notice. Clothes in those days were treated more the way overalls are treated now."

Keeping pets

It has often been said that the popularity of pet keeping increases in direct proportion to the wealth of a nation. Britain was cash-strapped in the 1940s and 1950s and fewer people than today kept pets as a result, and the days of exotic pet keeping – lizards, parrots and snakes – were still a long way off. Dogs were kept on farms, it is true, but these were usually sheep dogs or retrievers – primarily working dogs rather than pets. Likewise people often kept cats simply to keep the rats and mice at bay. Attitudes to animals were very different, too. In cities and towns it was common to see dogs roaming the streets and occasionally causing accidents. Today the sight of a dog wandering

Stray dogs
The increased affluence in 1950s Britain also saw an increase in the number of pets that the nation owned. Attitudes towards pets were slowly changing, but there were still an alarming number of stray dogs left to roam the streets. In London alone in 1950 over 20,000 dogs were picked up by wardens.

Bob-a-Job
The growth of dog keeping in urban areas provided a lucrative opportunity for the Boy Scout movement. Introduced in 1949 as a way of testing initiative and raising funds, "Bob-a-Job" week would generally take place once a year. Boys from the local groups would be paid a bob (one shilling) in return for carrying out jobs such as chopping firewood, cleaning windows or, as seen here, walking the dog.

on its own is unusual. The laws have also been changed to protect animals from neglect, but it wasn't always like that, as John Quinn recalls.

"My family and I were all fond of dogs but we weren't sentimental about them in the way people later became. We didn't buy special food for them or take them regularly to the vet for jabs and check-ups – those lines of specialist tinned foods didn't exist. We used to feed ours on offal from the butcher or on our scraps. People just liked to have dogs around but the dogs had to take their chances – if they got ill and it didn't look as if they were getting better a farmer would usually shoot a dog rather than take it to the vet. It was the same with cats – my mother had a cat she loved but she fed it fish heads and never once took it to the vet. Times were hard and there was no spare cash for vet bills or pampering."

But where pets were kept they still captured their owners' hearts occasionally, as Kevin O'Brien recalls.

"We had a dog called Nipper who was a stray with a lovely comical nature. At first when he started to hang around the house we tried to get rid of him but he always came bouncing back, and he was so charming that eventually we found we'd let him slip into our lives, and when he didn't appear at the back door one day we went out to look for him. We didn't find him but he was back next day and we were so relieved we let him into the house, and he stayed for ten years till he died."

"... my mother had a cat she loved but she fed it fish heads and never took it to the vet."

Pam Tarlton recalls some rather more unusual pets from her country upbringing.

"We always noticed that the gipsy children who passed through the village had dogs that ran by the sides of the caravans, but the boys would often catch thrushes or crows and keep them as pets with bits of string tied to their legs to stop them escaping. I remember, too, that the local gamekeeper kept a fox cub he'd found abandoned. He used to call it and it would come like a dog. It even got on well with the keeper's Labradors. What was really odd was that the keeper spent a great deal of his time snaring and shooting foxes so they wouldn't take his pheasants, but he wouldn't hear a word against his pet, which he called Puss. As it grew it spent more time away from the keeper's cottage, and eventually it vanished."

Green fingers

Working people had always grown fruit and vegetables in their gardens but the popularity of allotments, which grew massively in the war years, gave them the chance to produce a surplus that could be sold or bartered, especially during the lean years or rationing, as Tom Shackle recalls.

"We were very lucky to get an allotment. I can't quite remember how it came about

"We became very good at making compost heaps and using scraps to fertilise the ground, because it was hard to get artificial fertiliser then."

Fierce competition
Allotments were features of great pride to both the gardeners and the locality. This was recognised by local councils who would organise annual village shows, such as the one seen below which features Alfred Cole, head gardener at Buckingham Palace, judging an allotment competition in Fulham.

Honey ration
Sugar was one of the first items to be rationed in 1940. This led to many people turning to honey as a substitute and, in turn, becoming amateur beekeepers. During World War II there were some 70,000 beekeepers in Britain, compared with just over 44,000 today. Honey was eventually rationed just after the war as demand outstripped supply.

"Dig for Victory"
During both World Wars the allotment became the focal point on the home front, as families took part in the "Dig for Victory" campaigns. During World War II allotments were estimated to have contributed some 1.3 million tons of produce from 1.4 million plots.

but I think a friend gave his up on the grounds of ill health and we took over and repaid him with a regular supply of produce. We became very good at making compost heaps and using scraps to fertilise the ground, because it was hard to get artificial fertiliser then. People were very kind and really did help each other in those days. A number of those with allotments that we knew about made sure elderly people round about received some of what they grew. We also had an arrangement with a local beekeeper who wanted extra space for his hives – we provided the space and he gave us honey in return! A wonderful thing when sugar was rationed.

We also had a garden at home filled with roses that my mother loved, and we grew vegetables in the garden too. I'm sure they always tasted better than the bought variety. Having raspberries in the summer during the war was a rare treat too

Show cancelled
Events such as Southport Flower Show (above) were cancelled during the war years as all efforts went into the "Dig for Victory" campaign. All spare plots of soil were turned over to food production rather than flowers, and any produce that was grown was reserved for human consumption rather than prize-winning.

and we tended our raspberry canes with enormous care. I can recall too that for the roses my mother would always listen out for the occasional horse passing by and someone would then be sent out to shovel up any manure that it had left in the road – it was so good for all kinds of flowering plants."

In these rather drab years the garden could also be a source of enjoyment, at a time when few could afford much in the way of entertainment. Pam Tarlton recalls the pleasure her garden gave.

"We had a very large garden – well, it would be large by today's standards I suppose – and a gardener who got paid a little but was also paid in kind. He kept a percentage of the vegetables he grew for my parents and seemed delighted at the arrangement.

One of the nicest things we also did – and we continued with it even during the war – was to have a summer flower and vegetable show in the village. We felt we should try to keep some things going as they had been before the war to show Hitler that we were not going to be defeated. We gave small prizes for the best and biggest blooms, the heaviest vegetables and so on. Even those who didn't compete – and it was all very informal – enjoyed it hugely, because there was so little to enjoy in those years for most of us."

Panking pole
To earn some extra money in the apple orchards women would often collect fallen apples for a shilling a sack, or £1 a ton, after the fruit had been shaken off the trees with a panking pole. Around 60 per cent of Britain's orchards have disappeared since 1950.

EVERY HOME SHOULD HAVE ONE

Labour saving devices

Despite the huge cost of fridges, washing machines and other labour-saving devices – in real terms they were far more expensive than they are now – the postwar world couldn't resist equipment that made life easier. This revolution was largely driven by women who had seen their mothers struggling with hot tubs and hand wringers, coal-fired ranges and open fires. A new generation was determined to have nothing to do with the back-breaking work of the past.

Kitchen appliances
As any families grew more prosperous in the 1950s, the possibility of affording shiny new kitchen appliances for the first time became real. Refrigerators, washing machines, vacuum cleaners and food mixers were among the most popular.

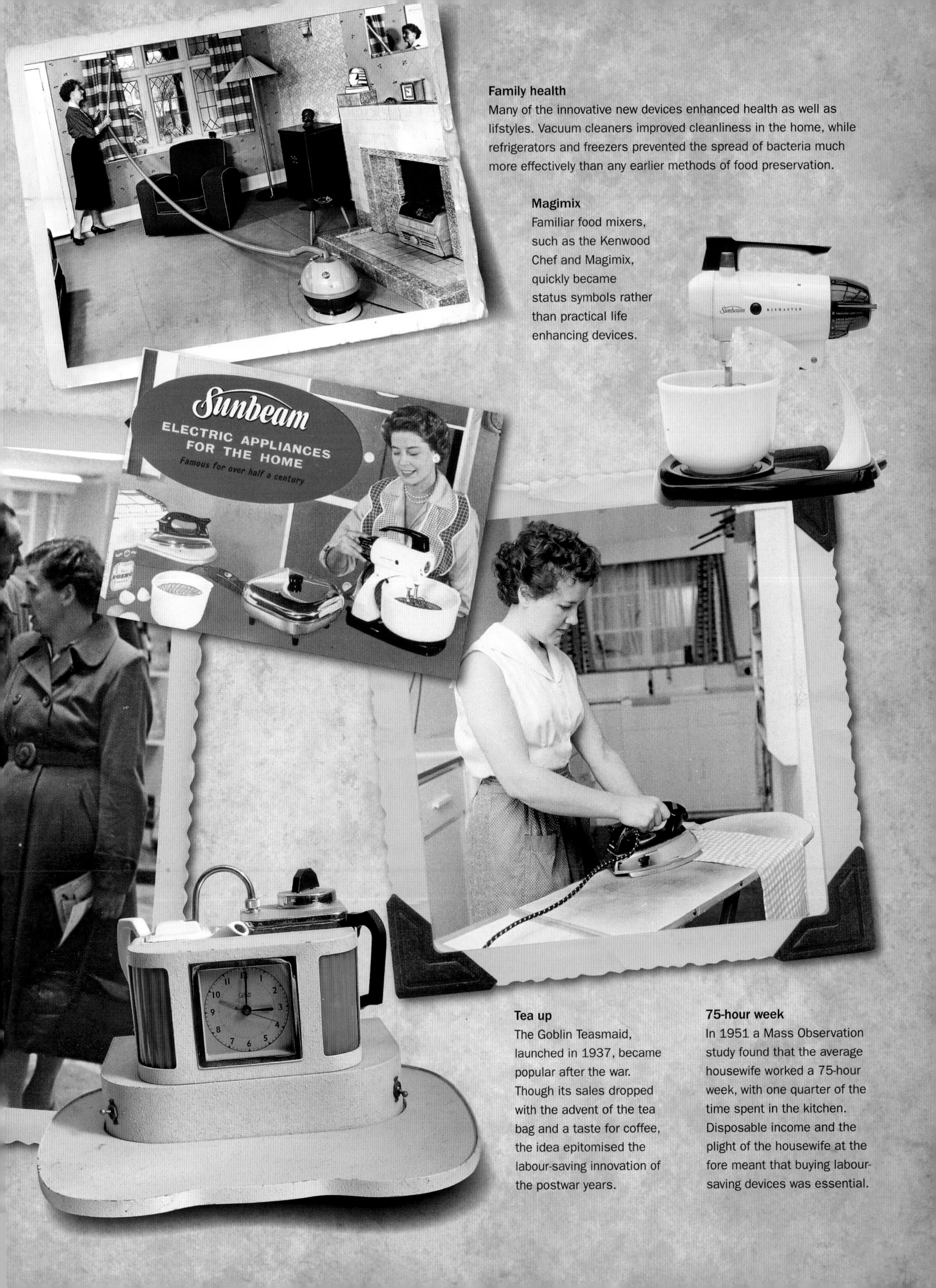

Family health

Many of the innovative new devices enhanced health as well as lifstyles. Vacuum cleaners improved cleanliness in the home, while refrigerators and freezers prevented the spread of bacteria much more effectively than any earlier methods of food preservation.

Magimix

Familiar food mixers, such as the Kenwood Chef and Magimix, quickly became status symbols rather than practical life enhancing devices.

Tea up

The Goblin Teasmaid, launched in 1937, became popular after the war. Though its sales dropped with the advent of the tea bag and a taste for coffee, the idea epitomised the labour-saving innovation of the postwar years.

75-hour week

In 1951 a Mass Observation study found that the average housewife worked a 75-hour week, with one quarter of the time spent in the kitchen. Disposable income and the plight of the housewife at the fore meant that buying labour-saving devices was essential.

In with the new

Christian Dior's 1947 "New Look" collection was received with excitement in postwar Britain. Between ten and twenty-five yards of material had been used for the day dresses, and as much as eighty yards in the case of the evening dresses. This was a striking contrast to the war time necessity for economy and utility.

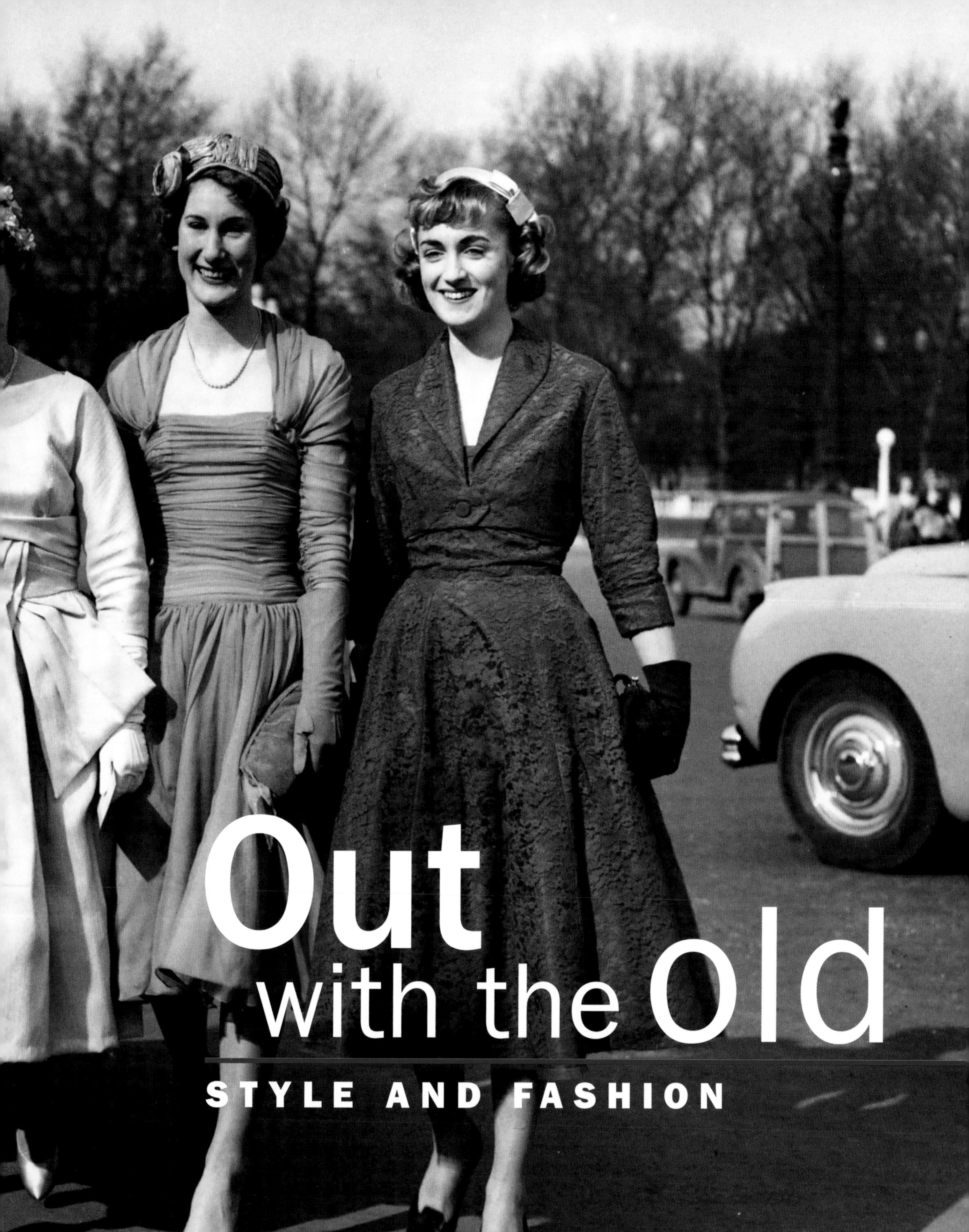

Out with the Old

STYLE AND FASHION

Bikinis, beehives, stilettos, plastic, nylon and jeans: the post-war world loved anything and everything that was new and stylish even if, as in the case of the famous Dior New Look, it wasn't really new at all! But as we gained a bright new world of labour-saving devices, easy-care fabrics and functional furniture, so we gradually lost much that had formerly been *de rigueur*. Where hats had once been almost universal for both men and women they slowly disappeared never to return, along with fans and even gloves.

New Look

The end of World War II brought a huge desire right across Britain to dispense with almost every aspect of what was seen as the dim, dull, discredited past. There was little nostalgia even among the old for the past, because the past had let people down and it was associated with dreariness and deprivation.

And there was another issue. During the war ordinary people had their first glimpse of how Americans lived – their cars, their televisions, their freedom from the old proprieties, their love of the new. Younger people in particular were entranced by new clothing and design fashions from the other side of the Atlantic. This love of anything bright and new was fuelled, too, by technologies developed largely during the war that made artificial material – nylons and plastics – widely available and at low cost. What started as a trickle of enthusiasm had become a flood by the end of the 1950s.

Growing up in Cardiff after the war, Gwen Morgan remembers the first great shock of the new:

> "People were so fed up with old-fashioned clothes – the sort of utility war look – that they jumped at the chance of anything new. Slightly older women really went for what was called the New Look, but teenagers were completely hooked on American fashions. The clothes might not have been that different but we could suddenly have bright colours after years of drab."

Setting an example

King George V forbade princesses Elizabeth and Margaret from wearing the Christian Dior "New Look" (seen left, being unveiled). He was worried that it would set a bad example to his public at a time when rationing was still in place and people were short of money.

Back to femininity

The New Look's concept of traditional femininity suited the political agenda. Women had been mobilised during the war to work on farms and in factories, but in peacetime those women were expected to return to passive roles as housewives and mothers, leaving their jobs free for the returning soldiers.

The New Look was a Dior creation that took Britain by storm in February 1947. It was a design with narrow shoulders, small waist, slightly padded hips and a skirt that ended well below the knee. It was in fact not new at all. It was a conservative look based on designs that Dior himself remembered his mother wearing when he was a child. Hemlines had become shorter during the war and the New Look was actually a return to a more demure look, but it was different from what had gone immediately before and it was French – that was its main attraction. But by some people the New Look was reviled for wasting too much material (the longer skirt) during a period when clothing material was in extremely short supply.

Gwen Morgan remembers her enthusiasm for this fashion.

> "We loved the New Look, but younger women tended to go for the other new look – a full skirt that flared out from the waist with a top that was cut to emphasise the bust – I think it was called the Princess Line. The New Look that Dior came up with had to be worn with a corset!"

Pam Tarlton has similar memories.

> "All ages are naturally conservative, so when the New Look came in younger women tended to like it while older women thought it was vaguely scandalous, I think partly because it was French and frivolous. France was still seen by the older generation as somehow permanently immoral.
>
> But the real outrage was reserved for the teenage look – Teddy Boys with drainpipe trousers, long tailored jackets with velvet collars that looked disconcertingly Edwardian, and what my father called cads' shoes. He meant those big crepe-soled shoes that Teddy Boys wore. My father thought anyone who wore them was definitely common and almost certainly criminal!"

A look to be desired

The British Guild of Creative Designers did not agree with the New Look, believing that many women were glad of just any clothes. But a study revealed that 10 million women either had or desired the "needless luxury" of the New Look.

"The clothes might not have been that different but we could suddenly have bright colours after years of drab."

TEDDY BOYS

The Teddy Boy look had really taken off by the mid 1950s and was combined with quiff hairstyles for boys – masses of greased-back hair but with a floppy bit left high above the forehead – and with new dances that must have seemed incomprehensible to a generation brought up on the foxtrot and the waltz.

Pam Tarlton remembers how the younger generation avidly adopted styles in clothes and music that seemed to go against everything their parents believed in.

"Until jeans and T-shirts arrived teenage boys' clothes were so dull ..."

'Teds'
Neo-Edwardians, or "Teds". as they became known, were a new teenage generation that longed for elegant attire. They wore Edwardian-style velvet trimmed skirted coats, usually costing up to £100 when custom tailored.

"Younger women and girls had their hair in pony tails – perms were so old-fashioned by then – or towards the end of the 1950s they'd started to put their hair up in a beehive. We wore big circular skirts with nylon petticoats, stockings and suspenders (no one had heard of tights!), white blouses and kitten-heeled shoes. Cardigans were worn backwards with the buttons down the back and maybe pearls or a scarf. Girls never wore trousers or jeans in the early 1950s or late 1940s. The music we loved was Bill Haley and Johnnie Ray, Elvis Presley, Buddy Holly and Eddie Cochrane – all American, but then the way we looked and danced was American too. We copied the look of our heroes, if you like. Just like every generation, we wanted to look like the people who played the music we liked. Unless you were there you just can't believe how much teenagers looked to America for everything.

Until jeans and T-shirts arrived teenage boys' clothes were so dull – they wore neat trousers in grey flannel, sports jackets and all in the most boring colours imaginable, but then their parents above all wanted them to be respectable."

For young men, the end of the war meant being demobbed and a major change of style from uniform to civvy street, as Eric Gray recalls.

"When you left the services you could have a full suit – that meant jacket and trousers, waistcoat, shoes and hat, and it was known as the Full Monty after Montague Burton, who started Burton's menswear. Burton also happened to make most of the demob suits. He only made them in a few sizes, which meant they usually didn't fit properly and the colours were really boring. I looked a right clown in mine!"

Make-your-own

For all but a privileged few, money was tight in the 1940s and 1950s, and as a result far more women made their own dresses and skirts or knitted scarves, socks, hats and jerseys for themselves and for friends and family. The really enterprising even made shirts and occasionally trousers for their husbands and their children, but most men still bought their suits from local tailors or from the newly emerging High Street clothing chain stores, most famously Burton's.

Lisa Edwards recalls the frenzy of activity among the dressmakers at home.

"My mother and my aunts all made their own clothes – and each other's! The point was that something expensive like shot silk could just about be afforded if you bought a bit of it but didn't have to pay to have it made up. And people back then really minded if someone else had the same dress on, so they'd buy a pattern from one of the famous pattern makers of the day – Vogue, Butterick or Simplicity – and then add something unique, such as a fake flower or a few fake cherries. The patterns poured out, I seem to remember, because the pattern makers knew that after the war there was a real clamour for new fashions and new bright materials.

There were professional dressmakers all over the country before the war – in little shops but more often at home – but they had all but vanished by the mid 1960s. The sense that everyone had to pull

Patterns galore
The austere years of the war had left women yearning for glamour. Dressmaking pattern manufacturers and women's magazines all responded by creating stylish dress patterns that could be made at home. Accessories and embellishments would be added for originality.

Ready-to-wear
Advances in textile mass production contributed to the development of the female ready-to-wear market. Companies such as the famous Horrockses Fashions supplied the female consumer with good quality cotton dresses in stylish designs. A girl's best dress was a Horrockses dress.

together in difficult times reduced the amount of snobbery about clothes – well-off middle-class women no longer thought that doing a bit of sewing was beneath them, so working-class women and the well-off were buying the same new patterns and creating a huge new market and a new look that spread quickly everywhere. Popular pattern fabrics were stripes and spots and checks, and there was something called the Cotton Board that tried to promote cotton, which was not so popular back then. People preferred the new exciting fabrics like nylon and Crimplene, and anything in nylon was seen as the best. Cotton was for poor people, which is a complete contrast with more recent years where everyone wants cotton and other natural fibres and everyone hates man-made stuff.

It's funny because looking back, a lot of the fashions made women look bottom-heavy because so many wide flaring skirts were worn with hoops – we were like those Victorians with their bustles!"

Dressmaking as a pastime also increased because patterns took more account of

amateurs, not professional dressmakers, and the boom in pattern sales coincided with a whole range of new sewing machines that could do so much more than the old prewar models, as Lisa Edwards remembers.

> "They could do zigzag stitch for buttonholes, for example – and sewing got so popular that you could take your half-made garment to a Singer sewing-machine shop and they'd do the buttonholes for you! A lot of women had their old treadle sewing machines converted to run on electricity too."

But at the top end of the market clothes were still largely handmade, particularly for men. Casual clothes were rare and men simply wore their suits for everything. And for women the casual look simply didn't fit the desire to look glamorous; the groomed look for the mature woman was everything, with carefully tailored detailing – flap pockets and three-quarter sleeves were among the most popular details – and a universal yearning for style.

Hats off

Anyone who had predicted back in the 1940s or 1950s that hats and gloves as regular everyday items would have largely vanished within 30 years would have been laughed at. Hats and gloves were a way of showing who you really were; they were the detailed accessories that said grace and elegance.

"A lot of women had their treadle sewing machines converted to run on electricity ..."

Sewing machines
The only equipment that some women had was a needle and thread, while others would use hand sewing machines or treadles (although some had their treadle machines converted into electric models). The Singer sewing machine (below) recovered quickly from the war years when production was stopped, and 1952 saw the launch of its first machine that was capable of zig zag stitching.

"... in summer it was always a straw hat and in winter a trilby ..."

Hollywood style
Hats became increasingly prominent in men's fashion thanks to the American influence of the grey flannel suite. In 1940s Hollywood characters would often wear a fedora hat (shown above), particularly when playing film noir characters.

In his book *Hatless Jack* Neil Steinberg argues that it was the young glamorous President John Kennedy who sealed the hat's fate by refusing to wear one. Kennedy may well in fact have been following rather than starting a trend, but his influence was still a decade away when Will Constance bought a new hat in the autumn of 1954.

"We all still wore hats back then. You felt naked if you went out without one and in summer it was always a straw hat and in winter a trilby or something similar. I bought a lovely trilby in 1954 I remember and it made my day. When I was working in the fields I'd wear a straw hat or a flat cap but I can't ever remember not wearing one or at least not owning one. Seems so odd now looking back, that hats were so important, because I quite liked the freedom when I stopped wearing them."

For Rose Plummer hats were part of the fun of dressing up to go out.

"We loved all the new styles of hat, even though we couldn't really afford the really posh ones. The pillbox was the most popular hat of the 1950s. Girls loved it because it was so flattering, and for special occasions you'd wear it with a bit of a veil. We had other hat styles too – some covered in flowers, folds of tulle or other bits of material, or with bits of net sewn on rather than half-covering your face.

We looked at all the fashion magazines we could get our hands on and fantasised, as all girls do, over the various styles. Berets were really popular too and a bit cheaper, but a really good one would cost a pound or a guinea – which was a lot of money back then."

Hats vs hair
The reprisal of hats, particularly for women, was relatively short lived. By the end of the 1950s hair styles were becoming more elaborate, and took precedence over headgear.

Fashion accessories
Utility regulations – which were were set in place by the British government in 1943 to enforce the economical use of materials and labour – all but put paid to fashion during the war years. With clothing restricted, women would use hairstyles, make-up and accessories to be as fashionable as possible.

Gender roles
Gendered representations structured British society by encouraging particular feminine roles. Most magazine publications for women in the postwar era conveyed the ideals of domesticity and femininity through articles on home-based craft, housework, fashions and childcare.

dewees

As the 1950s wore on younger women started to wear their hair in pony tails or in delicate perms. As a result hats started slowly to go out of fashion. This was partly because the natural look was beginning to grow in popularity and partly because hair styles such as the beehive just did not work with a hat.

FASHION ACCESSORIES

The idea of glamour wasn't confined to hats. Even spectacles got the full glamour treatment, producing a style that came almost to define the 1950s and early 1960s: who can forget those spectacles with wings arching up and away from the sides of the frames and perhaps studded with semi-precious stones or bits of glass or glitter?

Gloves too, though more restrained in style, were another feature vital to the 1950s look, as Sheila Kehoe recalls:

"Gloves were probably the most important accessory for a woman in the 1950s – if they were beautifully white and ultra-clean it was a way of saying, 'Look at me. I'm a lady'. It really was.

The rich had leather or kid gloves but we made do with cotton gloves, and everyone loved nylon gloves when they came in – they were cheap and you could get them in all sorts of lovely colours. The best and most expensive gloves were made by companies such as Pittards or Dents."

But like many women Sheila's real passion in her early days was for the new styles of make-up. New brands from make up manufacturers, such as Max Factor, were designed to hide blemishes, and a much wider range of colours and styles of eye shadow and lipstick gradually became available, as Pam Tarlton recalls.

"We looked at all the fashion magazines and fantasised, as all girls do, over various styles."

A gloved hand

Clean gloves were the characteristic of a lady and without them she was not properly accessorised. The gloves were usually made of cotton because it was more affordable than leather or the newer nylon fabric, and they could be easily washed. Many women would still own a pair of leather gloves for special occasions.

Facial accessories

Eight million pairs of spectacles were provided in the first year of the NHS in 1948. The choice of frames was limited to just two, however, as the concept of wearing fashion-orientated eyewear was largely unheard of.

"Young girls were not usually allowed to wear bright red lipstick as it was considered a bit fast, so when the big make-up firms introduced soft peach colours and pastel shades everyone was delighted."

One fashion accessory that was hugely popular in the 1950s but has now all but vanished is the stole. Even young women wore fur stoles if they could afford them, and fox stoles with the fox's head, legs, tail and feet carefully preserved and allowed to hang around the shoulders were still frequently worn by older women. Handbags with grip clasps were also very popular – particularly Hermès bags,

Hollywood look

Cinema screens accentuated the unblemished appearance of stars and led to the invention of pimple-concealing foundation make-up.

Hazardous fashion
Italian designer Roger Vivier produced the stiletto to accompany clothes designed by Christian Dior. Like other fashions of the time, stilettos were not at all practical. Although they highlighted women's femininity, they were a safety hazard and damaged floor surfaces to the extent that they were banned by some airlines and buildings by the end of the decade.

after the 1950s glamour icon and former Hollywood star Princess Grace of Monaco was photographed carrying a Hermès bag.

Shoe styles in the early 1950s were high and with rounded or peep toes. Cuban heels were common, as were sandals, but by the mid 1950s kitten heels and metal-tipped steel stiletto heels began to replace styles that owed more to the so-called New Look of 1947. The stiletto had a deliberately sexual air about it. As if to match the spindly heel, umbrellas were elongated and given fearsome-looking six-inch steel spikes. For men, winkle-pickers – shoes with impossible long thin fronts – were popular by the mid 1950s. But the trademark shoe of the 1950s was the stiletto, first seen in 1952 at the Dior fashion show.

And then there were stockings, as Lisa Edwards recalls.

"How we put up with them I just don't know, but we did. All the paraphernalia you needed to hold them up was such a pain, when I look back, and because we

Shoe X-ray
The 1950s saw the end of the shoe-fitting fluoroscope. The small X-ray machine would check the placement of feet inside the shoe to ensure that they fitted correctly. The machines were removed after it was decided that the threat of radiation was more severe than that posed by poorly-fitted shoes, and shoe fitters reverted to the traditional way of doing it by hand.

didn't like the first seamless stockings that appeared on the market – they lost their shape really quickly – we needed to check every minute that our seams were straight. I don't remember there being any idea that stocking were sexy back then, because everyone wore them because there was nothing else. It was only when tights came in much later that stockings started to get their sexy image. We used to get our stockings in Marks & Spencer."

Perhaps the most scandalous fashion innovation of the 1950s was the bikini. Invented by Frenchman Louis Réard, it was named after Bikini Atoll, the Pacific island that was constantly in the news during the 1950s as a result of the atomic bomb tests held there.

Pam Tarlton remembers her brief encounter with the two-piece swimming costume.

"I wore one on the beach once – I wanted to seem dashing and glamorous – and it was very exciting, but I was terrified because I thought that anyone who saw me might call a policeman, so after about 10 minutes I covered myself up!"

"I was terrified because I thought that anyone who saw me might call a policeman ..."

Swimwear

In July 1946, at an open-air swimming pool in Paris, French engineer Louis Réard displayed the first skimpy swimming costume. He called it the "bikini", after the US nuclear test on Bikini Atoll in the Marshall Islands that had taken place four days earlier. While the bikini became ever more popular, fashion designers continued to revamp the more traditional beachwear.

Design for living

The great building innovation of the postwar period was the bungalow. Built along prefabricated lines and foreshadowing the great 1960s system-built tower blocks, the 1950s bungalow was usually kitted out with the latest no-nonsense interior design, as Pam Tarlton recalls.

"When we moved to the south coast in the mid 1950s we bought a brand-new bungalow overlooking the sea. It was kitted out with the latest wallpaper, flooring, furniture and fabrics. We didn't want any of our parents' old things even though they'd be viewed as valuable antiques today – to us back then they seemed like something out of a horrible gloomy mahogany-dark ages.

We had a new fitted kitchen in green – my mother was horrified. The cupboards were metal and there was a big old green fridge, a terrible waste of money according to my mother. There were fitted carpets in the sitting room, steel Crittall windows and a pink bathroom suite. It was a revolution! We were one of very few houses with a fridge. We had a Formica-covered table with tubular steel seats and plastic covers – we thought they were the height of fashion, but they'd look awful now. All the doors were flat – no panels to collect dust as you'd get in an old house – the fireplace was square and functional – no coloured tiles or ornate surround. The staircase was absolutely plain. The idea of all this was to make the house easy to run – the house itself became a sort of labour-saving device, because although women were still

Bring on the plastic
Formica and cheaper plastic laminates were used to inject bold colours into dull kitchens and dining rooms. Formica could be easily cut and applied with contact adhesive and, as well as looking good, it resisted scratching and staining.

Kitchen layout
The growth of both gas and electric labour-saving appliances started to alleviate the toil of household tasks, making the kitchen the focus of an intense deliberation about how best to organise its layout. Careful consideration was taken to take full advantage of the new materials, fittings and appliances.

Home ownership
In 1900 90 per cent of houses were rented, but by 1950 approximately 60 per cent were owner-occupied. By 1955 nearly half of all houses were at least 65 years old and in need of renovation, but labour was expensive and one of the only options left was to do-it-yourself.

expected to stay at home the idea was that the modern successful man got his wife all the latest things (including the latest modern bungalow) so her work was reduced. The idea of the bungalow itself fitted this – with no upstairs you didn't have to worry about getting tired going to bed at night!"

Elsewhere older houses were rapidly being divided into flats; old fireplaces which had served so well began to be ripped out as central heating gained a tiny foothold towards the end of the 1950s, as Libby MacIntyre remembers.

"Our Victorian terrace – we only lived there for a short while, thank God – was given a bit of a makeover in the late 1950s. We had the staircase with its elaborate turned balusters boxed in with hardboard, the panelled doors were covered with plywood to make them look flat, we covered the black and white ceramic tiles in the hall with green lino and bought an electric fire for the sitting room. The fireplaces were either blocked up or taken out. Looking back it was amazingly destructive really,

"Where we'd had old dusty furniture before we now had collectables ..."

and we felt a bit silly when in the 1980s people started putting back into houses all the things we'd taken out! But back then we were the envy of our neighbours. We also threw out a Victorian table and chairs as well as a grandfather clock, and bought a plastic table with chrome legs and some very smart high stools."

MAN-MADE FIBRES

In tandem with houses that forgot their past was an enthusiasm for man-made fibres that now seems baffling – nylon and Crimplene for clothes, curtains, upholstery and bedding, and plastics, fake laminates and steel for furniture. The new materials not only had the supreme virtue of being new but they were also cheap and fitted new ideas about functionality; they were simple, didn't gather dust and looked forward into an idyllic future not back into the gloom and austerity of the war years.

But what was happening in the suburbs of the big cities it wasn't necessarily happening everywhere, as Will Constance explains.

DIY magazines The demand for DIY instruction was fulfilled by magazines such as *The Practical Householder*, which first appeared in October 1955. Step-by-step instructions showed how just about anyone could build their own refrigerator, television and even a fitted kitchen.

Home improvement Encouraged by the government building programme to replace bomb-damaged housing and to clear the slums, people in the early 1950s aspired to owning their own homes or tackling home improvement. Because it was hard to get hold of tradesmen as most of them were busy with reconstructing war-torn Britain, home improvement soon swept across the nation. Many companies capitalised on wartime advances in plastics and adhesives, transforming them into commercial products for consumers.

"Going out and buying new furniture and lights and doors when we had stuff that had lasted a century and more would have made us a laughing-stock – things changed slowly in our part of Norfolk and by the time the fad for new things had come and gone our old furniture, the stuff people threw out in the 1950s, had suddenly become fashionable again. Where we'd had old dusty furniture before we now had collectables, and the knockers started to come regularly to the door to try to buy our old stuff for the London markets."

As long as it's new

Most people are surprised at how early plastic furniture and man-made fibres started to be used for everyday items of clothing and furniture. What might seem typical of the 1960s and 1970s actually began to spread deeply into our lives in the 1950s and in some cases even earlier.

Plastic moulded chairs, prefabricated concrete buildings, nylon and Crimplene sheets, chair covers, stockings and pullovers – all gradually became available in the 1950s. Their unique selling point was that they were hard-wearing and easy to look after – nylon shirts didn't need ironing, for example. Most of the new fabrics were created using petrochemicals and in the early days they were expensive simply because the process of synthesis by which they were produced was still in its infancy. But very quickly polyester, acrylic and nylon became widely and cheaply available – acrylic could be spun into yarn to make jerseys that never seemed to tear or wear out and they were even moth-proof.

Sheila Kehoe remembers using early nylon and acrylic products.

"That really got going in the early 1960s, but I do remember in the mid and late 1950s that a few items began to appear. We all thought that nylon sheets were

Plywood design
Designers Ray and Charles Eames began plywood experimentation during World War II, first fashioning plywood leg splints for wounded naval officers, then designing airplane parts from moulded plywood for the US Airforce. After the war they used their innovative designs from their research with the US navy to design the Eames Lounge Chair Wood (LCW) involving the naturalistic curvature of plywood splints, as in the picture above.

A new kitchen
During the 1950s the kitchen became a multi-functional living space and one of the main attractions of the house. It was enjoyed rather than endured due to introduction of modern electric appliances, as well as the availability of new materials and finishes, changing the look and layout of the kitchen for good.

wonderful and paid extra for them, but it's amazing how long it took us to realise that they made you sweat horribly. My first experience of nylon came when my brother in America sent me some nylon pyjamas. I thought they were like silk! The cotton makers must have been panicking, because cotton was suddenly seen as old hat and boring and difficult because it creased so badly. A lot of people in those days still ironed their sheets – but if nylon sheets were bad, just think of nylon shirts. The whole thing has come full circle now and very few of us would dream of wearing a nylon shirt or an acrylic pullover – even to have a bit of nylon in your shirts is considered such a bad idea.

"In those days if it was modern we wanted it, even if it didn't work as well as the things we got rid of."

We also had loads of aluminium because it didn't rust – aluminium saucepans, aluminium knives and forks, aluminium door handles. In those days if it was modern we wanted it, even if it didn't work as well as the things we got rid of. Door handles as opposed to knobs for example – the handles were really annoying and not nearly as good as knobs, but we all had to have them. Silly really."

Furniture design began to change too, as Pam Tarlton recalls.

"We had a sofa with arms just like the wings of a Zephyr – that was a late 1950s car. The wings of the sofa also looked a bit like the butterfly wings you see on those classic 1950s spectacles."

Robert Fox taught woodwork in the 1950s in an inner London school. He remembers how the new materials of the 1950s made old skills more or less redundant.

"Being a bit of an old buffer even then I couldn't see why it was better to glue and screw everything – the new way – rather than cut proper joints when you were making a bookcase or whatever. I loved the smell of the old horse-hoof glue we used to boil and the smell of oak and elm being sawn by the boys, but that suddenly went out of the window in the late 1950s and we had to use chipboard and chemical glues, Formica – a sort of nasty artificial veneer – screws and nails. Dove-tail joints and mortise-and-tenon joints were suddenly redundant. It was all so cheap and nasty, but because it was new people didn't look at it properly and ask if it was really any good. I'm glad the fashion for all that tat didn't last too long!"

The Ideal Home
Exhibitions around the country inspired people to create the perfect home. The Ideal Home Exibition, which started in the 19th century, inspired visitors with innovation, and introduced them to the latest must-have products with which to adorn their homes. With the postwar focus shifting towards fashion and style in the home and inventive labour-saving devices, these exhibitions were more popular than ever before.

SUGAR

STYLE MEETS FUNCTION

The Festival of Britain

The 1951 Festival of Britain deliberately echoed the Great Exhibition of a century earlier. Like its predecessor it was a celebration of the best of British design and technology but it also marked a turning point in Britain's attitude to the new. Exhibitions were organised nationwide from Bristol to Birmingham, Manchester to Glasgow. Deputy Labour leader Herbert Morrison put the official view when he said the Festival was "a tonic for the nation".

Pleasure gardens
As part of the festivities, Battersea Park was transformed into the Festival Gardens, laid out as a pleasure garden with riverside walk, funfair, Oystercreek Railway and restaurants selling canned peas.

Urban design
Construction of the South Bank site opened up a new public space, a riverside walkway, which had previously been warehouses and working-class housing. The layout was intended to showcase the principles of urban design that would feature in the postwar rebuilding of London and the creation of the new towns.

Dome of discovery
The main attraction at the Festival of Britain was the Dome of Discovery, designed by 39-year-old Ralph Tubbs. This featured a planetarium, reached by an "Escalator to Outer Space", a Polar Theatre and a life-sized reproduction of Captain Cook's *Endeavour*.

Science and technology
Although the Festival took pride in Britain's past, most of the exhibits looked to the future, where science and technology featured strongly. In one of the pavilions, many Londoners saw their first ever television pictures.

Tonic for the nation
Over the summer of 1951 the Festival of Britain was publicised in shops, at events, exhibitions, radio programmes and concert halls. By September 1951, over eight million people had visited the South Bank exhibition.

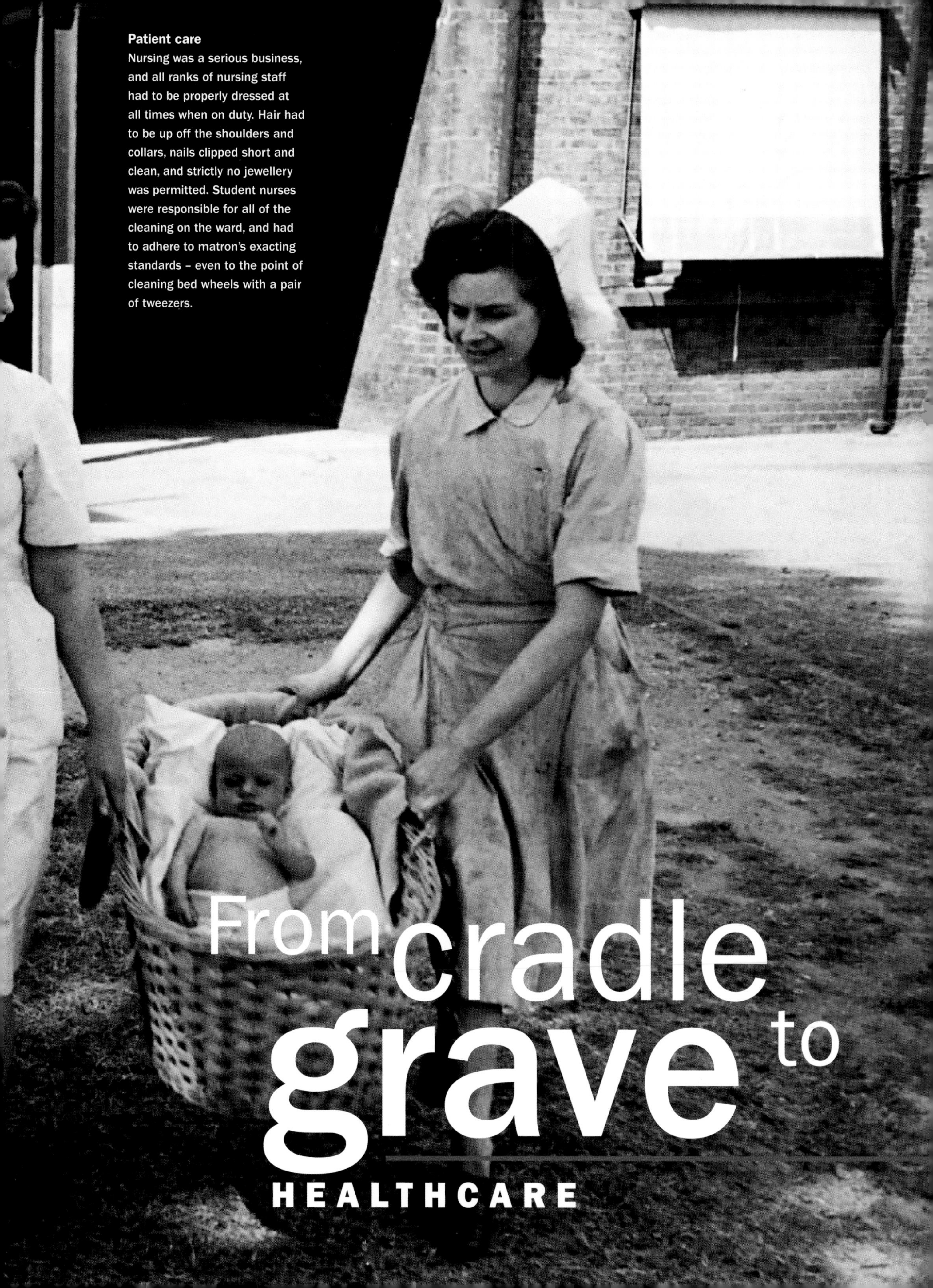

Patient care
Nursing was a serious business, and all ranks of nursing staff had to be properly dressed at all times when on duty. Hair had to be up off the shoulders and collars, nails clipped short and clean, and strictly no jewellery was permitted. Student nurses were responsible for all of the cleaning on the ward, and had to adhere to matron's exacting standards – even to the point of cleaning bed wheels with a pair of tweezers.

From cradle to grave

HEALTHCARE

Two extraordinary changes in healthcare made the postwar world profoundly different from any previous era. The first was the widespread use of penicillin which helped defeat TB, one of history's biggest killers; the second was the launch of the welfare state and, more particularly, the National Health Service. Under the new Labour government the poor would no longer be allowed to suffer and die simply because they could not afford a doctor; nursing, general practice, surgery and dentistry were transformed. Britain was to become not just a land fit for heroes but also a place where heroes had a right to a decent, healthy life.

A doctor calls
The NHS was born out of a long-held ideal that good healthcare should be provided, regardless of wealth. Britain was the first country in the world to offer free healthcare to all.

Precarious health

Anyone familiar with Somerset Maugham's first novel, *Lisa of Lambeth* (1897), will remember his heart-rending description of a poor man seeking help at St Thomas's Hospital in London, where Maugham had trained as a doctor towards the end of the 19th century. The patient clearly had consumption or TB, for which at that time the only cure was rest and a stay in a warm country. How, asked Maugham, could a London labourer with many children be told to go abroad? It was stories like this that fuelled the increasing clamour for a health service that did not depend on how much money one had.

The inadequacy of the health system before the Beveridge Report and the National Health Service that followed it in 1948 is difficult today to comprehend. But while the politicians were broadly in favour of a new system of health care precisely because things were so bad for the poor under the old system, the medical profession was resolutely against it. Doctors felt their status as independent practitioners would be undermined. In the wider world there was scepticism, and for years after the NHS was set up older people remained suspicious.

Will Constance, living in rural Norfolk, recalls a typical pre-NHS world.

> "I had four brothers and three sisters who all died in infancy. Most families round about had lost little children – disease was everywhere in the 1930s, particularly TB and smallpox – and of course if you had no money you could not easily get a doctor, even if you were dying. A relative of mine cut his leg on a fence and died from gangrene – there was nothing anyone could do.
>
> My father ran four miles for the doctor soon after my sister was born and the doctor brought my father back with him in the pony cart. I remember that as if it was yesterday. He was a kindly doctor but they weren't all like that – some would want to see your money before they'd even look at you. Mind you, a lot of the older people hated the new system. There was a woman in the village who worked as a midwife who also made up potions – I think they were pretty harmless but I doubt if they did much good, but even after the NHS came in, the older villagers went to her for medicine for coughs and colds. I remember an elderly woman who absolutely refused to go to a doctor even after she became very ill because she said he might ask her to take her clothes off! She eventually died at home and untreated, so stubborn was she."

John Adams, a doctor working in Devon in the 1930s, remembers how erratic medical provision was in those days, and some of the strategies employed by people who needed care but could not afford to pay for it.

Home care
Many doctors feared that they would lose their independence if a national system was introduced, while some older people were suspicious of the state's involvement in medical provision. But the benefits were indisputable – the poor, who often had to go without treatment or rely on dubious home remedies, now received the same level of care as the wealthy.

> "Well, it wasn't just that a lot of our remedies were inadequate – remember this was in the 1920s and 1930s, before antibiotics – it was also that we often had to treat patients who couldn't pay. We didn't like it I must admit, but it was very difficult to turn them away – some doctors did but then they'd go to the next doctor and very few had medical insurance in those days. I was paid all sorts of things in lieu of cash – baskets of fruit, a violin, a painting. One chap offered to work in the garden for a few days in return for help.
>
> The big killers were diphtheria, scarlet fever and, most dreaded of all, TB.

"Of course if you had no money you could not easily get a doctor, even if you were dying."

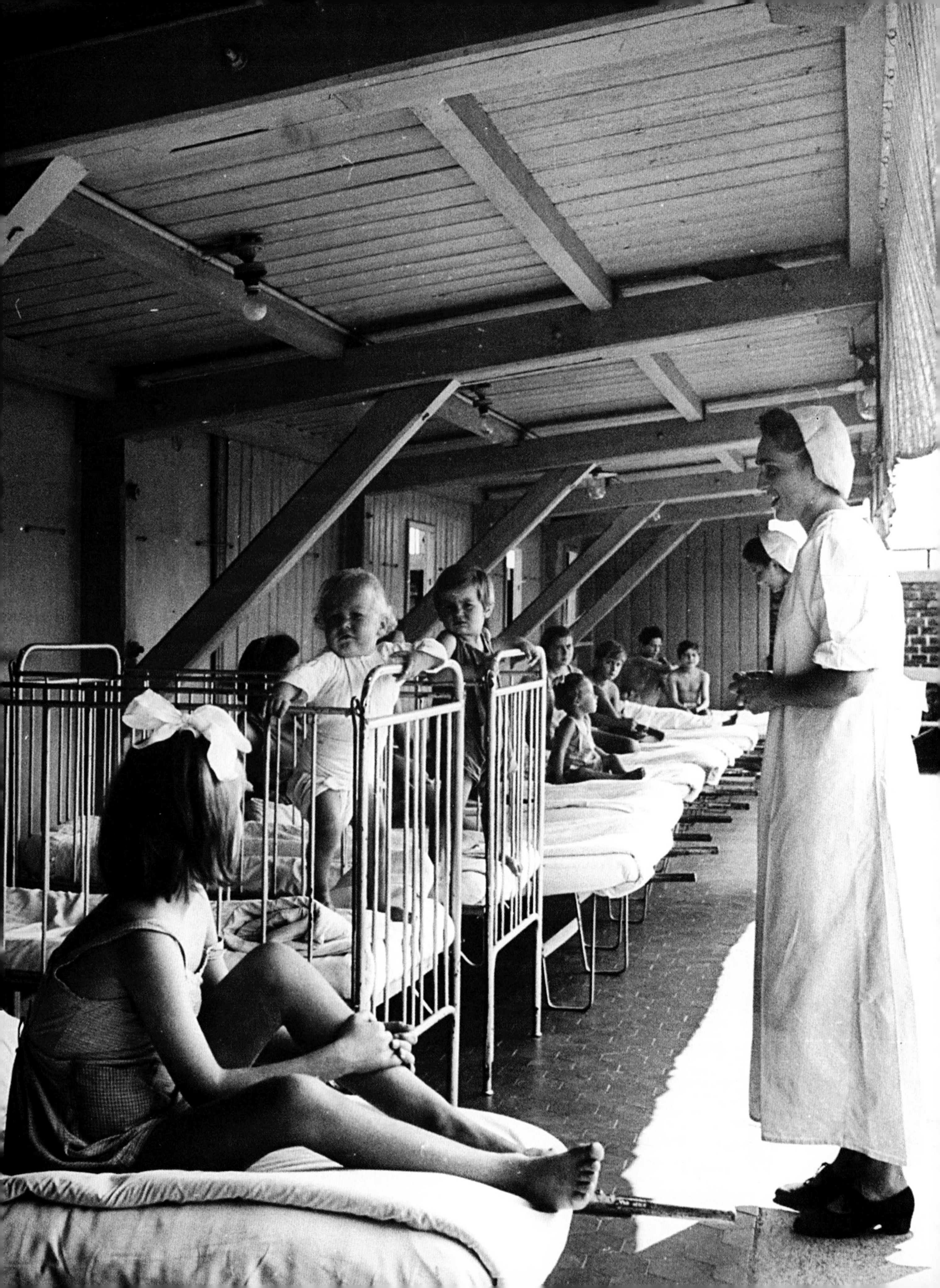

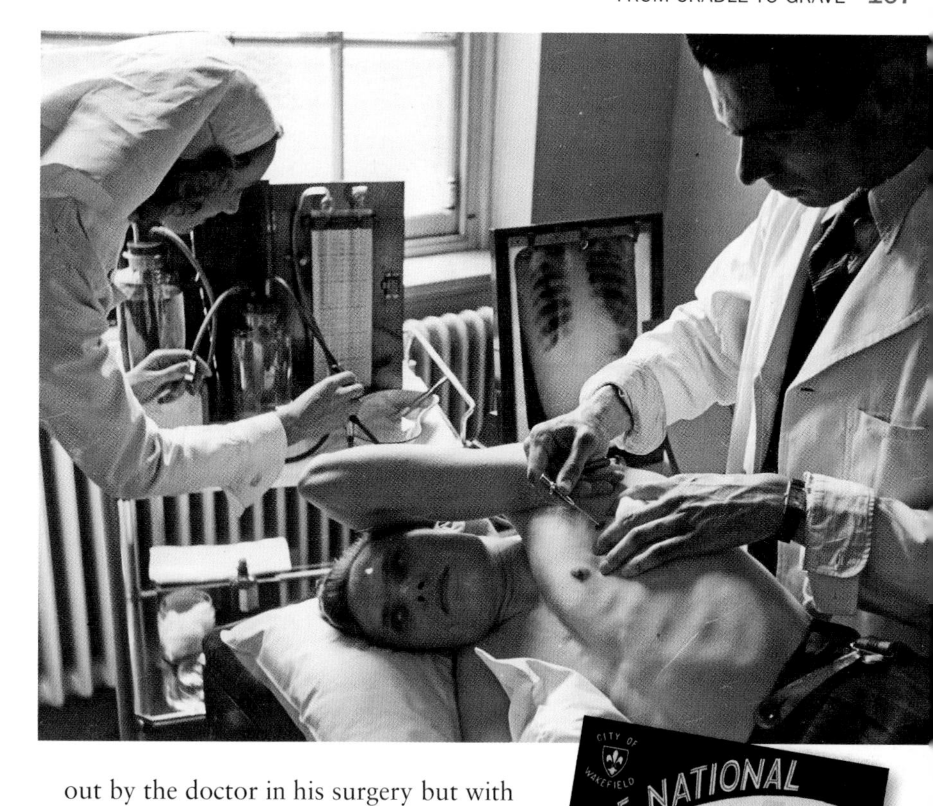

There were voluntary hospitals, hospitals for infectious diseases and a sort of ramshackle regional responsibility for health care, but the bottom line was that in the vast majority of cases if you couldn't pay you'd probably not be treated properly. Working-class patients were often treated with thinly disguised displeasure; middle-class patients with more courtesy. The upper-middle classes reversed the whole thing and treated doctors like a sort of slightly superior domestic servant. Thank God that whole world has been swept away!"

LIVING WITH ACHES AND PAINS

For Reg Dobson it was the bravery of people in the face of medical procedures that was impressive.

"People put up with pain – toothache and arthritis and all kinds of things and never had painkillers to deal with it. I remember once my dad was kicked in the face by a pony, breaking his jaw. He went into the house, holding his jaw without a sound. The doctor came out and reset it and not once did Dad even flinch. And he still didn't flinch when the doctor discovered the jaw wasn't setting properly and it had to be broken again by the doctor and reset – and all with no anaesthetic."

Denys Watkins Pitchford recalls being operated on with chloroform as the anaesthetic, which was reminiscent of pre-war medical treatment.

"They just put a drug-soaked cloth over my mouth and did the operation on the scrubbed kitchen table – many years after World War II in remote rural areas things hadn't changed a bit! The only progress was that often the operation was carried out by the doctor in his surgery but with no proper anaesthetist, nor heart monitors or back-up if things went wrong."

Free for all

The NHS came in the wake of a huge number of political and social reforms, including the taking into public ownership of gas and electricity, coal and steel production. The private mine owners had run what were seen as nationally important sectors for personal profit, and Labour was determined to stop them. They were also determined to stop medicine being available only to the rich. But the nationalisation of health didn't appeal to doctors, as Mark Brown recalls.

"It's odd that so many doctors and the medical establishment generally were so against the NHS – they felt that it was a sort of communist conspiracy and felt that they would get a terrible deal out of it and lose their professional independent status. As it turned out we did very well out of the change, both financially and in terms of status. But there was really just a nervousness about such a big change. The old system could be pretty heartless too, because if you were a GP you expected patients to pay for a consultation and for

Lots of fresh air
In the early 1950s there were 50,000 annual cases of tuberculosis, but improved living conditions and vaccine development were beginning to bring the numbers down. It was particularly prevalent in young people, and sanatoriums for both children and adults were common. While some patients recovered, relapsing and dying wasn't uncommon. Fresh air clinics were advocated as a way of treating the disease and controlling its spread.

Treating TB
Early experimental treatments for TB were lengthy, painful and ineffective. It wasn't until 1943 that Selman A Waksman found an antibiotic treatment for the disease. It was administered to its first patient a year later. The Bacillus Calmette-Guérin (BCG) vaccination programme against TB was introduced for children by the NHS in 1953. It continued to be used until 2005 when recorded instances of the disease fell to their lowest levels.

Healthcare for everyone Park Hospital, Manchester, was the first NHS hospital. It was opened by the service's founder Aneurin Bevan (above, at the hospital) on July 5, 1948.

"Dozens of patent medicines contained cocaine and no one thought anything about it."

Not free for long The Labour government introduced the idea of prescription charges, but Aneurin Bevan argued that they were contrary to the "universally free" principle of the NHS, and resigned when colleagues forced the proposal through. Labour was voted out of power before the charges could be implemented, but 1s was then levied by the Conservatives in 1952.

medicine, and if they couldn't pay they knew they couldn't come to see you. The poorest people definitely died because they couldn't afford care. Some doctors did a lot of pro bono work through charities but it was never enough.

My memories of the early NHS are of green-painted wards, strict hospital matrons who ordered nurses (and sometimes doctors!) about as if they were in the army, and also of the old-fashioned nature of everything – mahogany cupboards and brass microscopes were still in use. And those big apothecary's jars in rows in wooden cupboards. Amazingly, dozens of patent medicines contained cocaine and no one thought anything about it. For aches and pains we prescribed White Horse embrocation; for colds and flu we suggested sticking your head over a bowl of hot water and menthol. There were very few of the fancy medicines there are now."

William Beveridge's celebrated report recommended a welfare state that would care for everyone regardless of means. Minister of Health Aneurin Bevan, the great architect of the new National Health Service, said he thought the NHS would create an atmosphere of "greater security and serenity up and down the country for families faced by anxiety and the distress of illness."

A HEALTHIER NATION

It was felt that as the health of the nation improved the cost of the health service would be reduced because people would be healthier and less prone to illness. This failed to take account of increasing longevity and improvements in technology – expensive improvements. But in the early days optimism was high. Victorian hospitals run on a charitable basis were often underfunded. In some areas provision was good, in others appalling. Bigger hospitals were often filled with cockroaches and mice and many – particularly in London – damaged by bombs. The visionaries of the new system wanted to sweep all this away.

Rose Plummer recalls how ordinary people felt about the new service.

> "When we first heard about it I think we thought it all sounded wonderful but we doubted it would be much different in practice – we all just thought it was more promises that wouldn't be kept, but I remember having to go to my local doctor in 1949 and it was completely different from when I'd last visited before the NHS, which was probably in 1946. The surgery

In demand
From the outset there was huge demand for the services provided by the NHS. The buggest rushes were for drugs, spectacles and false teeth, which led to long queues in surgeries and clinics around the country. NHS numbers were issued upon joining the local doctors' surgery; babies were automatically issued them at birth.

Baby boom
Attitudes towards childbirth started to change shortly before the end of the war, adopting a medical focus where previously it had been seen as merely a natural event. More women opted to give birth in hospital – at a cost of about five guineas before the NHS – and the new maternity wards quickly filled up.

looked pretty much the same as I recall, but there had been two entrances – one for private patients and the other for the poor. In the past you'd been made to feel like a second or third-class citizen and I suddenly realised all that had gone. It might have been just because we all felt more confident having won the war but the atmosphere had changed too – the doctor was definitely friendlier, less inclined to look down his nose at you. I think they didn't like treating the poor before the NHS because they worried about not being paid, and sometimes to be honest they didn't like treating people who didn't have baths at home and had to work long hours labouring. Doctors were middle class and I think they resented having to look at a labourer's feet! After the NHS started none of that seemed to matter any more – they treated us all the same."

A new world for the old hospitals

When the NHS started life in 1948 it was faced with a number of daunting tasks including the seemingly impossible business of restoring hundreds of badly run-down hospital buildings.

The old hospital system had been run on voluntary lines and many of its buildings were poorly maintained and seriously in debt. The government could take over the debt, but what of the buildings? These were often damp and vermin-infested or had been damaged by enemy bombs. It was undoubtedly the spirit of optimism and political will that saved the day, as John Quinn recalls.

"The politicians were 100 per cent behind the new NHS because there was an attitude generally held that the state had let people down in the past and that was never going to be allowed to happen again. It was a sort of brave-new-world view but it galvanised people into action, particularly as regards hospitals. Doom-mongers said it wouldn't work but it did.

I had to go into hospital for a hernia operation in 1950 and I remember being amazed at the efficiency and politeness of the staff, but I also remember how carefully the hospital was cleaned – every day from top to bottom, it seemed, an army of staff was constantly scrubbing and mopping. Windows were cleaned regularly too and the whole place had an absolutely spotless air. There were workmen constantly hammering and sawing too, trying to make something modern out of a big draughty old Edwardian building. The paintwork was a little dreary it is true – I remember ghastly creams and browns and old dark mahogany doors, but most houses, offices and shops were like that too back then. I think they made a wonderful job of transforming those old hospitals, although of course almost no expense was spared at the time and it is a process that continues to this day."

Attitudes to patients and to medicine in general were very different too in the late 1940s and 1950s, as Dr John Adams recalls.

"Hospitals took no risks back then, which meant that patients typically stayed in hospital far longer than they did 30 and more years later. In the early 1950s the average length of stay in hospital for a woman after giving birth was just under two weeks. By the year 2000 that was down to two days. Or take cataract operations, which were already fairly common in the 1950s. You had to stay in bed for a week without moving and with your eyes bandaged after the op. By 2000 a cataract patient would come into hospital in the morning, have the operation and be home the same day. Anyone who thinks the NHS has not been a success should remember that life expectancy is now 10 years longer on average than it was in 1948."

New hospitals
The lack of suitable buildings was a major problem for the fledgling NHS, which led to "emergency project" hospitals, such as the Alexandria in the Leven Valley, Scotland (above), to be quickly built in 1955. It wasn't until 1962 that the Hospital Plan, proposed by Enoch Powell, addressed the issue with a 10-year building plan.

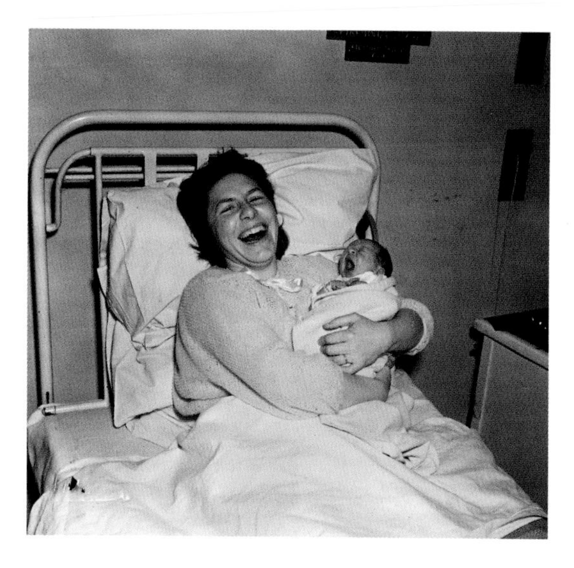

Bonding time
Infant mortality rates fell in the postwar years as a result of improved quality of living and medical care. The government had also recognised the importance of nutrition for expectant mothers. There was still no question of the father being present at the birth.

The family doctor

General practitioners have always been the first line of defence in the health-care system, but the new NHS brought in changes that sometimes tested doctors' patience to the limit. John Adams recalls the start of the new era.

"The biggest thing I recall about the early days was record keeping. It had been almost very imprecise before the arrival of the NHS because it was completely up to the individual GP – some kept good records, some didn't. We had to sort that out and it was a Herculean task to do it. Other GPs might disagree with that, but we certainly hardly kept any records in my practice – and it was quite a big practice – because we knew everyone by name and we knew their medical history without having to look it up. But what you have to remember is that in the early days a lot of medical people carried on pretty much as they had before the NHS. It was only gradually that meticulous record keeping became compulsory. There were no national targets, no nationally agreed procedures or strategies – we just carried on as before, except that now the government paid our salaries and we were paid for having a certain number of patients on the books.

I had friends who were doctors in big cities and I remember them telling me that the number of patients went up continually after the NHS came in because people began to realise that they no longer had to worry about money first and their health afterwards. In big city practices when surgery was open the patients would queue patiently in a line that stretched half way down the street sometimes.

Prescribing was very different then. We had far fewer drugs and our greatest new weapon, penicillin, was one of a very small number of antibiotics we were able to

Doctor on call
Advances in technology during the war years enabled the first radio-telephone equipped cars to be on the road in the early 1950s. They were generally used by doctors on call. The radio was powered by the car battery, but it was basically a complete telephone unit mounted on the dashboard and proved to be cumbersome and impractical.

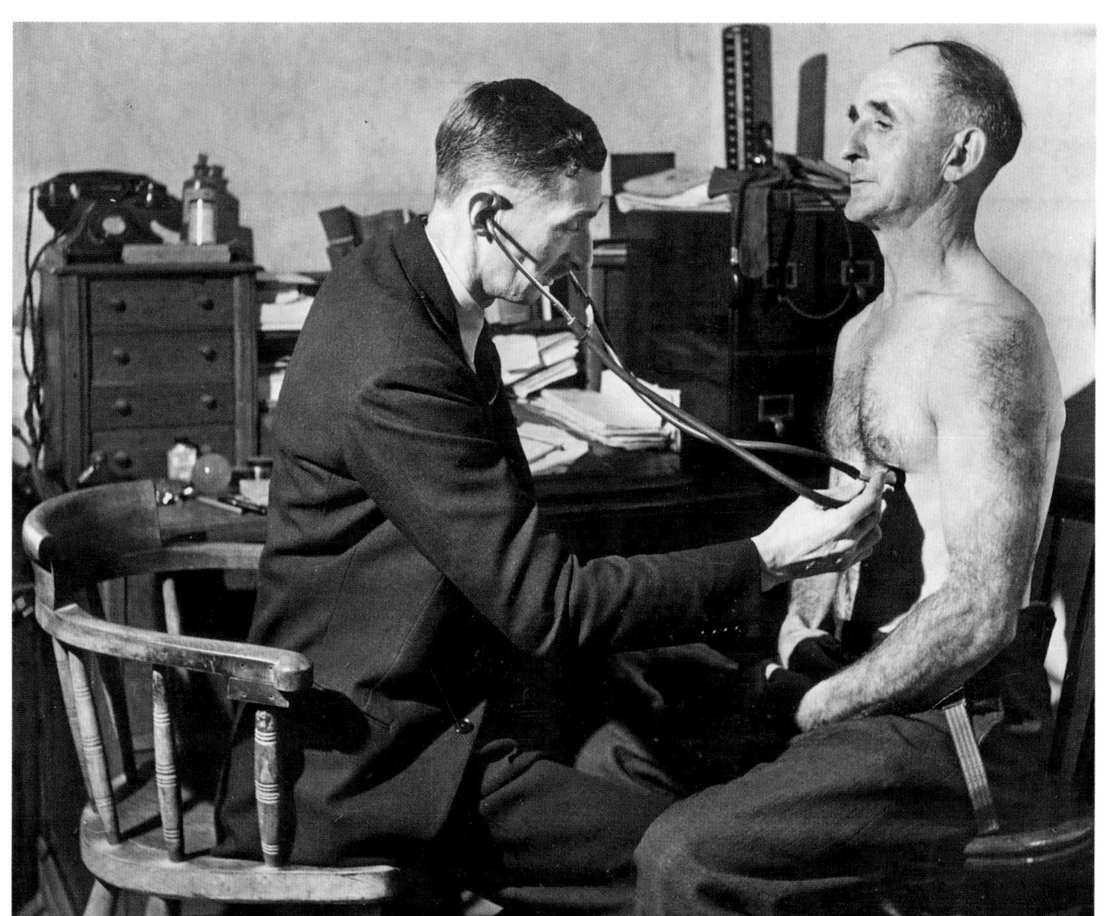

Health check
Despite the wartime changes in lifestyle and diet, death rates from coronary heart disease in middle-aged men and women continued to rise in the postwar period. The 1950s diet contained a lot of meat, and was high in fat.

Paying for it
Before the NHS access to GPs had been free for workers on lower incomes, but this did not extend to their wives or children. It was this group of people, as well as the poor who were out of work, that the service was primarily aimed at. Access to a GP prior to this had to be paid for, and most GPs could earn a good living from their patients alone.

prescribe. Within 20 years there were dozens of new ones and they are still being developed all the time. There was a greater element of caution then too – we recommended bed rest for almost everything where much later that idea was discredited largely and we tried to get everyone out of bed as fast as possible!

The same was true of pregnancy. I'm afraid we all treated pregnant women as if they were ill – after giving birth they might stay in hospital for a week or two! But delivering babies was the thing I missed after the health service became increasingly specialised. GPs were always summoned when a woman was giving birth but that mostly stopped when the local maternity ward opened.

A modern GP would be astonished at our other duties – we mixed medicines as if we were pharmacists, we did minor surgery if someone had an accident that wasn't quite bad enough for the hospital, and we seemed to be endlessly on call. But back then it was more of a vocation than a job, I think."

"I'm afraid we all treated pregnant women as if they were ill ..."

Open wide
"A nation of people with bad teeth" was how the writer and social observer George Orwell caricatured Great Britain in 1940. But with the introduction of the National Health Service, which, for the first time, included free dental checks, British teeth and gums began to improve.

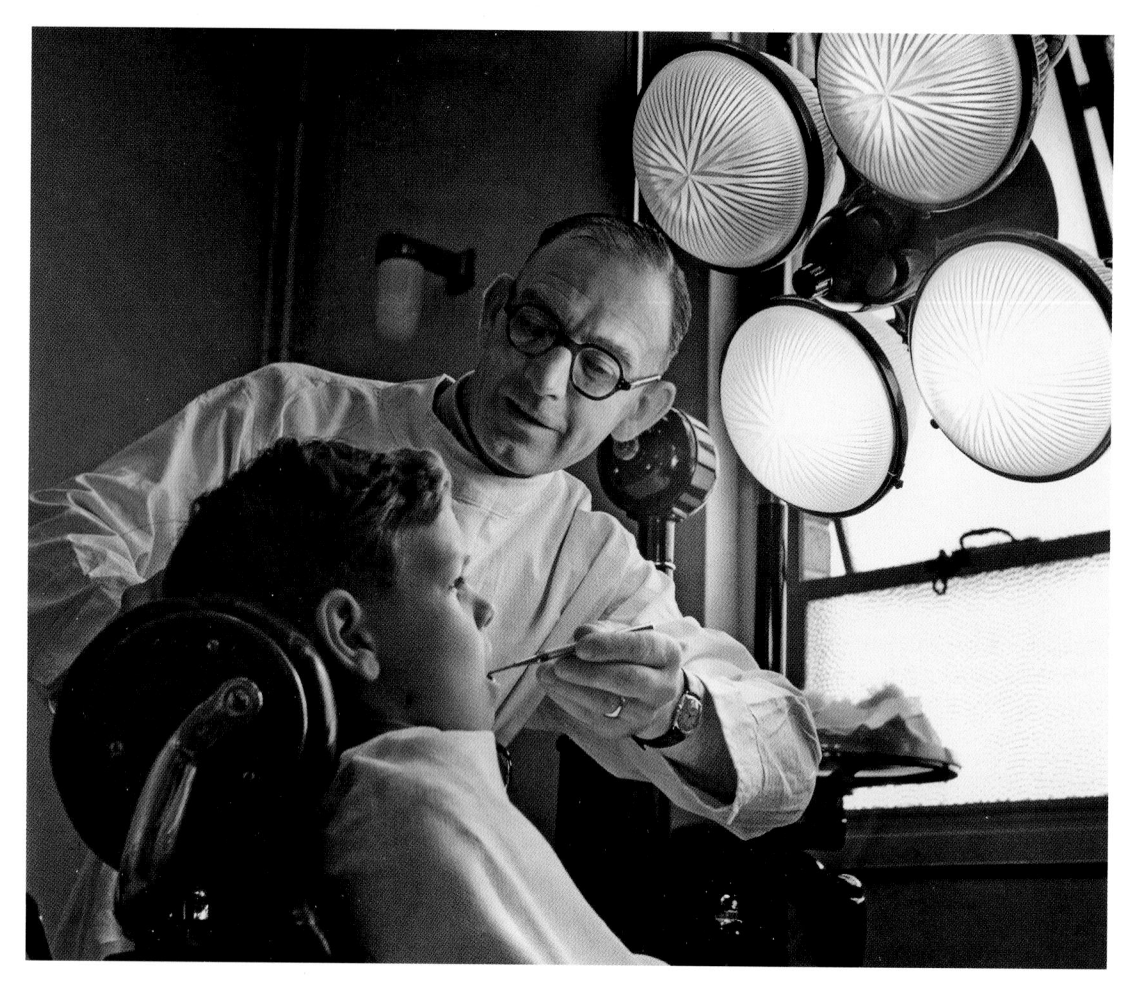

The dentist's chair

Before the NHS, dentistry was difficult to obtain for the poor and, like medicine more generally, it was a ramshackle affair where relatively primitive general anaesthetic was administered by the dentist himself, a practice that is now banned, as Richard Green recalls.

"We did indeed administer general anaesthetic ourselves and by today's standards it was probably dangerous and there were a few cases where patients died. But then dentistry was generally rather primitive back then. I recall that poor people almost always wanted extractions when there was the least trouble with a tooth, while the rich generally could afford fillings. Fillings, it goes without saying, were not the invisible modern white ones but the old amalgam that looked like metal. People also sometimes got their friends and family to knock their teeth out – the old story about a piece of string tied to a decayed tooth and then to a door that was slammed is not pure invention.

"Poor people almost always wanted extractions when there was the least trouble with a tooth, while the rich generally could afford fillings."

In those pre-fluoride days too, people's teeth were generally in a much worse condition than they are now. Oddly, no one seemed to mind much. I think people were more fatalistic about what happened to them. One terrible practice was the routine removal at the age of 18–21 of all a girl's teeth. It was never common I

Overwhelming demand
At the start of the NHS it is estimated that only a quarter of Britain's dentists had signed up to offer free treatment. Public demand shocked everyone however, and most dentists went from treating 15–20 people per day to up to 100. Many dentists worked over the 35 recommended hours per week to try and keep up, and seven practices opened days a week.

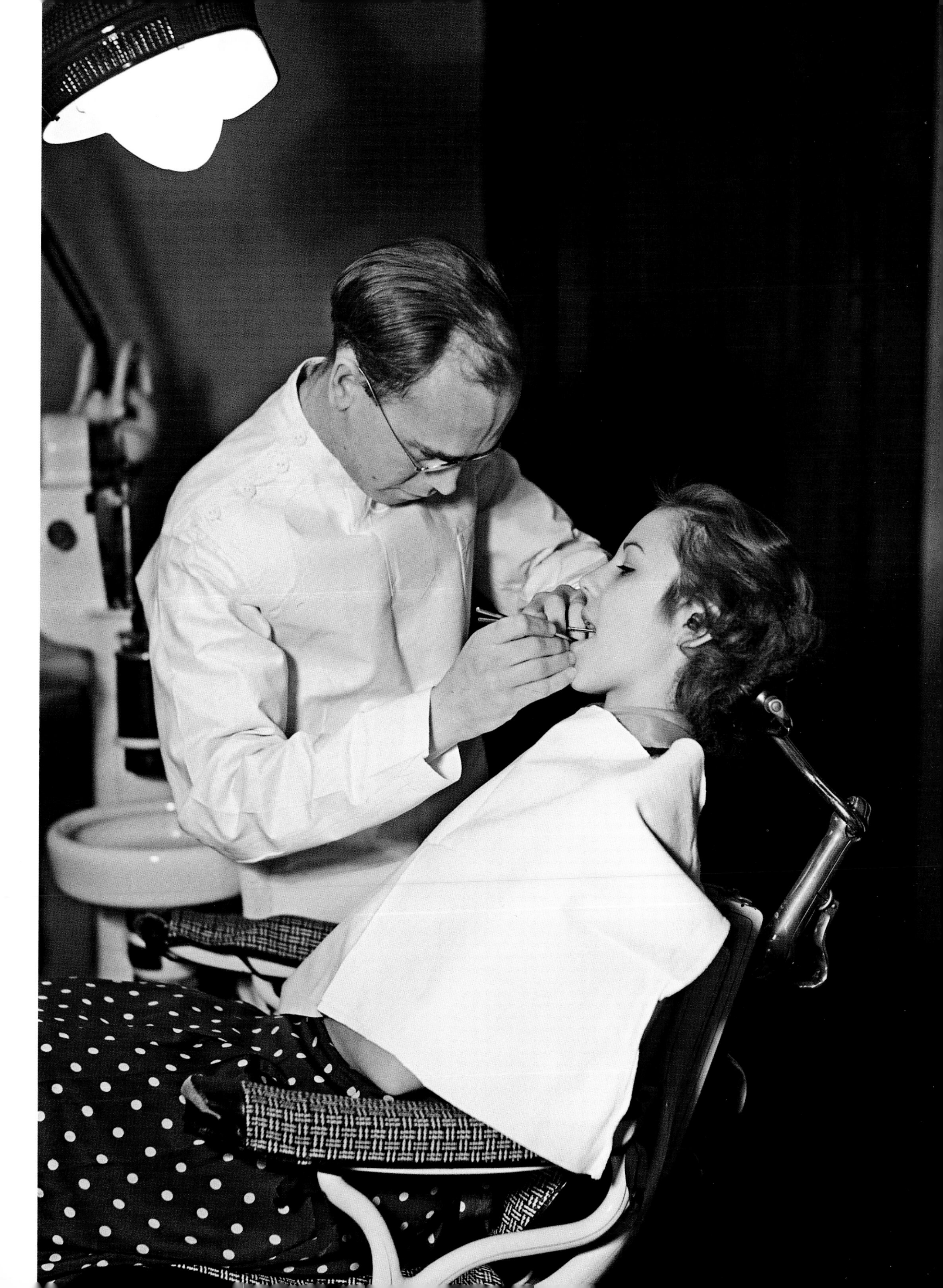

suspect but did happen in some areas. The idea was that if she had all her teeth out and got a set of false ones there would be no further bills for dentistry for her husband-to-be. Terrible."

But from the patient's point of view the dentist was as much to be avoided as the doctor, as Sheila Kehoe recalls.

"People would do anything to avoid going to the dentist because it was very expensive for ordinary working people, quite apart from the pain. I was always amazed, too, at how gloomy the dentist's surgery was – battered old leather armchairs, a bad-tempered receptionist and only one poster on the walls, which suggested you should eat an apple each day rather than biscuits or sweets. In those days of course no one thought that the dentist's surgery should be a pleasant place. It had to be purely functional and it was – at least in London. We sat, all of us, children and adults, in a silent miserable row waiting for the dreaded call! In a small country town I suspect it was often very different – more relaxed, and there was a far better chance that you would know the dentist well."

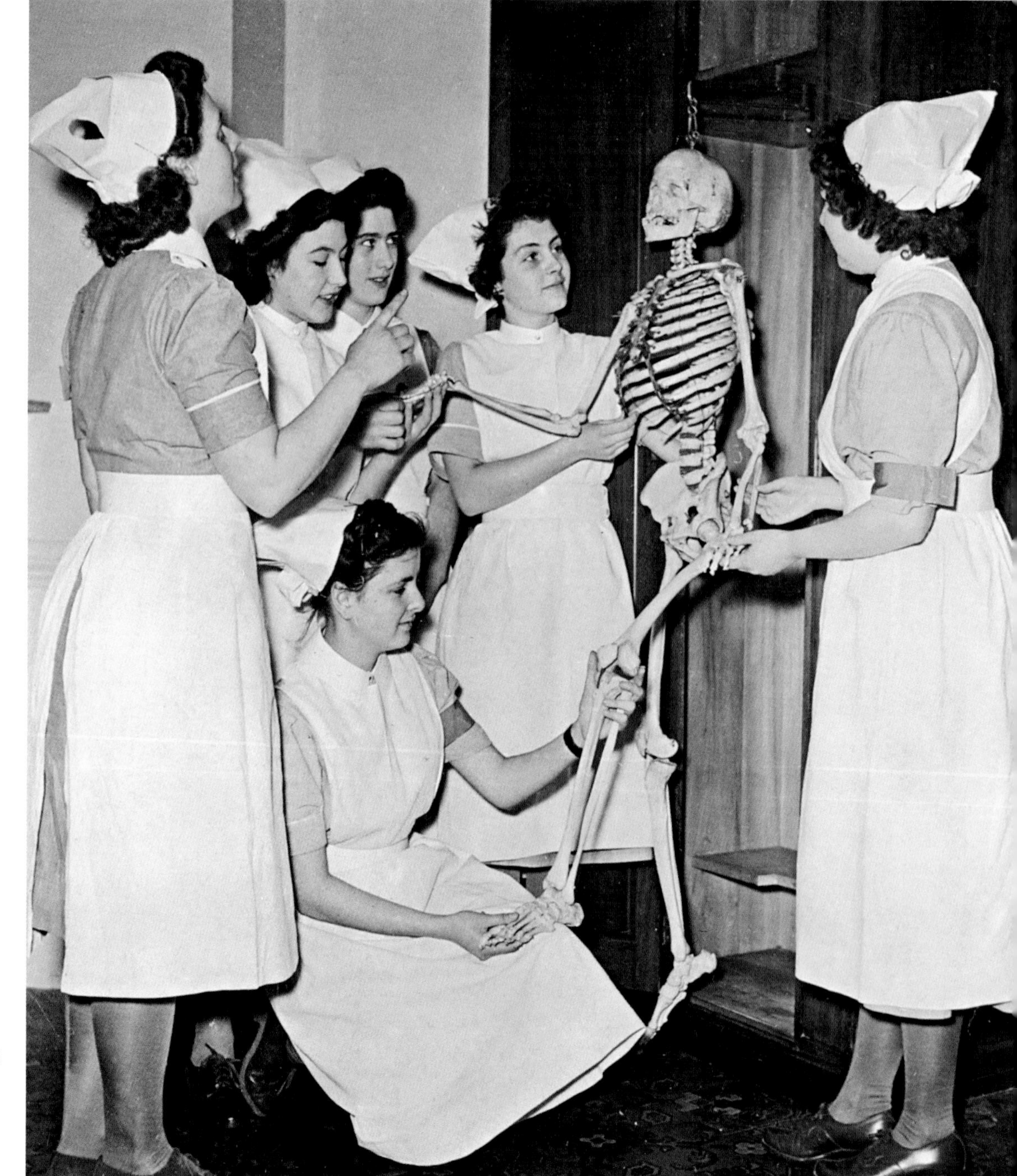

Nurse training
Student nurses had to train for three years to become a state registered nurse (SRN), or for two to gain the status of state enrolled nurse (SEN). The late 1940s saw the number of male nurses increase as demobilised servicemen with medical experience joined the profession. Student nurses worked long hours, mostly learning on the job, but were also expected to attend compulsory lectures on a range of topics to help their studies, including anatomy.

An army of nurses

The most enduring symbol of the early National Health Service is that of the matron – the fierce no-nonsense martinet immortalised by Hattie Jacques in the *Carry On* films. Certainly the early NHS was run on strict, almost military lines, but then the 1950s was still a time of great formality – patients were exactly that and the idea that they should be consulted and kept informed about their treatment would have seemed dangerous, not to say revolutionary.

Frederica 'Freddie' Walsh trained as a nurse just after the war and worked throughout the transition to the NHS, eventually becoming a ward sister and then matron at a large teaching hospital in West London. She recalls a remarkably different world from that of modern nursing.

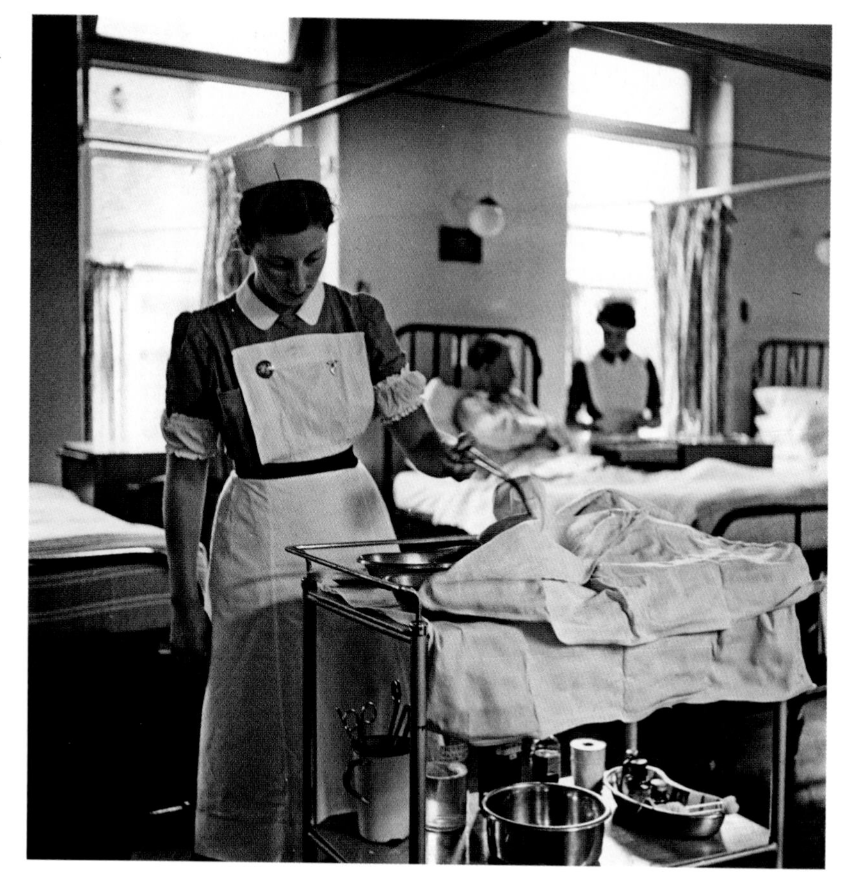

"Becoming a nurse when I started out was a bit like joining the army – in fact I really think the structure and organisation were based on military ways of doing things. In 1945 I had to sign a contract that said that I had to remain a nurse for a minimum of four years – the contract also said that if you wanted to get out early you had to pay. Just like the army.

Training was a shock because most girls of 18 back then had never seen a man with his shirt off, let alone naked, but the ward sister would stand no nonsense and you had to empty bedpans and do bed baths right from the start. The formal nature of everything and the fact that ward sisters were also strict with the patients also helped. But we had to work very long days – the day shift was 7am until 9pm. The day was long because most girls who went in for nursing were working class and it was expected that they should work longer hours than middle-class girls, who became secretaries or air stewardesses.

"Most girls of 18 back then had never seen a man with his shirt off ... "

Training was on the job but there were regular compulsory lectures – we had to go even if the lecture was being held during our statutory two hours off a day. When you were due a day off you were allowed to leave at 6pm rather than 9pm the previous evening so you could get home before the day off, which was decent of them I suppose.

Chronic shortages
A dearth of nursing staff in the NHS is not a recent phenomenon. It was common for beds to lie empty despite waiting lists for people needing treatment, as there weren't enough nurses to tend to the patients.

A woman's job
In 1951 86 per cent of women in work were in female-dominated occupations, a figure which had changed little since the turn of the century. Midwifery was an obvious women-only profession, and it would have been unheard of for a male to deliver a baby.

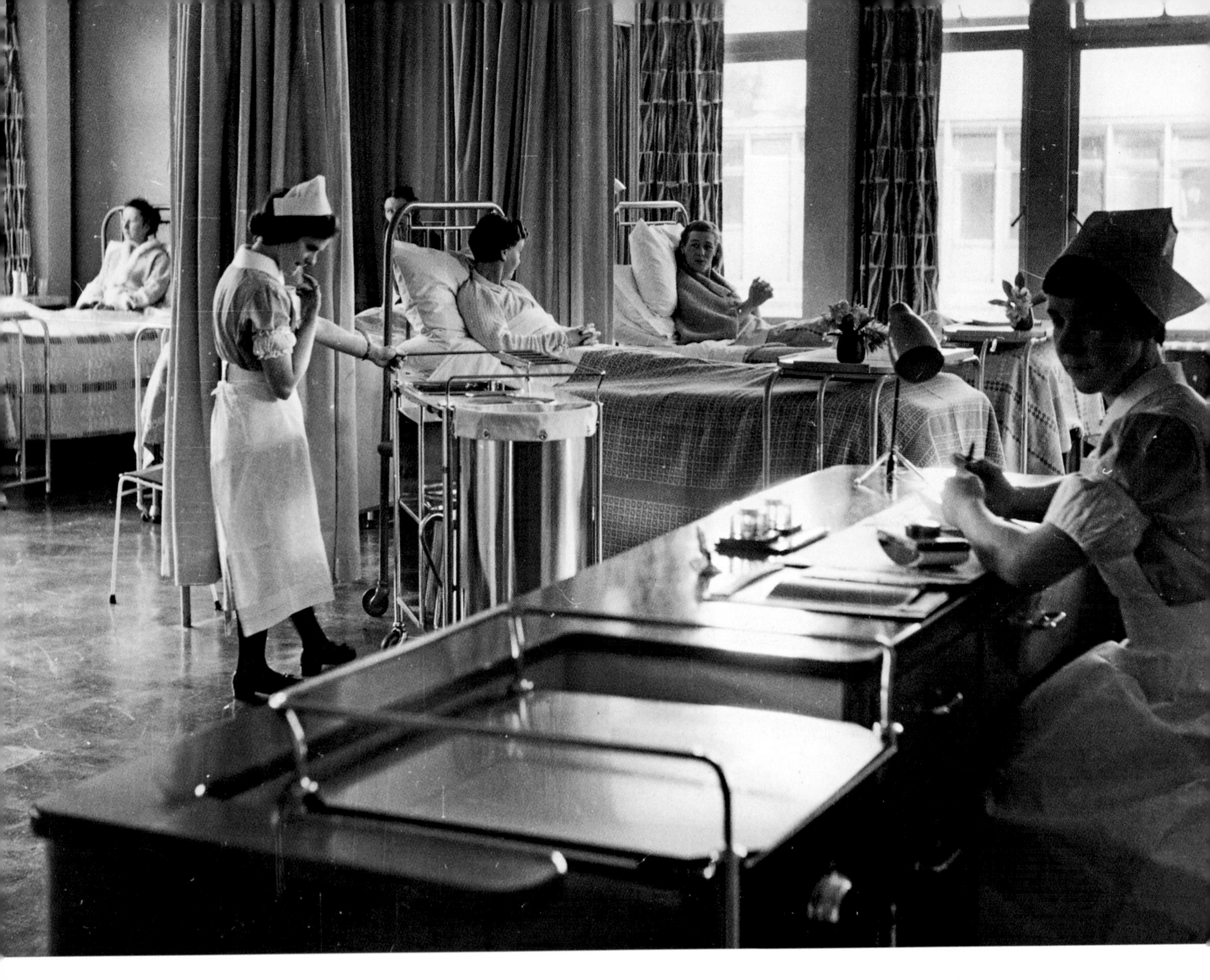

Those are the rules
Discipline in hospitals in the 1950s was strict. Visiting hours were fastidiously adhered to, and segregation of the sexes was stringently observed. Visitors were rarely welcomed by the ward sister and matron, being viewed as nuisances who broke routine and brought in bacteria. There was no sitting on the bed allowed, and even the patients had to be properly in bed, or sitting in a chair.

As you went through your training you earned your stripes – one a year for each of your four years, and they were worn on your sleeve. Again it was just like the army. At the end of the four years you got a badge to say you were qualified but you couldn't train as a nurse at university as you can now – there were no nursing degrees, just training on the job. The doctors often looked down on us, which wouldn't have happened 20 or 30 years later, but we always had a good image with the public.

Night shifts were worse as you started at eight in the evening and had to work through till 8am, but whether you were doing days or nights the rules about uniform were absolutely rigid. Before the NHS we wore dresses that had to be a regulation three inches below the knee. Regulation blue and white came in after the NHS began I think, and with a starched white apron, black laced shoes and severe black stockings. The matron's uniform was green and matrons were incredibly strict in those days – absolute punctuality was demanded and our hair caps and general appearance were constantly under scrutiny. You had to wear your hair precisely three inches above your collar and our caps were more elaborate than they are now and needed careful folding. It was all the starching that seemed silly to me – with stiff white cuffs and collars – but smartness was seen as really important, though I don't think anyone really stopped to think why it was so important. Patients were always addressed as Mr or Mrs or Miss – never by their first name. You weren't allowed to sit on a patient's bed while you talked to them and even the patients weren't allowed to sit on their beds! They had to lie in bed or sit on a chair or matron would be after them. We worked a 48-hour week with two weeks holiday a year!

There were some really mad rules too – all pillows had to be placed on the beds so that their open ends faced away from the door. What on earth was that for?"

Hierarchy was strictly adhered to in the nursing world. At the top was the famous, or infamous, matron who oversaw everything in the nurses' daily lives. Then there was an assistant matron, a housekeeping sister who sorted out the nurses' food and, finally, a home sister, as Freddie Walsh explains.

"The home sister made sure we all behaved in our free time because she looked after the nurses' home where we had to live. In the dining room matrons ate on one table, first-year nurses on another and so on. They were also obsessed with what they called our moral welfare – you could barely get into the nurses' home at night without being searched, and there was absolutely no chance of taking a boy to your room – not that many of us would have wanted to. The housekeeping sister would not even allow you to take a boy to the nurses' annual ball unless you could prove that your parents already knew and approved!"

Personal service

The NHS meant nursing became a single entity with a national pay structure instead of local agreements. But midwifery was always slightly on the edge of things – before the NHS it was regulated separately by the Midwives Act of 1936. Midwives round the country would deliver as many as 100 babies a year but in a carefully circumscribed area where they would know most of their clients. There were no male midwives – the idea would have seemed incomprehensible at the time – and most midwives travelled by bicycle. They used knowledge and techniques – perhaps primitive by more recent standards – that had developed over centuries. With the start of the NHS more maternity wards opened and fewer babies were born at home, but the midwife was still key to the whole process of childbirth, as Julia Willock recalls.

"There were some really mad rules too – all pillows had to be placed on the beds so that their open ends faced away from the door."

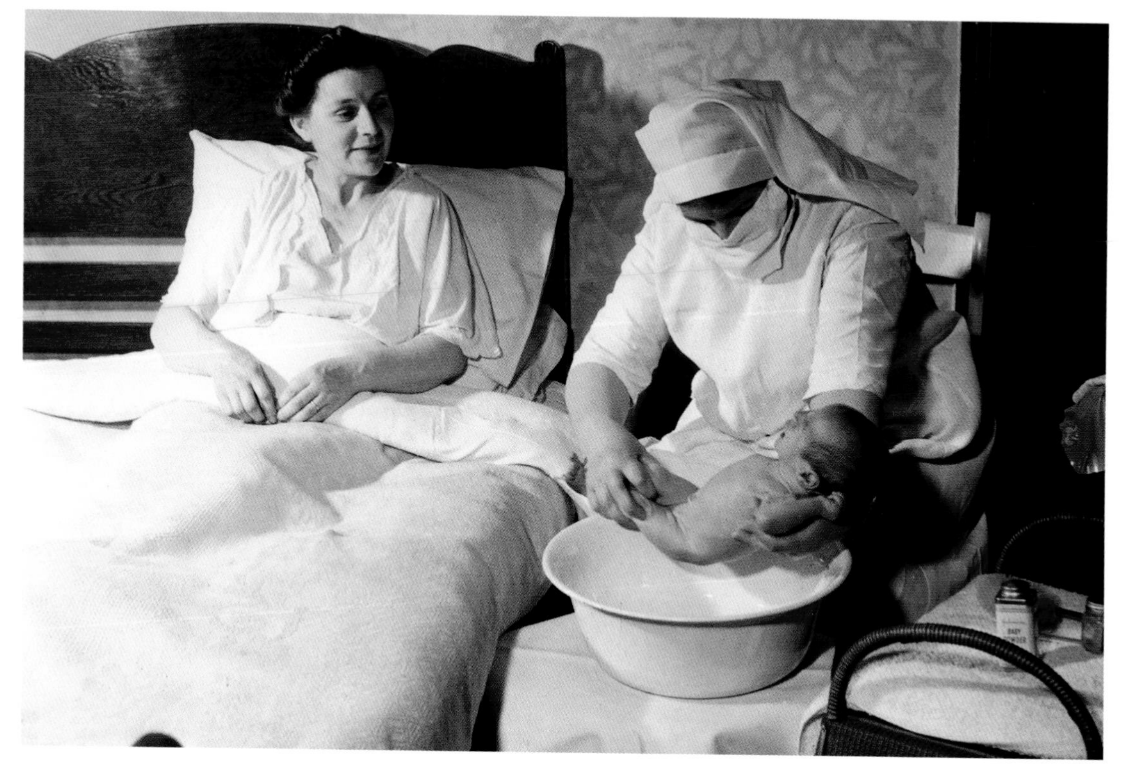

Home visits
Bed rest for ten days was considered to be the minimum confinement period necessary following childbirth, with two weeks being the ideal and most common amount of time. For those who gave birth in hospital this usually meant staying on the ward, in bed, for the whole period. Those who chose to have their babies at home with the help of a midwife would have daily visits from the nurse for the two week period. This service, which would traditionally have been paid for, was provided free of charge under the new NHS.

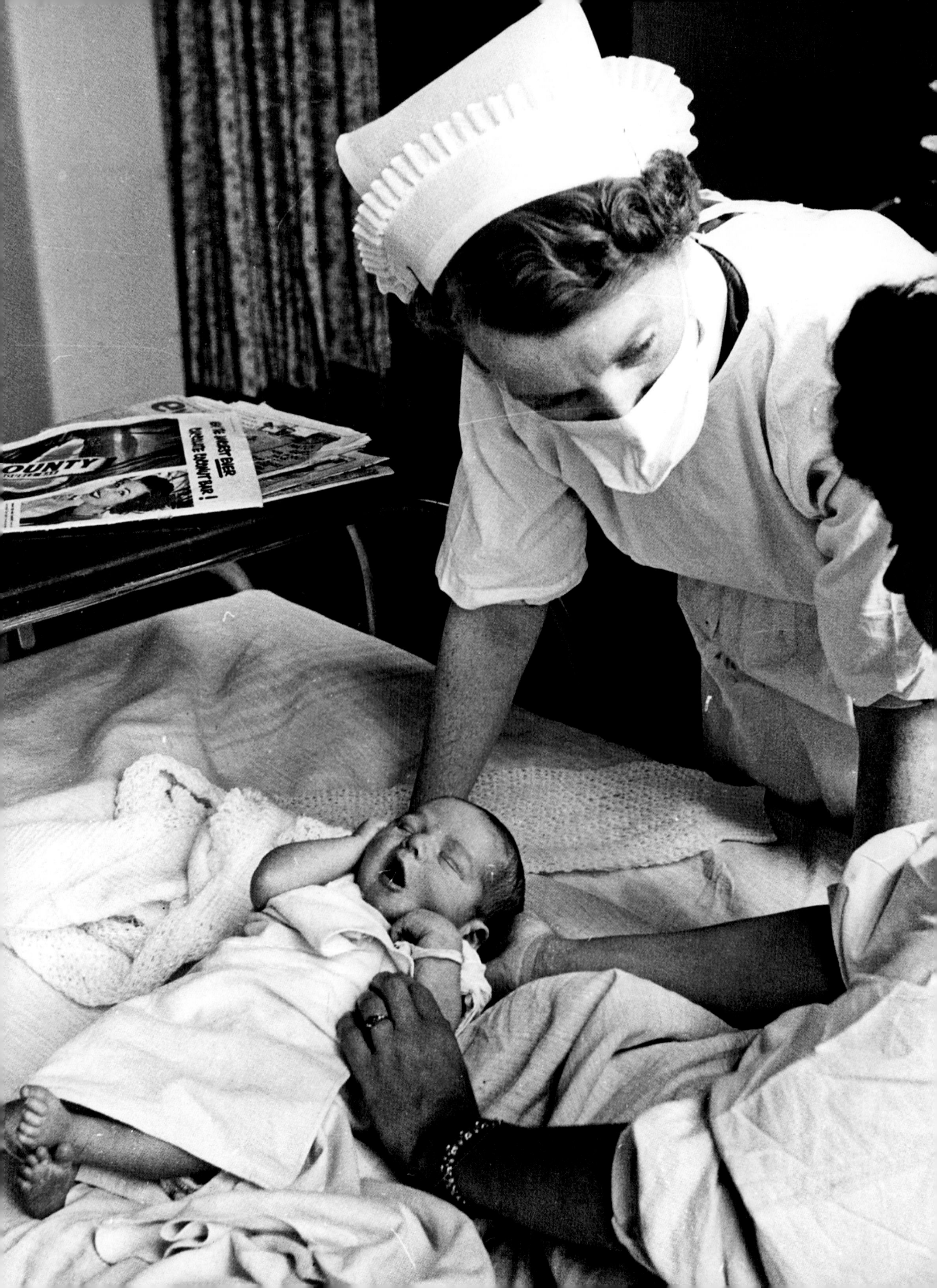
OUNTY

"My patch was Islington in North London. The worst part of my work and the part of it I remember best is the smogs – they were terrible. So bad sometimes that I'd have to push my bicycle or risk a bad fall. I remember the bombed-out houses, the piles of rubbish and badly damaged factories – all the damage lasted until well into the 1950s and beyond.

I remember helping a woman expecting twins who'd been told that her house was potentially dangerous because the house next door had been hit during the war. I sort of admired her really because she was still there in 1950 and the house still hadn't fallen over!

Most of what we did I think was support mothers-to-be, but attitudes were different then and some midwives treated mothers quite harshly – they didn't ask them questions; they just told them what to do, but our training encouraged that sort of thing. We were told that we were the experts, which is funny really when you think how little we had in the way of technology to help us. It was still the days of plenty of hot water and clean towels! But no one today I think would be able to believe the conditions in which a lot of Londoners lived in those days. I helped women give birth lying in freezing rooms on filthy mattresses with no furniture. On one occasion I helped a woman who was lying on a mattress on the floor and all she had to cover her was old coats. Many flats in the old tenement buildings had broken windows, no locks on the doors, hardly a stick of furniture, yet many of the parents were very caring despite their poverty, and I know some of the children who I helped into the world went on to become well off and happy. But a lot more babies died then and I know that many of the women I helped had to work as prostitutes and had no idea who the father of their child was. For us the main rules were scrupulously clean hands and aprons, and always treat the women with respect. My memory is that even under the worst conditions people always smiled and offered you a cup of tea."

"Most of what we did I think was support mothers-to-be, but attitudes were different then and some midwives treated mothers quite harshly."

The National Health Service gradually improved the life of the midwife and by the mid 1950s most hospitals were able to boast that they could get a team of doctors and midwives to any emergency within half an hour. But in more remote rural areas the midwife on her bicycle lasted well into the 1960s.

A surgical procedure
The shift in attitude from birth being a natural event to a medical procedure was reflected in the obligatory attire of the delivery team. Surgical garb was essential (in white to emphasise cleanliness), and masks and gowns compulsory to stem the spread of disease. Maternal death rates stood at just 87 per 100,000, which the Ministry of Health attributed to "better management of pregnancy and childbirth by routine antenatal supervision and greater obstetric care".

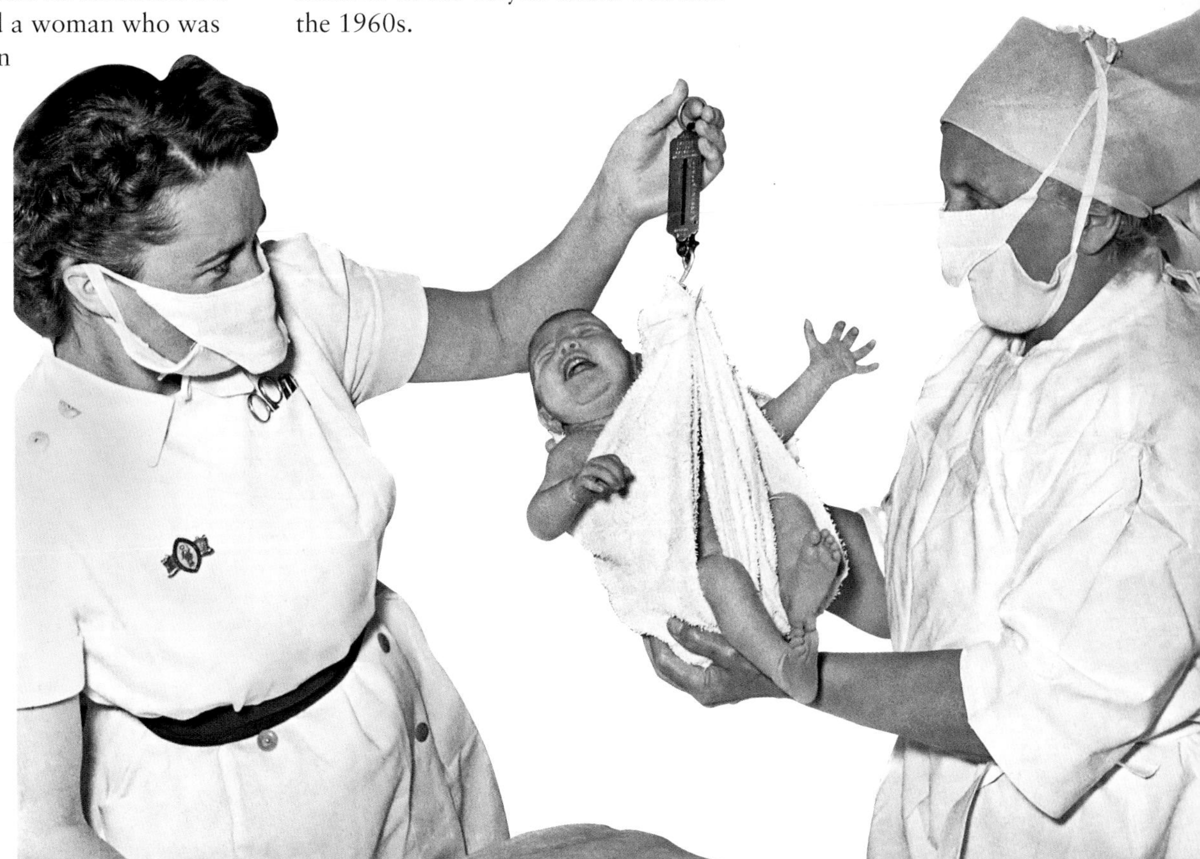

Preparing for birth
As part of the preparations for the birth of a baby the midwife would provide a list of what it would be necessary for expectant mothers to bring into hospital with them for their confinement. For the mother the list included pieces of old linen and 1lb of cotton wool, while for the baby nappies, nightgowns and matinée coats were advised.

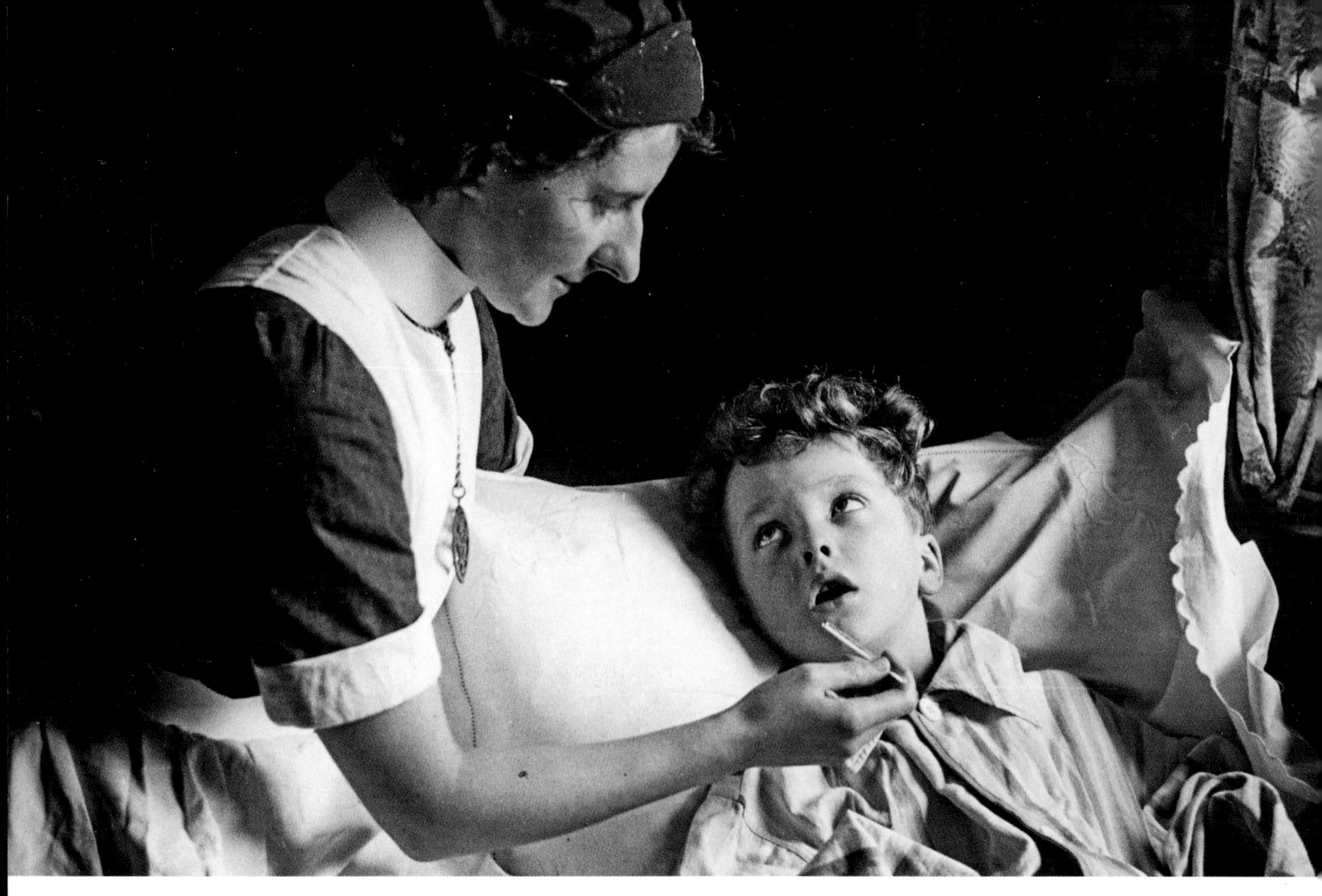

A friendly face
District nurses played a vital role in the community, regularly seeing ill and elderly patients and providing a level of care well beyond that of a GP. Trainee nurses had to work for 48 hours per week, were paid £10 a month and received two weeks annual leave.

DISTRICT NURSES

District nursing was a key element in the new NHS. Each district nurse was issued with a blue bag containing a tin, which in turn contained soap, a towel, disinfectant, artery forceps, rubber gloves, syringe, nailbrush, gauze, cotton wool and sterilised dressings. That may sound like a limited kit but it was the skill of the district nurses that really mattered, as Freddie Walsh remembers.

"When I moved over to district nursing I loved it – but then I loved everything I did in my nursing career. The funniest thing I remember is that when we attended a patient who needed sterilised dressings we had to get a clean baking tin or saucepan from them and put the dressings in it and then ask them to put it in the oven. The idea was that the heat would sterilise everything. Forceps and scissors would be boiled in a saucepan – cleanliness was everything in those days!

I don't remember any nurse having a car back then but we were all issued with bicycles, which was fine with me as it kept me fit and I'd always cycled anyway.

We looked after bed-ridden patients and the elderly and disabled mostly. We gave bed baths at home as well as doing minor surgical work, changing dressings and so on, but we became friends with our patients, organising visits for them on Christmas Day if they were elderly and alone and often lighting their fires – no central heating back then – and making tea and lunch for them each time we visited. They'd leave a key under the mat or under a flower pot or they'd give you a spare key. A district nurse was truly a pillar of the local community, but we were paid only two pounds and ten shillings a week. Women's jobs were always paid less

Strict hygiene
It was obligatory for a district nurse to wear a white apron when treating patients. These, items and the other contents of their bags, would be boiled at the end of each day. District nurses would call on patients as often as their condition required. Few had driving licences, let alone cars, so were issued with a bicycle.

than men's and looking back I'm amazed that we just accepted that was the way it had to be."

Home remedies

For centuries people in Britain relied on a range of home and folk remedies. A visit to the doctor with all its cost was usually a last resort. Folk remedies in rural areas included feeding boiled sheep brains to ailing children – because the brains were soft it was thought they would be easily digested – and drinking nettle tea or greens water, water that cabbage had been boiled in.

Kent farmer Aubrey Charman recalls how drinking TB-infected milk was seen as a way to protect against TB, one of the biggest killers before antibiotics.

> "As a child I was given a glass of milk for supper every night, and I must have drunk many a gallon of tubercular milk. I have remained very healthy. We didn't know all the science back then but over generations people had instinctively learned that some things worked well in terms of protecting from serious illness."

"I remember an elderly neighbour used to say that a hot drink with the right herb would cure anything."

Other remedies were freely available without a prescription from chemists. Many of these would now be illegal since they contained opium or cocaine. Until World War II more than 100 patent remedies for everything from coughs to colic included a small amount of cocaine or opium and it was undoubtedly the cocaine that made people feel better, as Fenland eel-catcher Ernie James recalls.

> "We used to give the children a popular medicine called Daffy's Elixir – it helped colicky children get a good night's sleep, but I heard later that it had a tiny amount of laudanum in it, which is an opium derivative. No wonder it worked so well!"

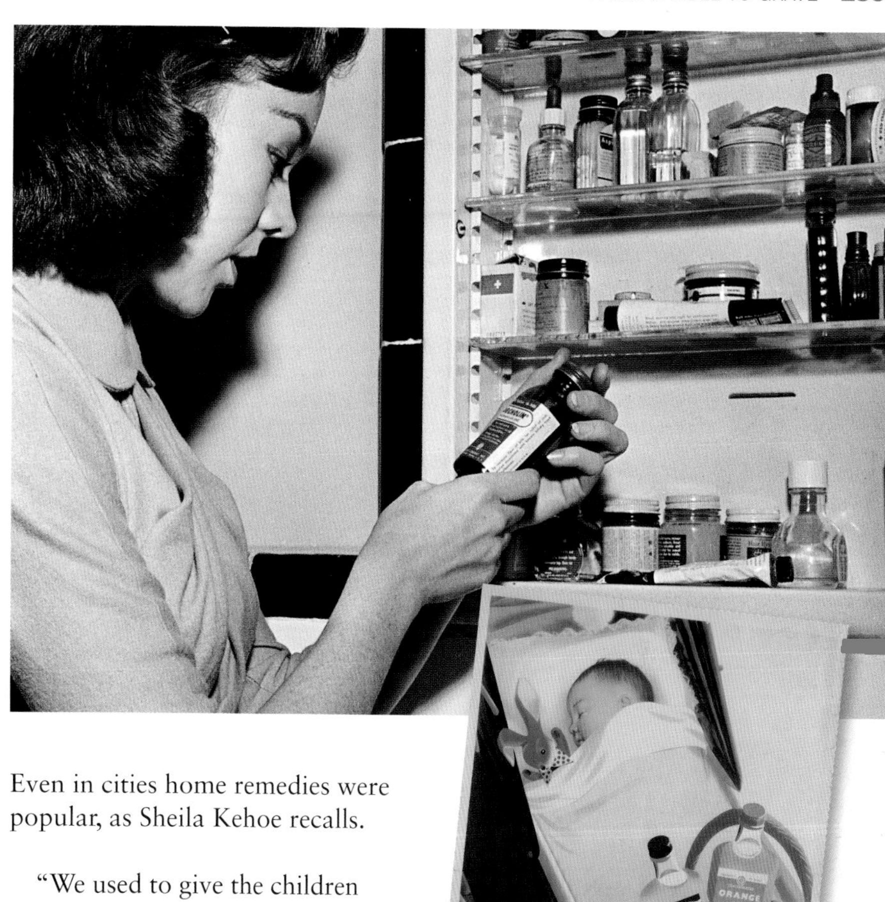

Even in cities home remedies were popular, as Sheila Kehoe recalls.

> "We used to give the children rosehip syrup every day as well as cod liver oil. I was furious if they wouldn't have it – they actually hated it – because I worried they would get colds and flu. Actually I can't now remember why we were so convinced that cod liver oil worked for colds but from what I've read recently about how good fish is for you in lots of different ways I think we were doing the right thing.
>
> But I remember an elderly neighbour of ours used to drink nettle tea for her arthritis and mint tea to aid her digestion – she used to say that a hot drink with the right herb would cure anything. She was also always gargling with ordinary Saxo salt – she swore that it kept colds at bay. If you do it at the first sign of a cold it does kill the virus in the throat. But those were the days when people were definitely more superstitious – lots of elderly people wore rabbits' feet for luck or copper bracelets to keep off the gout, or ate liquorice to help with constipation. Personally, I think they just wanted an excuse to eat the liquorice!"

A spoonful a day
Expensive private healthcare and lack of access to medical personnel – particularly in rural areas – resulted in credence being placed in natural remedies and old wives' tales. Cod liver oil was recommended daily for babies and children as a way of supplementing meagre diets and boosting immunity. The real benefits of the fatty acids it contains were not fully understood until the mid-1950s.

BAD AIR

The London smogs

By the mid-19th century London's factories and domestic fires poisoned the Thames and filled the air with noxious fumes. For Charles Dickens in *Bleak House* the "London particular", as the fog was known then, was a symbol for all that was rotten and corrupt in England. As London grew the fogs became steadily worse until, by the late 1940s and 1950s, a bad one could virtually bring the city to a standstill. The fogs finally vanished in the 1960s.

Weather fronts
The Great Smog which shrouded London for five days in December 1952 was caused by an area of high pressure that settled over southern England for an unusually long time. Due to a combination of freezing temperatures and a lack of wind, the smog became thicker than ever.

Smog masks
Harold Macmillan understood the need for officials to look proactive in the face of civilian catastrophe, so ministers decided that doctors should prescribe up to two million gauze "smog masks" to people with heart and respiratory diseases – even though they knew the masks were useless.

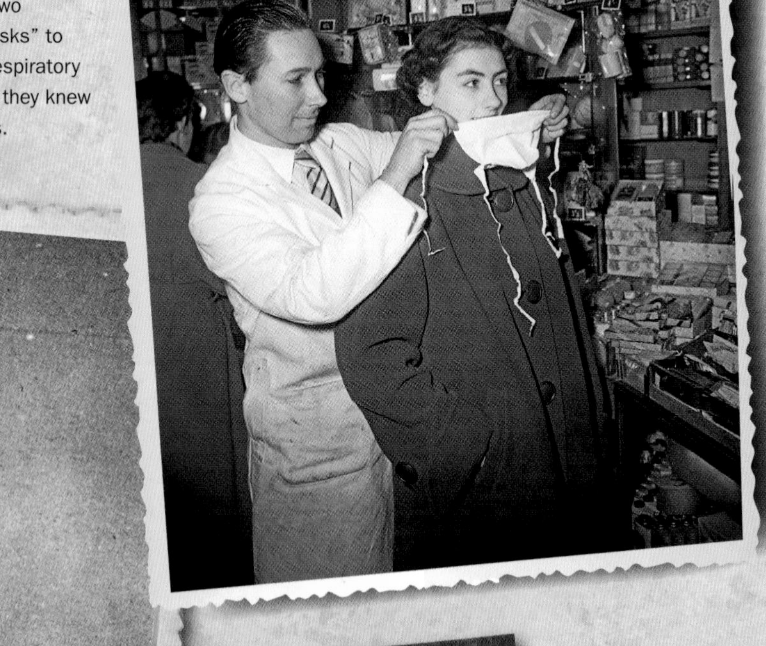

Deadly smog
The smog caused the premature death of up to 4,000 people. Many had suffered from lung-related illnesses, but many Londoners also died because of low levels of visibility. People could not see further than a few feet in front of them, which led to road accidents and drowning when people fell into the Thames.

Clean Air Act
To alleviate the congestion two Clean Air Acts were passed in 1956 and 1968, following the Beaver Committee Report. These Acts aimed to control domestic sources of smoke pollution by introducing smokeless zones. Although the Clean Air Act focused on reducing smoke pollution, the measures actually helped to reduce sulphur dioxide levels at the same time.

"Only a gesture"
Health minister Iain Macleod told Macmillan that the distribution of masks was "only a gesture" and that there was "no known mask" which would protect those at risk. Despite the Clean Air Act of 1956, air pollution in London continued to be a problem in the 1960s, particularly for those suffering from lung disease and asthma.

Cleaning up
Decline in manufacturing, combined with the rising popularity of central heating and smokeless fuels, meant that the effects of the pollution eventually began to subside. The acrid smell that was associated with the London fogs became a thing of the past.

A few precious hours

LEISURE TIME

The big screen
Cinema-going was a fundamental part of childhood in postwar Britain. The only prerequisite to join the local Saturday morning film club was that you had to be at least five years old.

After the long years of World War II and continuing austerity, having fun seemed like a distant memory. With Britain on the verge of bankruptcy few had the money for holidays or expensive radios and TVs. Good times, it seemed, were always just around the corner. But as the 1940s turned into the 1950s Britons almost imperceptibly transformed themselves from dour worried people into a nation of rock and rollers who fell in love with irreverent radio shows, crammed themselves into dirty cinemas and bingo halls, danced the night away, saved for TVs, cars, motorbikes and holidays and began to think that life might not be so bad after all.

TV and radio

Broadcasters today make desperate efforts to attract the youth market, but a time traveller going back to the late 1940s and 1950s would be astonished at how serious and middle-aged programming was at that time.

Sheila Kehoe remembers her favourite radio and television programmes.

> "People in their late eighties and nineties like me were so amazed when radio and later television became widely available that we would have watched or listened to anything. Things that wouldn't seem at all funny or interesting now were put out hour after hour – well, until the famous white dot appeared. This was what the picture diminished to if you left the television on after broadcasting finished at about midnight. Now of course, television is on 24 hours a day, seven days a week."

Most radio shows were broadcast live rather than pre-recorded, which means that little of BBC radio's output from the 1940s has survived. The 78rpm disc recording technology, which was all that was available prior to the development of tape recording, resulted in

Light relief
1945 saw the launch of the new BBC Light Programme, with announcer Roy Williams. It took over the longwave frequency used before 1939 by the BBC National Programme and offered an alternative output for listeners. The Light provided music and comedy not heard on the speech-based Home Service, giving a welcome light relief for listeners.

sound quality that was significantly worse than a live broadcast, so it was better not to fill the air-time with recordings.

Being a non-commercial broadcaster the BBC had no financial incentive to preserve its output.

"I loved *Mrs Dale's Diary* and *The Archers*, which was just getting going then, but BBC radio was all there was! No commercial radio at all and the BBC only had three wireless stations – everyone called it the wireless back then."

There can be no doubt that World War II changed the sound of BBC radio dramatically, the Light Programme being very much based on the informal American style of the Forces

"Things that wouldn't seem at all funny or interesting now were put out hour after hour ..."

Programme. This new station offered general entertainment, with shows not heard before the war on the old National Programme.

"The Home Service and the Third Programme were a bit more serious than the variety shows and plays on the Light Programme – there were lots of talks, news broadcasts and so on. We used to say that you'd need a Nobel Prize to understand any of the talks and classical

Needle time
Restrictions were imposed by the Musicians' Union and the BBC to ensure the continued employment of large in-house BBC orchestras, for light and classical music output. The BBC was also subject to "needle time" restrictions, limiting the number of records it could air in one week. However, all output from across the corporation was routed through the Central Control Room in Broadcasting House (pictured here).

Developing technology
When the BBC resumed transmissions in 1945 it had to work with the same antiquated equipment that was used before the war. Progress was slow in these early austere years, and transmission was initially restricted to a radius of 25 miles from the main transmitter. The first great success story was the televising of the Olympic Games at Wembley in 1948, and by 1949 there were some 90,000 television sets in homes across the country.

music on the Third Programme. It was always Bertrand Russell talking about philosophy or J.B.S. Haldane discussing science. However, there was a Home Service quiz called *The Brains' Trust* where you could send in a question and a panel of experts would answer it on air. People would ask questions like, 'Does burned toast make your hair grow faster?'"

But already there were signs of the kind of anti-establishment satirical and anarchic television and radio programmes that typified the 1960s and 1970s.

> "When I first heard *The Goons* in 1951 – or the *Crazy People* as it was originally called – I thought the world had gone mad. It was so zany and silly but you couldn't help listening to it after a while – the characters were so good. I remember Bloodknot, Bluebottle, and Eccles and the funny catchline 'He's fallen in the water!'"

WAITING FOR THE GLOW

Television wasn't quite in its infancy by 1950 – a few hundred people even had television in the 1930s – but it was still all broadcast live and it was exclusively black and white. Early sets were built into mahogany or walnut cabinets and took a considerable time to warm up. With no microcircuits they relied on valves, which were rather like light bulbs. People would stare into the ventilation grills on the back of the sets – needed because the valves produced a lot of heat – waiting for the glow in the valves that signalled that the picture was about to appear. Famous television makes of the time included Baird, HMV, Marconi and Pye.

Rose Plummer recalls:

> "When I first saw television it was on a screen about a foot wide and built into a wooden cabinet! I've since seen one in a museum and when I told my granddaughter that we used to watch a TV like that she just didn't believe me. But we were dazzled by it. It cost a fortune, far more expensive than a giant plasma flat screen would cost today, but it was magical for people who, like me, had grown up when the only entertainment was the radio or nothing at all!"

From the first main BBC transmitter at Alexandra Palace in north London, others began springing up across Britain as the popularity of television continued to grow. By 1952 aerials had begun to appear on rooftops in Scotland, South Wales and the West Country, and the prospect of owning a television became everyone's dream. However, the tone of the programming remained élitist; the BBC – which was deemed custodian of public morals – considered regional accents inappropriate, and broadcasters' voices were closely scrutinised until 1955 when the Independent Television Authority (ITA) was launched and attitudes began to relax.

> "Everyone on TV spoke with a posh accent – I heard that poor old Wilfred Pickles, an announcer from Lancashire, was sent to have elocution lessons to get rid of his lovely Lancashire accent. But everyone else really was posh. Announcers on the TV wore dinner jackets and black tie – looking back it all seems so bizarre but the BBC were definitely part of the Establishment and I remember lots of debates among politicians about how careful broadcasters had to be. The Establishment thought that television was much more powerful than it really was. They thought that if they didn't keep a

tight control of it there would be a revolution! It was all very moral by the standards of today – *Dixon of Dock Green* always started and ended with a moral lesson given by the friendly bobby who was the central character. Yet in 1958 there were signs that things were changing when *Armchair Theatre* started – that was much more about real life as we knew it."

Let the music play

During the war and late 1940s Britain was largely starved of culture. With the closure of most concert venues music was particularly hard hit. Concerts did continue in London – most notably Dame Myra Hess became famous for her piano recitals at the National Gallery – but with theatres and halls closed for the duration there was a real thirst for entertainment after the war ended and well into the 1950s.

Robert Sharpe recalls his solution:

"I was an avid record collector – I loved jazz, which was the equivalent to heavy metal in the 1970s and punk in the 1980s [sic]. It was the music of rebellious youth because rock and roll still hadn't penetrated Britain that much."

Production limits
The shortage of manufacturing materials postwar meant that the government kept a tight control on the usage of raw materials. With this in mind, production of televisions was limited to 78,000 in 1946. Considering that only 20,000 sets had been produced in three years before the war, this figure seemed rather generous.

Lunchtime culture
British concert pianist Myra Hess organised a series of concerts at the National Gallery (above) throughout the war. To avoid blackout restrictions the concerts were held at lunchtime, and Hess performed in many of them herself. The galleries had been emptied of paintings to protect them from German bombs. Hess was later appointed a DBE for her contribution to boosting the country's morale.

Enriching cultural life
The first Edinburgh Festival took place in September 1947 as part of the resurgence of culture and entertainment in Britain. Its remit was to "provide a platform for the flowering of the human spirit" and to enrich the cultural life of Scotland, Britain and Europe. Here, Artur Schnabel (centre right) rehearses for the inaugural festival with (from left to right) Hungarian-American violinist Joseph Szigeti, Scottish violist William Primrose and French cellist Pierre Fournier.

The 78-rpm disc reigned supreme as the accepted recording medium for many years despite its tendency to break easily and the fact that longer works could not be listened to without breaks for disc change.

"Looking at my old collection now I can't believe that I once saw them as part of a young vibrant world! My grandchildren can't believe that these heavy clumsy discs (made from shellac) were once as hi tech as an iPod! We used to play them at 78 revolutions per minute on a player that had needles you bought loose in a brown paper bag. Diamond styluses didn't come in until later but when I got my first electric player I was in heaven. Before that I'd used a wind up model. With my electric player – a cabinet with a record player and speakers built in – I was the envy of my friends. They would all come round and we'd smoke and listen to it very seriously."

LEGENDARY CONCERTS

But if listening to music at home was becoming easier and less expensive for younger people, the habit of concert going which had largely vanished during the war years made a welcome return. There were a number of legendary venues up and down the country that opened their doors once more to the public, such as Manchester's Free Trade Hall – home to the renowned Hallé Orchestra for many decades – and London's Wigmore Hall, as Pam Tarlton remembers:

"Oh it was marvellous to be free again to go out when the war was over. We saw some of the great pianists who were just starting to properly rebuild their careers – people like Solomon and Rubinstein. It was so lovely to see concert halls like the Wigmore Hall filled with life again. I suppose by today's standards the Wigmore was rather stuffy as it was always full of older people but then I revisited the

"... it was marvellous to be free again to go out when the war was over it was so lovely to see concert halls filled with life again."

Wigmore recently and it was just the same – mostly older people!"

Manchester was heavily bombed during World War II and the Free Trade Hall suffered significant damage. It reopened in 1951 with a newly reconstructed interior. Over the following decades it became a legendary venue not only for classical music, but also for contemporary rock and pop.

John Quinn recalls the upset caused by the bombing of the Free Trade Hall:

"It had been the centre of musical life in the city; the Hallé Orchestra had been performing there since the 1850s so when the front became badly damaged we thought that it might be the end. Luckily it quickly got going again after the war and the atmosphere was simply marvellous. There's nothing quite like being deprived of music for a few years for you to really appreciate it!

A night at the Royal Albert Hall

Austrian Vic Oliver – founder of the British Concert Orchestra and seen conducting at the Royal Albert Hall in 1946 (right) – believed that orchestral concerts should be entertaining and fun for the audiences. Postwar Britain saw the emergence of talented musicians and artists and, with funding once again available for major events such as the Proms, life was beginning to look good again.

78
ONLY
78
His Master's Voice
PARLOPHONE RECORDS
His Master's Voice

During the worst years a few friends and I used to play quartets when we were home on leave. That continued into the 1950s until my best friend Ernie, our viola player, died suddenly. During the war and then on into the 1950s, people all over Lancashire, Yorkshire, and the rest of the country I shouldn't wonder, organised their own musical evenings until records and record players became more affordable."

Without high quality recordings or broadcast music, playing an instrument at home was a far more common means of entertainment than it is now. Even poorer families would save up to buy that quintessential parlour instrument, the upright piano. A boom in popularity and manufacturing at the end of the 19th century saw pianos being made in their millions; second-hand pianos were still readily for sale in postwar Britain for just £5.

"Until the 1950s almost every pub and house in the country had at least an upright piano. We had regular singsongs round our old upright until the 1960s but by then everything had changed. You could buy a reasonable upright in a Manchester auction room for anything between five shillings and five pounds – you couldn't give them away because everyone wanted guitars or records or TV by then."

Dance crazy

The late 1940s and early 1950s were probably the heyday of the dancehall in Britain. At the start of the decade the young often danced to the Big Band sound typified by Glen Miller, but ten years later rock and roll made the waltz and the foxtrot seem positively antediluvian.

Sheila Kehoe remembers the heady nights at one of the best known dancehalls in the country: the Hammersmith Palais.

Listening booths
It was quite common for avid music fans to spend an afternoon in the soundproof listening booth at their nearest music store. The 78-rpm discs of the latest releases were played on individual gramophones attached to each booth.

The rock and roll years
Typified by hits such as *Rock Around the Clock* by Bill Haley and the Comets (seen here performing at the Hammersmith Palais), the worldwide popularity of rock and roll was undeniable. Bill Haley is often dubbed the pioneer of the music genre that went on to influence fashion, lifestyles and language well beyond its early years in 1950s Britain and America.

No dancing allowed
The "Boogie-Woogie" rhythm arrived with the Americans joining the Allied cause, as demonstrated by Ronald Ali and his jitterbug partner at the Feldman Swing Club, 1947 (right). A 30 per cent tax was levied by the British Government on "dancing" night clubs. Although the tax was later reduced to 20 per cent, "No Dancing Allowed" signs went up all over the country at places that hadn't paid the premium.

"The management liked to pretend that the Hammersmith Palais was something exotic from the Continent – hence the full name Hammersmith Palais de Danse, but after the war and well into the 1950s it was as British as you could imagine. The men lined up on one side of the hall and the girls on the other and you waited to be asked to dance – if you weren't asked to dance, you didn't, because you couldn't just hop around on your own! The men wore the suits they wore during the day – most only had the one!"

Dancing was an escape from everyday life during the war, and the craze for the dancehalls naturally continued afterwards. For women all over the country part of the thrill was the chance that you might meet Mr Right.

"It's very hard to explain how much we loved going dancing. For us girls it was the most exciting thing possible – I still look back on those nights dancing as the happiest of my life. We danced for hour after hour and the excitement of getting together in a huddle with your friends all dressed up and then wondering which handsome boy would ask us to dance just can't be imagined."

"The men lined up on one side of the hall and the girls on the other and you waited to be asked to dance – if you weren't asked to dance, you didn't ..."

ACTING THE PART

Looking right and having the latest clothing was important too as of course it is in all ages, but for Sheila Kehoe there were particular problems to negotiate:

"There were some silly things – girls were always horribly embarrassed if they had big feet in those days. I was a size seven and I hated it so I used to buy shoes which were too small for me and be half crippled after a couple of hours' dancing. My best friend was a German girl and she was a brilliant dancer, but she would never say a word about the war, even if you asked her a direct question about it."

Girls who grew up in rural, middle-class environments were expected to learn a wide range of social graces. Pam Tarlton admits that her background was decidedly 'country' and recalls rather grand affairs.

"As children in the countryside we were taught all sorts of reels and dances so that we could participate when we went to stay with our rather grand relatives in Scotland. Dancing the Gay Gordons and doing it well was very important at a country house party, but we also went up to London from our house in Gloucestershire for the season. I remember endless balls but very few public dances. It was rather like coming-out balls – you were introduced to the London season as a débutante if you came from a certain sort of background. You went to a series of grand balls in London and at one of these you curtseyed to the young Queen and that was it – you'd 'come out'. The idea of all these balls was simply to find a husband from the right set. It all seems so unreal now."

Glasgow's first dancehall was the Albert Ballroom, which opened in 1905. Secretary Libby Macintyre remembers it well and, like most of her friends, she felt that dancing gave

Dancing soldiers

Dancing was an integral part to people's social lives but it was disrupted by two world wars. Many of the top men in the ballroom dancing fraternity of the post-war years had excellent wartime service careers behind them. Victor Silvester Junior was an officer in the Hampshire Regiment and became a partner in his father's dancing business after the war. Sonny Binick, who went on to win both the British and International Professional Ballroom Dancing Championships in the 1950s, was in the Paratroops taking part in Operation Market Garden (Arnhem) in 1944.

her the chance to escape and be herself, to forget the everyday cares of growing up in Glasgow when money was tight and chances to have fun were few and far between.

"They used to say the most popular activity bar none in Glasgow was dancing. The girls loved it and the place to go in the late 1940s and 1950s was the Albert. It was marvellous. I met my husband there and we got on so well because he was a great dancer and I'd just been trodden on by my previous three partners. I was so captivated that when he asked if I would go out with him I said yes. The Albert burned down in 1953 but was quickly re-opened simply because the owners knew that the demand was so huge. On a Saturday night it would be a sea of moving heads – it was one of the few dance halls that had a reputation for staying sober, so mothers weren't too worried about their daughters going there. A reputation for sobriety in Scotland is a rare thing, as you can imagine!"

Off to the rep

Before television really took hold one of Britain's great entertainment traditions was repertory theatre. But repertory theatre also offered a peculiarly British theatre experience, since older plays would generally alternate with new ones, and old favourites were constantly revived to fill seats that were in danger of remaining empty if a new, unknown play was attempted.

Steven Day lived in Bristol and worked as a civil servant. He remembers visits to the Bristol Old Vic, one of the most famous repertory theatres in the country.

"We didn't have television in the 1940s and 1950s and no one we knew had a set. Though I loved radio and we listened to it a lot, it was nowhere near as exciting as a

The original "Blonde Bombshell"
US actress and singer Betty Hutton rehearsing with US group the Skylarks at the London Palladium in October, 1952. Critics described her as "a big strong, lively girl, always eager to please" but complained that her voice was so loud that she "deafened the first two rows of the auditorium."

"Though I loved radio and we listened to it a lot, it was nowhere near as exciting as a trip to the theatre."

trip to the theatre. The Bristol Old Vic was, and still is I believe, one of the best repertory theatres in the country and it has a reputation for trying new, even experimental things. That wasn't the case after the war because audiences wanted something respectable – in fact there was an obsession with respectability in entertainment during the late 1940s and 1950s. In those days we all accepted things the way they were and I remember going to the Bristol Old Vic with my aunt dressed up to the nines with a whole fox fur (including claws and head!) draped round her shoulders."

SIMPLE ENTERTAINMENT

The plays themselves, however, were often far less highbrow than one might imagine.

"We liked plays by JB Priestley with a strong moral theme, or by Terence Rattigan, whose *The Winslow Boy* was one of my favourite plays. Best of all I liked *The Admirable Crichton* by J.M.Barrie, better known of course for *Peter Pan*. The great thing was that the plays were rotated – that was the essence of repertory. It wasn't a long season of just one play; it was a string of them so that you could go back and see several different plays in successive weeks.

It was a marvellous experience to see drama brought to life in the days before television made such things so commonplace. Now we have so much living drama brought into our sitting rooms that we take it for granted, but the local rep theatre was our escape out of everyday lives."

Steven also valued the theatre building itself, and this at a time when many theatres had been demolished or allowed to fall into decay.

The golden age
The postwar years marked the beginning of the golden age for musical theatre in Britain, which spread from Broadway with *Oklahoma!*. American musicals were hugely popular and London's West End was soon overflowing with musical productions. In contrast, play-going was a formal affair and very much for the middle classes who, aware of their status, wouldn't be seen in the stalls without a jacket and tie, and women would dress as though they were going for an evening at the grandest opera.

As seen on Broadway
Local regional theatre generally had a resident company that produced a different play each week, making it a relatively inexpensive evening for the public. It occasionally attracted stars from London, or plays that had already succeeded in the capital such as Arthur Miller's popular *The Crucible*, seen left, being performed at the Bristol Old Vic in 1954.

"The Bristol Old Vic is in a lovely Georgian building and we never thought for a minute that this was in any way inferior to theatre in London. People say it's sad that rep theatre has suffered because of television, but I think that given the level of competition from the little box it's amazing that repertory theatres have survived at all!"

An evening at the local

In the years after the end of the war and well into the 1950s people would have been astonished if they had been told that a time would come when village pubs all over the country would close for lack of custom.

Half a century ago almost every village and hamlet in Britain still had at least one and often two or three pubs. Even Great Dunham in Norfolk (for example) had its little alehouse, and Great Dunham was a village with barely a dozen houses. Why were there so many pubs? Will Constance recalls:

"When I was in my late teens I started to go to Diss at weekends to whist drives and dances, so we had some fun. We went to pubs too, but I always remembered my father's warning that 'pubs were for man's use not for man's abuse'. Pubs were dingy old places – full of smoke and rarely a woman in sight.

Every pub looked more or less the same when you went in. A big fire in winter, a few scrubbed deal tables, dark low ceilings and a few old boys sitting round with their mugs of beer and smoking hard. Besides that there was nothing much to see in most pubs – no juke boxes, no hot meals, no music at all except when a local fiddler called in on an occasional Saturday night. People were there to drink alcohol and play cards or dominoes – dominoes was very popular with the old boys, and a few of the younger ones were beginning to play darts."

"Pubs were dingy old places – full of smoke and rarely a woman in sight."

BAR GAMES
In poor areas people made their entertainment with whatever was to hand, such as sticks and stones for the old-fashioned game of jacks, or an iron ring and stake for the popular game of quoits. In a countryside still dominated by the horse and the blacksmith's shop the raw materials for a game of quoits would not have been hard to come by.

"Quoits was a wonderful game that has vanished almost completely. Quoits matches were always being played in every pub yard. A quoit is a ring of iron weighing as much as 11lbs. There was an iron peg with a feather stuck in it that was driven into the centre of what was called the quoit bed. It was a clay area that was designed to make the quoits slow down or

A pint of the usual
Before the 1960s a visit to the local pub was the focus of many leisure activities. Even remote villages would have an alehouse, providing a social centre for its regulars. However, pubs had to change so that they became "fit for women" when they saw an opportunity to cash in on family drives into the country at weekends.

stick a bit. No money was ever bet, but a gallon or two of beer might go to the winner of a game and the loser then bought the beer. You had to throw your quoits eighteen yards and each man had two quoits. Four men would play at any one time. The last place I saw it being played was at Billingford Common in the 1950s. It just seemed to reach the end of its days and it disappeared, but the men loved it all over Norfolk. The men who'd played it had played it since they were young and they still enjoyed it, but as they died out their sons had other interests – motorbikes and cars."

"... you could watch the film and then stay in your seat and watch it again."

At the pictures

The postwar years were a boom time for cinema. Film-making had continued throughout the war, with Britain alone managing to produce some 500 films. Such was the public's passion for the cinema that people would rarely evacuate the theatres when the sirens went during a raid, choosing to take their chance and stay and watch the film, rather than go down to the air raid shelters. The careers of famous actors, such as Richard Burton, Peter Finch and Christopher Lee, were launched in this time, and cinema squared-up to its newest rival: television. For some however, nothing could compete with the glamour and excitement of the silver screen, as John Rogan recalls.

Junior film club
Saturday morning film clubs would show cartoons, serials, spy films and the inevitable cowboys and Indians flicks, encouraging their young audience members to excitedly re-enact what they had just seen in their play time. The clubs were hugely popular, as seen (right) at the Gaumont State Theatre in Kilburn, north west London.

Courting couples
It was common for the last two rows in the darkness at the back of the cinema to be designated for couples. Arm rests were removed between intermittent seats to create "couples' chairs", as seen (left) at the Western Talkie Theatre in Bradford.

Cardboard glasses
Bwana Devil (1952) was the first US feature film to be shown using Polaroid's dual-projector 3-D system. Written, produced and directed by Arch Oboler, the film was slated by the critics but was a runaway success with audiences, and paved the way for the golden era of 3-D.

"We used to go every Saturday to the Willesden Odeon here in north west London. It's now long gone but in those days it was packed every night and every weekend in the days before television. My mum and dad never went to the theatre – that was up west (the West End) and they didn't have the money. No one we knew had money for the theatre but you could get a seat for the Saturday morning kids' cinema club for three old pence and, best of all, you could watch the film through and then stay in your seat and watch it again. We were never thrown out and they usually showed the film at least twice in a morning. We were supposed to leave after seeing it but the management never thought that anyone – not even a child – would want to see the same film twice in a row, but we always did. There was always a two-film programme. You saw the B movie first and then the main feature. The B movies were always made to be just fillers with low budget and B list stars, but I always enjoyed them."

The thrill of going to the cinema often masked the disrepair and general neglect that the buildings had fallen into during the war.

"I remember the cinema always smelled very badly of cigarettes and dirty water, probably from all the rain brought in over the years by the customers. The seats were in a bit of a state too from all the kids bouncing up and down on them but no one seriously or deliberately vandalised

Coffee bars
In 1948 Achille Gaggia produced a form of espresso coffee that could not be recreated domestically, placing it at the centre of a "drinking out" culture of consumption. This prompted the revival of London coffee houses as centres of culture and civilization. While the public house of the postwar era had a largely male, beer-drinking clientele, women could now take refuge in a number of small, independent coffee bars.

anything. We were too hungry to throw popcorn or sweets around if we could ever afford them. My favourite films were cartoons and *Sinbad*.

Later we moved to Brighton and they had an even better Saturday morning film club for kids – I recall we'd see a cartoon, a serial such as *Flash Gordon* and then a full-length feature. And you could get to the cinema on the bus, have an ice cream and some popcorn, and get your ticket all for under a shilling."

NEWSREEL

Before everyone had access to television news the cinemas showed newsreels as well as feature films. Lisa Edwards remembered the small cinema in London's Victoria Station:

"This was a newsreel cinema that never showed proper films, although it became a cartoon cinema in the late 1950s. The old Pathe news was really popular and people would pop into the cinema to see what was happening around the world. It was far more interesting than reading the newspapers, but Pathe was largely killed off by TV and the cartoon cinema was later demolished. But it was an amazing little building – very small and built in an Art Deco style above the station concourse with special insulation so that you didn't hear the trains."

Eating out

After the war and until the early 1950s going out for a meal was a rare event for all but the very rich, and even for the rich it was hedged with difficulties, as Pam Tarlton recalls.

"I remember a young man who I was absolutely mad about taking me out in London – to the Savoy I think or possibly the Café Royal or the Ivy – and he was so embarrassed because the food was terrible.

We had to have what was called the five shilling dinner. It got its name because the government passed a law saying that no restaurant at that period of rationing could charge more than five shillings for dinner. It didn't matter whether you were dining at the best or the worst sort of place. The expensive places got round the rule by charging the earth for a bottle of absolutely terrible wine, putting the cost of dinner up to ten shillings!"

Food rationing was first introduced in January 1940 and didn't end until 14 years later. Rationing was vital if the country's food resources were to be fairly distributed, but that didn't lessen the pain and inconvenience of trying to get by on your allocation, which many saw as starvation rations. Restaurants also had to survive under these extremely difficult conditions.

"Everywhere had such a down-at-heel look too – I ate out in Oxford, Bath and London and everywhere seemed really grimy. Bomb damage was still visible well into the mid 1950s and all of the buildings, whether in Oxford or London, hadn't been cleaned in 50 years or more so they were black with soot from millions of coal fires. We took all of that for granted and we all smoked continually too – the idea that it was a dirty habit would have made people laugh then. I remember we used to blow cigarette smoke into our boyfriends' faces – it seemed rather romantic!"

PIE-AND-MASH

Further down the social scale Rose Plummer remembers the pie-and-mash shops of the old East End of London. Pie-and-mash shops (which still exist) had fed London's poor for more than a century. They were hugely popular in the East End and only began to disappear as alternative restaurants started up. Like fish-and-chip shops they offered a diet high in carbohydrates but they also offered that London delicacy – jellied eel.

"We used to go to Cooke's in Hackney. It's gone now but it was a real treat for us. We had fish and chips a lot but you couldn't sit down in most fish-and-chip shops then. Cooke's was wonderful – it had marble tiles up the high walls to the ceiling and they were beautifully decorated with fish and crabs and eels. There was even a domed glass ceiling – like a mini St Paul's.

The Cooke family had run it since about 1870. Pie and mash would be one dollop

"We had to have what was called the five shilling dinner."

East end delicacy

Jellied eels were a delicacy in the East end of London – for years they had been the only edible bounty from the murky waters of the river Thames. Improved transport and storage methods meant that a wider variety of seafood – such as cockles, whelks and winkles – was available after the war, so the stallholders quickly started adding these to their menus.

"They were everywhere if you went out for lunch or tea you went to Lyons – they were like Starbucks and McDonalds."

Nippies
Lyons' Private Catering School for Nippies would set challenging exams for their potential staff, including checking for deliberate mistakes in a buffet setting. Always innovative and with an acute awareness of popular taste, Lyons brought a unique blend of showmanship, style and spectacle to its aim of combining high quality with value for money.

of mash, one meat pie (with a teaspoon of minced meat in it!) and a ladle full of liquor, a green sauce made from the water they boiled the eels in, flour and parsley. If you asked for double-double you got two dollops of mash and two pies. That was all they served – and jellied eels of course. For pudding they had apple pies full of lovely cloves. The pie casings were the same for the meat and the fruit pies. Everyone met up in Cooke's of a Friday night – sawdust on the floor, marble tables and spoons and forks. I don't know why but they never had knives!"

TIME FOR A CUPPA

At the other end of the country Libby Macintyre remembers Glasgow's teashops.

"In the 1950s we didn't eat out in the evening but if we were lucky we had occasional tea in the Willow Tea Rooms in Sauchiehall Street. It was such a treat for us. At the time we liked it but it was only later that we realised how special it really was – the Willow was designed by Charles Rennie Macintosh in about 1900 and it's still going today. Nowadays it is full of tourists but back in the 1950s it was just us Glaswegians!"

Sheila Kehoe in west London can clearly remember the Lyons' tea shops. These were famous for their efficient service, good basic food and for a genteel air that stopped well this side of grand. There were roughly two hundred Lyons' teashops and in the early 1950s they offered a large cup of tea for just 'tuppence ha'penny'.

"They were everywhere – I seem to remember them only on corners! If you went out for lunch or tea you went to Lyons – they were

like Starbucks and McDonalds combined! A cake would cost 2d, and cheese on toast 7d. Later on in the 1960s they changed the name and became Jolyon Cafés but that was the beginning of the end as they just weren't as good. I remember the nippies – that's what they called the waitresses. They were famous for their smart uniforms and polite efficiency."

Down the bingo

The kind of bingo that we know today only really got going towards the end of the 1950s when cinema attendances began to plummet. This was due to more of us buying – or more usually renting – televisions. Television expanded particularly with the start of Independent Television in 1955–56.
But bingo was the saviour of many early cinema buildings, which otherwise might have been demolished. In recent years a few of these have even been returned to their original use as cinemas. Once bingo took off it quickly became hugely popular from one end of the country to the other, as Rose Plummer recalls.

"We used to play when we were on holiday in Clacton in an old cinema. Don't let people tell you that Bingo is for idiots – we used to marvel at the old ladies with cigarettes hanging out of their mouths whilst rapidly filling in two or three cards at the same time. They were so fast – they put us youngsters to shame, but the thing about bingo is that it combines gambling with the chance of a good gossip.

Every Saturday in London we'd go up to the bingo at the Hackney Empire where you put your winning sheet on a wire that was pulled up to the front of the stage. We looked forward to it every week – it was our highlight."

Bingo at the Trocadero
Originally conceived as a fundraising event, bingo became so popular and commercialised that scenes such as this at the Trocadero in London's Elephant and Castle became increasingly common. Many of the bingo call names still used today provide an insight into popular language and culture at the time. Traditional call names such as Danny la Rue (52) and Dirty Gertie (30) reflect popular personalities at the time and are a barometer for 1950s Britain.

Playing bingo
The popularity of bingo and the simplicity of organising it encouraged the development of regular games in many parts of the country, often accommodating several hundred players. Here people are seen playing bingo (above) at a stall at the Festival Funfair in Battersea Park, London in June 1951.

Libby Macintyre remembers playing bingo where, if anything, the locals had taken to the game with even more gusto and passsion than their southern counterparts.

> "We always had fish and chips before bingo, but playing bingo was an absolute craze – I remember lots of cinemas being converted and people were out several nights a week. Winnings were usually ten shillings or a pound and a huge win was £25! But these days Glasgow is embarrassed about bingo and fish and chips – it wants to forget all that and be a city of culture, which is fine, but they shouldn't forget how the ordinary people lived!"

The Butlin's holiday camps that had sprung up in the years immediately before and after the war were quick to capitalise on the craze, as Amy Capper recalls:

> "We went to Clacton in Essex and Minehead in Somerset and they both had Butlin's. We used to play bingo practically every night but particularly if it rained – the joke used to be that bingo was a good way to stop all the holidaymakers getting bored and causing trouble. It certainly worked

– men and women would be glued to their cards for hours and there would be a huge cheer (and a groan) when someone won. But if you were lucky and had a win it might pay for half of your holiday."

Reading matter

Books were still relatively expensive in the 1950s and very much a middle-class interest, but public libraries made reading available to a much wider public than would otherwise be the case, and taking children to the library seems to have been almost universal.Pam Tarlton recalls book buying in London.

"You could browse but you needed to be socially confident to do it for long."

Book shops
1950s Britain was awash with independent bookshops – such as this one (left) on London's Charing Cross Road. With reading a popular pastime and money not being readily available, the second-hand book market was a profitable trade.

"We used to go to Heywood Hill's bookshop in Mayfair. It was very grand and the people who worked there knew far more about books than any of their customers – I'm pretty sure they were all educated at Eton and Oxford! I know Nancy Mitford worked at there during the war, but by the time we were going in the mid-1950s it was still very smart. You could browse but you needed to be socially confident to do it for long. In those days people were suspicious in all shops if you didn't immediately ask for help and in Heywood Hill's they expected to be asked for recommendations and would discuss books knowledgeably. My mother loved all of this and of course from a business point of view it worked really well because after chatting for half an hour you could hardly leave without buying something!"

Penguin Classics
A Mass Observation survey in the summer of 1947 revealed that, of the 1,000 Tottenham residents canvassed, three in ten of the middle class counted reading as a favourite hobby, along with two in ten of the skilled working classes and one in ten of the unskilled. Penguin Classics' iconic cover design led the 1950s market for popular fiction.

Quiet please
Libraries provided a vital service for both adults and children alike, giving them access to books and information that would otherwise have been cost-prohibitive or hard to get hold of. Scenes such as this one (right) at the "Toddlers' Corner" of Bermondsey Public Library in 1950 became even more common into the 1960s as children's book publishing boomed.

Stepford wives
Women's magazines encouraged women to stay at home and look after the family, while their men went back to work after being demobbed from the forces.

"It was rather a treat for me each Saturday morning to go to the library ..."

But the shrewd commercialism of bookshops was matched by an enthusiasm for both light and serious reading; however, the pleasures of the printed page would begin to pale beside the glitzy attractions of improving television.

"We all loved Agatha Christie for light reading and Elizabeth Bowen for the more serious minded. There were paperbacks

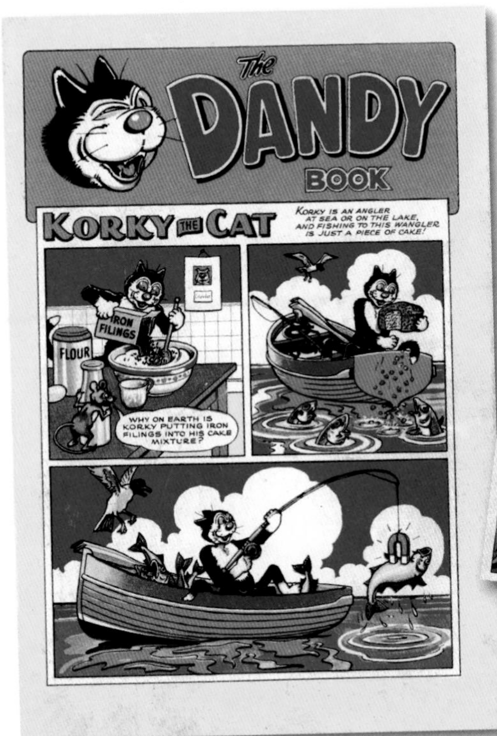

Comic strip
Paper was rationed in World War II, but comics such as the *The Beano* and *The Dandy* were still produced on low grade paper to entertain children. *The Dandy* poked fun at the Germans and the Italians, and Desperate Dan was shown punching Hitler out of Britain so hard that he landed in Germany.

but hardly anyone stocked them because they were associated with cheap, downmarket fiction and even pornography! A respectable book always had a hard cover – no one can believe me when I tell them that today!"

Sheila Kehoe was, by contrast, an avid library goer, and made good use of her local resource.

"It was rather a treat for me each Saturday morning to go to the Library in Ladbroke Grove, west London. The library, which is still there, was a lovely red brick building and very quiet – no computers and you were shushed instantly if you said a word!"

But libraries were not just important for adults – many remember the local library as the place where a lifetime's love (or loathing!) for books really began. Although children's books were not widespread until the 60s and 70s, postwar Britain witnessed a huge growth in the popularity of comics.

"We bought comics for the children – my children loved *The Dandy* and *The Beano* and were terribly upset if they missed a week. When they were a little older the boys read the *Eagle* and for novels they loved country books by BB and Dan Dare stories. There seemed far less for girls although I do remember *Bunty*. The funniest thing looking back is how posh all the children were in stories at that time. Enid Blyton children always said things such as 'I say you rotter, what a horrid thing to do!'. There really were very few magazines then. *The Lady* I recall – which was just for those looking for nannies and other domestic staff – *Country Life* and, at the other end of the social scale, *Titbits*, which has gone now. *Punch* was only read by upper-class men."

"... my children loved The Dandy *and* The Beano *and were terribly upset if they missed a week."*

There was an innocence about the leisure pursuits of the late 1940s and 1950s that has all but vanished today. People still remembered that during World War II they'd had to pull together to survive on virtually nothing, and this made them proud to enjoy their leisure time together. It was a theme that ran through everything, from meetings in tea shops and pubs, going to dance halls, listening to 78-rpm records with friends, or a whole gang of friends and neighbours gathering at the one house in the street with a television to watch that most momentous event of the 20th century – the coronation of Queen Elizabeth II.

TEENAGE KICKS
Rock and roll and the new youth culture

In the way we understand the term now, teenagers hardly existed before World War II. It was the influence of America that transformed the way young people in Britain looked and behaved. Out went sensible haircuts and clothes and the rules under which teenagers were respectful to the values and beliefs of an older generation. New styles came in, new music and above all new attitudes in a world of rock and roll, Teddy boys, Mods and rockers!

Little Richard
Little Richard was a key figure in the transition from rhythm and blues to rock and roll in the 1950s. Pioneering hit singles such as *Tutti Frutti* and *Long Tall Sally,* released between 1955 and 1957 helped to lay the foundation for rock and roll music, and influenced generations of rhythm & blues, rock and soul music artists.

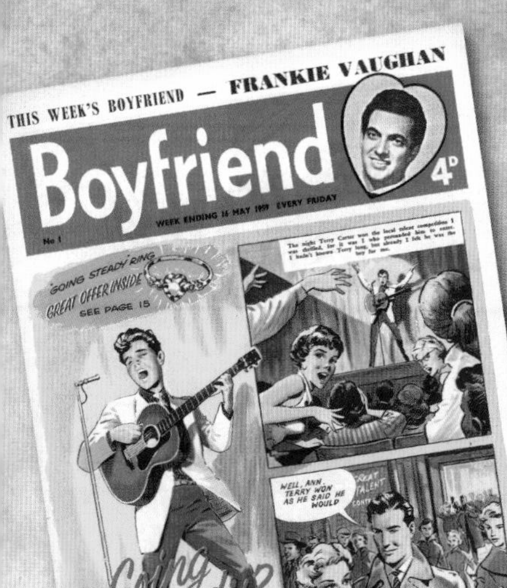

Music magazines

Boyfriend was launched in 1959 and was the first girls' magazine to put music first. Each week there would be a new "boyfriend" such as Russ Conway, or Johnny Mathis, introducing his life story. Cliff Richard was given his own column to introduce other stars of the pop scene.

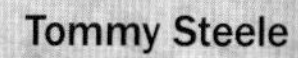

Listening booths

Going to a record shop to spend the afternoon listening to the latest tunes in a booth was a fashionable pastime. Music was a serious business, and the 7-inch vinyl of choice would be put on the turntable and listened to intently.

Tommy Steele

Britain's first teen idol and rock and roll star Tommy Steele rose to fame with a skiffle group, however Tommy's brand of rock and roll was nearer to easy listening than that of some of his American contemporaries

Bill Haley and his Comets

Shake, Rattle and Roll sold a million copies and became the first rock and roll song to enter British singles charts in 1954, leading to Bill Haley and his Comets being credited with popularizing that genre of music. Rock and roll was finally reaching a wider audience after years of being considered an underground movement.

Jukeboxes

The postwar years saw a nation desperate for entertainment, and factories ran at full capacity to produce 100 jukebox machines per day for 245 working days. The jukebox was the best way for the music industry to reach out to record-buying patrons. Any establishment with a jukebox was the best place for music lovers to hear their favorite artists' new recordings.

Football mad

The postwar era witnessed the popularity of English football reach its highest as the nation tried to shrug off its wartime restraints and tedium and return to the pleasure pursuits of peaceful times. During the improving economic circumstances many found in football a cheap and exciting way to pass their free time.

Play the game

SPORTS

The 1940s and 1950s were arguably the last decades to retain a Victorian belief in the virtues of sport as a way to build character. At private schools boys played rugby, at state schools football, but all children – including girls playing compulsory hockey – were expected to play in all weathers. Watching football was hugely popular among working class men, while the middle class passion for football was still decades away. Shooting, fishing and hunting were the favoured pursuits of the wealthy while the football pools had begun to define the leisure activities of the masses.

Sport for all

In the years immediately following the war, and for a decade and more beyond that, sport was still riven by class divisions. Rugby Union was played and watched by the middle classes in the south of England, while Rugby League was a uniquely working-class sport confined to the north of England. Football was largely a working-class interest, both as a spectator sport and as something to play – the chattering classes had as yet absolutely no interest in the game and it was definitely not yet big business. The first £100-a-week footballer didn't arrive on the scene until the 1960s and few footballers would have thought of themselves as celebrities. Cricket – the great game of the English summer – was still largely the preserve of the middle classes, as were trout and salmon fishing. The poor contented themselves with coarse fishing on rivers that were usually too polluted to maintain a stock of trout and salmon or on canals running through industrial areas.

At schools up and down the country the social divide was mirrored more or less precisely, with public schools playing rugby and state schools football, but the Victorian idea that sport was good from a moral point of view still held sway right across the board, as Malcolm Croft remembers.

"We had to play football every week at my state secondary school, whatever the weather. We had to wear shorts even if a blizzard was blowing – no track suits allowed even if you were the goalie – and they made more fuss if you missed what we used to call the Wednesday afternoon nightmare than if you missed a maths or an English lesson. In more recent years the idea has been to keep kids from putting on weight but back then it was almost as if

Eton games
One of the UK's top public schools played a different form of football called the Eton Field Game, which still continues to this day. The ball is one size smaller than a traditional football, but handling is still prohibited. The field rules are more similar to those of rugby. The goal is smaller, however, and there is no dedicated goalkeeper.

Rugby training
Playing rugby was seen as an excellent way of building teamwork, discipline and courage. A group of grammar-school boys use the scrummager during practice to make the scrum more effective (below).

"We had to wear shorts even if a blizzard was blowing – no track suits allowed even if you were the goalie ..."

we had to play sport in case there was another war, or just to be sure that if we had to defend the Empire we'd be fit enough to make a good job of it!

No one mentioned fitness – it was just that sport was good for your morals, like having a cold bath every morning. I must admit that I hated football and it was only later on I realised that the grammar school down the road from my secondary modern played rugby in winter in imitation of the big public schools.

In summer there were genuine difficulties with playing cricket because you needed a lot more equipment. My state school couldn't afford pads and bats and wickets so we didn't play, or if we did it was a simpler game with just one wicket chalked on a playground wall. Football was always the cheapest option because all you needed was the ball.

My memory of footballs in the 1950s is that they were impossible for a child to kick – they were solid leather and very heavy. If it rained they quickly doubled in weight and would nearly break your foot if you gave them a really hard kick.

Swimming was the other big thing – every child in my junior school was expected to swim a mile before they were 11. It was another obsession from earlier times, when travel was always by ship. They thought we'd have a chance if we could swim and the ship went down! We used to joke and say it was because the

Howzat
Playing cricket was popular at all levels of society. Even the hard pitch and the lack of properly-fitting equipment did not stop children from picking up the bat.

Learning to swim
Attending a school with its own swimming pool was for the wealthy only. Most children made a weekly pilgrimage to the local municipal baths to learn to swim. A treat for those with just a weekly tin bath at home, public baths were generally rather unhygienic places, and many remember the scum around the water line, and cockroach infestations.

"My state school couldn't afford pads and bats and wickets so we didn't play, or if we did it was a simpler game ..."

Summer days
Outdoor pools in cities such as London (right) were generally open from May to September; a ticket for the whole season was coveted by most children. Swimming caps – which were hard to come by during the war due to rationing of rubber – were obligatory not only for school girls, but also adult women who were desperate to preserve their all-important hair style. The 1950s saw floral swimming caps become *de rigeur.*

teachers were old enough to remember the sinking of the *Titanic* which, actually, they probably were!"

James Guest had similar memories of swimming sessions at his grammar school.

"There was a real passion for swimming back in the 1940s and even more so in the 1950s. Health and safety rules and regulations hadn't yet made teachers terrified of taking the kids to the local pool and it was cheap so we went every week.

There seemed to be endless competitions and every kid was desperate to get his or her bronze, silver and gold personal survival medals. As far as I recall, to win each medal you had to jump in with your pyjamas on and then, while treading water, take the trousers off, tie knots in the legs and turn them into a flotation device. It was hilarious! The other thing I remember was the complete chaos of it all – we had formal orderly races for the first part of each session but then we were allowed to muck about for the last half hour while the teachers went off for a cigarette! We used to dive in and bomb each other, run along the sides of the pool and scream at the top of our voices. That was all banned by the 1980s and 1990s and today you can't even dive in most pools. A pity really."

But if sport was good for boys things weren't nearly so clear-cut when it came to girls. Pam Tarlton recalls her experience at the Cheltenham Ladies' College.

"We played hockey and learned to swim, but the obsession with decorum and delicacy meant that our swimming suits were enormous and for hockey we had to wear four skirts and eight pairs of

A straight bat
Private schools were renowned then, as now, not just for an improved quality of teaching, but also for a focus on sport. Concern was raised in a House of Commons debate about the nation's sporting abilities, which lead to Prime Minister Clement Atlee outlining the brief of the Minister of Education with regard to physical education as "the development to the full of each person's physical potentialities and not the fostering of success at competitive games".

Season's climax
The 1948 FA Cup Final, at the Wembley Empire Stadium in London, was a thrilling Lancashire derby between Blackpool and Manchester United. It marked the season's end of the oldest and most prestigious domestic knock-out tournament in world football. By the 1950s, crowds of more than 100,000 routinely attended cup finals.

knickers. I exaggerate a little, but there was an idea that though sport was good for girls it was risky from a moral standpoint if any part of our flesh was exposed!"

Off to the match

Football was and is the great spectator sport. But in the 1940s and 1950s local people supported the local team, which was largely made up of local players. The whole point of it, as Nat Budgen explains, was that it was your home-town team.

"When I see Manchester United and similar teams buying players from all over the world I realise that football is not the football I once knew. If you lived in Southampton as I did you supported Southampton. That was the point of it. People would have thought you were mad – or didn't understand the point of football at all – if you lived in Southampton and supported Manchester United or any other foreign team.

It was wonderful to go on a Saturday when the weather was cold. We all stood then – the terraces right round the ground had no seats except a few for VIPs and when your team scored you could jump around like a lunatic, but it was dangerous with 30- or 40-thousand people all penned in together like that.

I remember we'd have a beer while watching and no one thought anything of it – again the alcohol ban was a good idea, because people stopped behaving themselves. In the old days when I went they didn't really mind if you drank because there were few fights, and no one minded if we invaded the pitch after the match because people only did it so they could pat their heroes on the back, not to try to kill the opposing team's players as they do now.

I went to a few rugby matches but it never had the excitement of football."

Tom Shackle recalls that other great spectator sport – horse racing – as well as the now defunct hare coursing.

"We went to Cheltenham every year. It was a great place to meet old friends who, like us, went every year – many over from Ireland – and you could enjoy a bet and a catch-up. I also went up to Liverpool each year to the Waterloo Cup. That was a coursing event. It was banned when they banned hunting. I think they were probably right to ban it but it was exciting to watch – two greyhounds were released each time a hare was let into the field and the greyhounds would try, and usually fail, to catch it. The best performing dog would win, not necessarily the one that caught the hare."

Pam Tarlton recalls more elevated sports.

"We went to stay with friends at Chiswick each year to watch the boat race and to Henley for the regatta. My parents knew so many people there, as I did. There was always some excitement about the boat race itself and people did take bets on who

Summer joys
Horse racing, both flat and over the jumps, was a passion shared by all classes. Various race meetings – such as Royal Ascot and Glorious Goodwood – were a feature of the fashionable season.

The river bank
Henley Royal Regatta, featuring rowing races on the River Thames, was one of the highlights of the upper-class season in early July. The event had the flavour of an Edwardian garden party, and the river banks were crammed with marquees and stands.

"No one minded if we invaded the pitch after the match because people only did it so they could pat their heroes on the back, not to try to kill the opposing team ..."

would win, but mostly for us it was a chance to meet friends and chat. At Henley I never remember noticing much on the river at all. It was all baffling – men in blazers drifting up and down apparently pointlessly, but I loved the Pimms!"

Hunting, shooting and fishing

Before television and the widespread ownership of cars country sports were important as a means to knit together the social fabric of the countryside. Hunting was largely the preserve of the rich simply because keeping a horse was an expensive business and hunt subscriptions were beyond the means of most country people.

Shooting was rather different. While the rich might shoot pheasants and grouse in season the more lowly farm labourer would find plenty of sport with which to fill his larder with rabbits and pigeon. Fishing was similarly split into fly fishing for trout and salmon the preserve of the wealthy and coarse fish – roach, perch, bream and carp – for the rest.

Will Constance remembers shooting in Norfolk in the 1940s and 1950s:

"The local toffs round Scole were the Mann family. They owned all the land round about and all the farmers were their tenants. I can't say they were bad landlords, but we only saw him and his family when they were pheasant shooting and we'd perhaps beat for them. To be fair, there was also an interesting tradition that on one day a season the toffs would beat for the beaters! That was our reward, if you like, for beating the rest of the season.

We also shot rabbits and pigeons and sometimes the landlord would give us the cartridges because they saw it as pest control. It was great fun for us though. I remember particularly out roost shooting at night and the pigeons coming in to the gradually darkening woods. It was a quiet time but good to be out with a friend talking quietly as the dark came in and we'd get a few shots and take a few pigeon home. They made very good eating."

The 'Glorious Twelfth'
The four-month grouse shooting season, from the "Glorious Twelfth" of August onwards, was a prestigious sport on upland moors. Bags peaked before World War I, and by the late 1940s each estate probably averaged a few hundred birds a year.

Rough shooting
Animals such as rabbits and pigeons were classed as vermin by landowners. They could be shot at any time of the year, and made a useful addition to a farm worker's larder.

For the pot
Country workers used their knowledge of nature and wildlife to add to their diet and income. Rabbits – a good and readily available source of protein – could be shot in the field, flushed out of their burrow with ferrets and netted at the entrance, or lamped.

VERMIN SHOOTS

Farmer Lance Whitehead also remembers happy days out shooting.

"My great hobby has always been shooting. We used to have wonderful days before myxomatosis wiped the rabbits out in the late 1950s – it was never as it was in Edwardian days on the grand shoots where they'd say about a duck or a pheasant, 'Up goes a guinea, bang goes a penny and down comes half a crown!'

We just used to get together with all the farmers round about for vermin shoots – you know, rabbits, jays, magpies and so on – and it was our bit of fun and way of socialising, because it's very difficult for a farmer to take a holiday, as you can imagine."

Taking something home for the pot was part of the huge appeal of shooting. Protein was hard to come by and people were grateful for a rabbit, a hare, or a pigeon, as Denys Watkins Pitchford recalled.

"In our part of Northamptonshire there were still a lot of very poor cottagers who struggled at the best of times so those of us who did a bit of shooting and fishing did what we could for them. If I'd managed to shoot a brace of pheasants or a few rabbits – they were everywhere in those days – I'd always keep one for myself and give the others away. No one was anti-shooting back then because we were so hungry for a bit of meat most of the time and people were grateful for what they could get. Farmers always welcomed us on to their land to shoot too because modern ways to scare off pests hadn't been invented and after the War rabbits and pigeons in particular did a lot of damage to crops.

But the real pleasure of shooting for me was just to walk the hedgerows with my old Labrador. That phrase about people never being so close to nature as when they are in pursuit of it is very true. I'd spot songbird nests, the occasional buzzard or kestrel and sometimes get so absorbed in all this that I'd get home and realise I hadn't fired a shot. It was lovely too when you met someone else from the village out shooting. You'd stop for a chat and then set off in different directions or walk the fields together for a while. It was all very relaxed and sociable. It was the social side of shooting I later missed."

Match fishing – a competition to catch the greatest weight of fish – really got going in the 1950s as city fishing clubs were more easily able to hire coaches to take their members out of the city to various rivers, as Nobby Clarke recalls.

"Match fishing with our club was brilliant. We used to meet outside a pub in the Portobello Road at six on a Sunday morning and go with all our mates out to Lechlade on the Thames or up to Norfolk to fish the Ouse. Match fishing in those days was about fun not money – the person who caught the heaviest bag of fish won about £10, which was a lot in those days but not enough to tempt you to cheat! You had to put all the fish back alive because these were coarse fish, not salmon and trout.

We'd go every Sunday, however bad the weather, and right through the winter. I used to take a gallon of maggots for the day and the best way to keep your hands

Match fishing
Coarse fishing had always been a popular sport, and the growth of motor transport after World War II meant that numerous members of city fishing clubs could line the banks of fishing hot spots at competitions to catch the greatest weight of fish.

Catch of the day
Local piers, wharfs and rock marks along the coast provided young boys with the perfect locations to catch fish from the sea, which could be taken home for eating or sold to get some extra pocket money. A simple handline was generally sufficient to catch a good head of mackerel or herring in season.

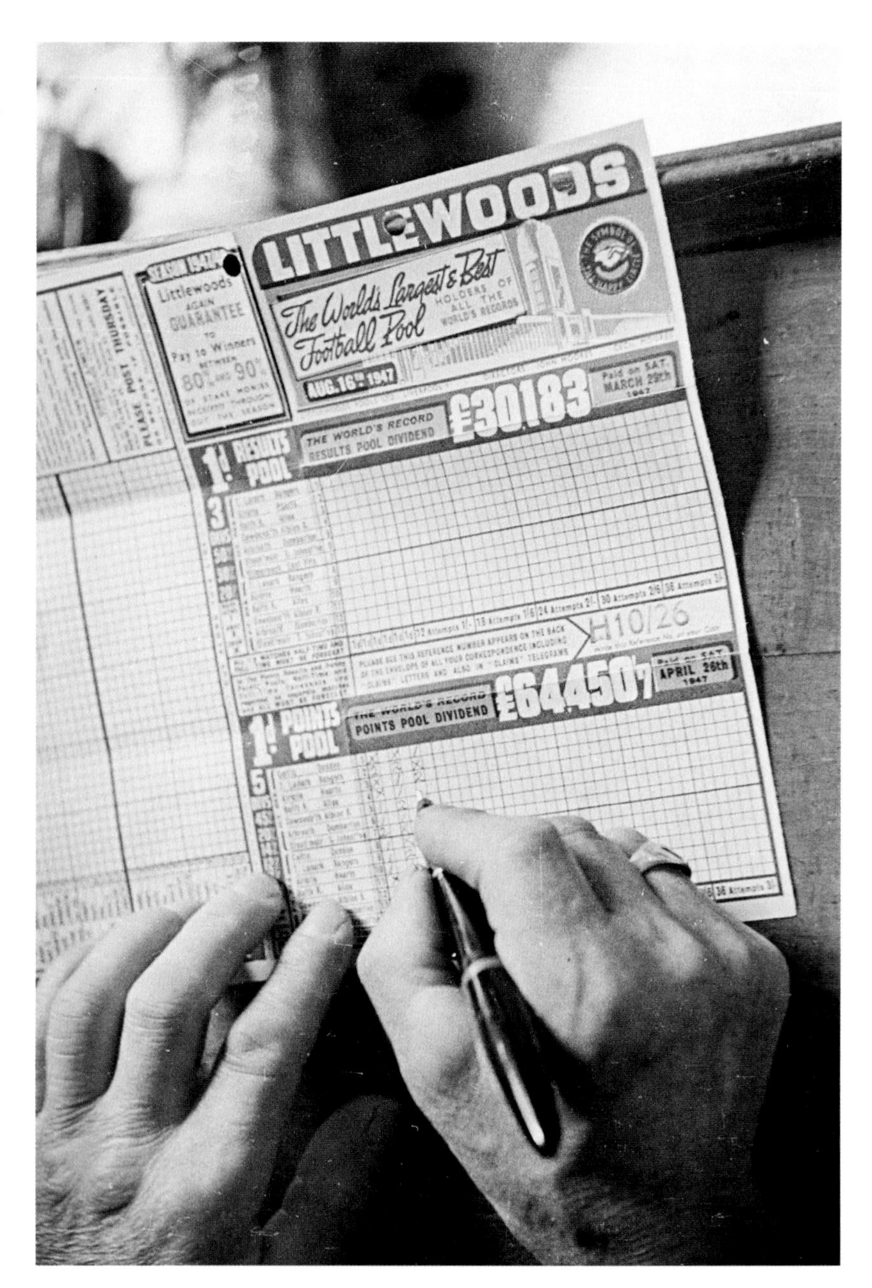

Doing the Pools
Littlewoods Football Pools were founded in 1923, and the famous"Treble Chance" game started in 1946. The Treble Chance was popular because it offered a single jackpot prize at a time when no other such prize was on offer. The Pools – which were based on predicting football match scores – did not fall under gambling legislation as they claimed to be a competition of skill, rather than chance.

warm was to push your hands deep into the mass of writhing maggots. They generated a lot of heat! If it was really frosty and the maggots weren't wriggling much we'd pop them in our mouths for a minute to liven them up. The things people do for a bit of fishing!"

After World War II, when systematic surveys began to be conducted into what ordinary people did in their leisure time, it was discovered that fishing was the most popular participant sport in the country. That situation remains unchanged – to the astonishment of those who find the idea of fishing both boring and incomprehensible. But the appeal in the years after the War was that whether you lived in town or country, city centre or remote hamlet there was always a pond a lake or a canal nearby where you could happily spend a few hours using, if you really were on your uppers, a few pieces of home made tackle, as Lofty Smith recalled.

"I was unemployed for about a year from the autumn of 1949 and at that time unemployment was awful because the dole as we used to call social security in those days was only just enough to live on.

I made a rod from a few bits of garden bamboo cane. I bought an old reel for a shilling and a few hooks and used to spend the whole weekend fishing the Grand Union Canal. It wasn't pretty but if you kept your eyes on the water you could imagine yourself anywhere, and anyone who enjoys fishing will know what I mean when I say that the hours pass very quickly and happily when you are staring at a float. They certainly passed far more quickly than the time on other days when I was searching for work.

Best of all the old canals were free fishing because no one thought for a minute that anyone would be mad enough to want to pay to fish there! I believe that all came to an end because by the 1970s every bit of water had been snapped up by various clubs. We used to joke that if you took a fish home for your supper from the Grand Union you'd be dead by morning!"

Putting money on it

Even though there was no National Lottery – such things did exist in many European countries at the time – gambling was big business in the UK after the end of the war.

Perhaps the most popular form of gambling was bingo, followed by the football pools, which were killed off by the National Lottery.

A social activity
Despite all forms of gambling being illegal until the Betting and Gaming Act of 1960, two private members bills had permitted the organising of "Housey-Housey" (an informal bingo game) ostensibly for the support of charities. The difficulty of enforcing the law, combined with the ease of organising a game meant that personal profits were made. The Act of 1960 enabled commercial bingo halls to be developed.

APRIL
JULY

Guess the weight
Gambling pre-1960 was illegal and widespread. Anything that could be gambled upon generally would be, such as here on the banks of the river Nene in Peterborough, where books are being run on bag weights at the National Match Fishing competition.

Sheila Kehoe recalls the pleasures of playing the pools every week.

"I did the Littlewoods Pools for years and although I never won winning always seemed more of a genuine possibility than it does with the Lottery. The trouble with the Lottery is that it's completely random. With the pools there was meant to be a bit of skill involved, because you were supposed to be able to work out and predict who would have a no-score draw, a score draw or a win. I was absolutely hopeless at it as I didn't have any interest in football itself. I just used to guess, but then so did all my friends. I think the pools were more of a woman's thing than for men – they were much more interested in watching football and betting on horses! Mind you, my other passion each year was for betting on the Grand National – all the girls used to bet and if anyone complained that it was unladylike to gamble on the horses we used to tell them that the Queen Mother was a gambler, so it must be all right!"

"... back in the 1950s you could still place bets on a photo-finish race while they were getting the film developed ... "

John Quinn recalls a long-vanished form of betting that actually improved the odds in favour of the punter.

"The best gamblers would get a position on the racecourse overlooking the finishing line and bet mostly, or only, on photo finishes, because back in the 1950s you could still place bets on a photo-finish race while they were getting the film developed, as it were. So if you stood on the line and watched as hard as you could you quickly got the knack of getting it right and ended up winning far more than you lost. I made a lot of money until the bookies realised

At the bookies
The Betting and Gaming Act of 1960 aimed to address the archaic laws surrounding gambling in Britain. After enforcement on May 1, 1961 betting shops opened at a rate of 100 a week for the next six months. Racecourse or trackside bookies were issued special licences from the Racecourse Betting Control Board.

Not a social problem
A government social survey of 1950 found that 80% of respondents had gambled and that 10–13% gambled at least weekly. One of the main conclusions of the survey was that, despite being largely illegal: "betting in Britain today is an almost universal habit", and recommended taxation and regulation.

that the finish-line business gave the punters a chance and banned it. Bets would no longer be taken in that short gap between the end of the race and the declaration of the photo-finish winner. After that a lot of us gave up because we realised that the bookies wanted it so weighted in their favour that you really had no chance of coming out on top in the long run."

FASTER HIGHER STRONGER

The 1948 Olympics

It was fitting that the 1948 Olympics should be held in London, the capital of the nation that had done more than any other to defeat Nazi aggression. This symbol of healthy competition between nations was also still a genuinely amateur affair. Few could have imagined that politics would one day mar the image of the greatest sporting events. In 1948 athletes still cobbled together their own kit, asking their mothers to sew national flags on to their shirts!

Olympic torch
There were three types of torches used during the the Olympic games: a standard torch, a torch with a gas recipient for the sea crossing and a torch for the last runner (above). The flame was magnesium to ensure that the spectators could still see it clearly during daylight.

Commemorative stamps
Special issues of 2½d, 3d, 6d and 1/- commemorative stamps went on sale at all Post Offices to honour the Olympic games.

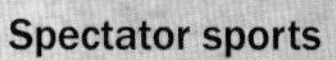

Spectator sports

The games began on July 29, 1948, with King George VI presiding over the opening ceremony in the presence of more than 80,000 spectators. At 4pm, the time shown on Big Ben on the London Games symbol, the King declared the games open, and 2,500 pigeons were set free as a symbol of peace.

A frugal event

The main athletics events were held in Wembley Stadium, where a temporary running track had been installed. An Olympic village had not been built, instead the foreign athletes were accommodated in old wartime barracks and schools across the city. The London-based British athletes stayed at their homes. The games saw some technological innovations, including the photo finish and starting blocks.

Relaxing pleasures
Blackpool in the early 1950s was the favoured holiday resort of millions. People travelled by train and coach to enjoy the miles of beaches, three piers, the Tower and Winter Gardens, the ballrooms and Pleasure Park, and a vast array of arcades, snack bars, restaurants and hotels. The town's autumn Illuminations, not permitted during the war's blackout conditions, were a great relief from post-war austerity.

Let the good times roll

HOLIDAYS

It is difficult today to fully appreciate the huge postwar desire of the British simply to have fun. After years of no fun at all, holidays were central to this new desire; the growth in their popularity and affordability was one of the wonders of the 1950s. The poor had to make do with an occasional day-trip to the seaside and only the wealthy could afford foreign holidays, but between these two extremes a vast middle market developed. These new holidaymakers were not prepared to endure a week in a dingy boarding house with a bad-tempered landlady; they wanted a week or two at the fabulous new holiday camps where the cares of everyday life could, at least for a time, be forgotten.

The birth of the holiday

Until 1871 the British worker had no right at all to holidays. It was the Bank Holiday Act of 1871 that turned a number of the old religious holidays into secular days off. Even if workers were not paid they now had the right at least to take some time off without running the risk of being sacked.

It took another 60 years and more for paid holidays to become part of everyday life in Britain. In 1936 the Annual Holiday Bill made a once-a-year paid holiday a statutory right. By this time of course it was much easier from a practical point of view to take a holiday than it had been a century earlier, because the railway had spread into the most remote parts of the country, although it was not until the 1950s that the majority of Britons could afford to have a holiday away from home.

Once seaside towns such as Blackpool and Cleethorpes, Minehead and Southend became accessible by rail the rail companies promoted them as day-excursion or holiday destinations, and the passion of the British for seaside holidays had begun. It was a passion that lasted right up until the mid 1960s and the advent of cheap flights and holidays abroad.

Donkey rides
Tractors and industrial-scale farming left an estimated 100,000 donkeys redundant in postwar Britain, but because of their quiet disposition and gentle nature donkeys became popular on beaches around the country. Donkey rides on the beach became one of the main attractions at tourist haunts such as Blackpool, Scarborough, Skegness and Morecambe.

Great British seaside

A picture of kiss-me-quick hats, donkey rides and ice cream: in short, the quintessential seaside holiday, but for individual holidaymakers back in the late 1940s and 1950s there was nothing nostalgic about a trip to the coast. Seaside holidays were new and exciting, even if they lasted only a day.

Rose Plummer remembers seaside trips that were the highlight of the year.

"We didn't have any of the expensive sophisticated holidays people have today, but when we decided on a seaside outing it was something to really look forward to. Children would be mad with excitement for weeks before and their mums would make loads of food to eat: we'd eat on the train and on the beach or pier. We took our food with us because even a day trip by train was likely to cost a poor London family more than they could afford, so they had no money for cafés and shops.

I remember going from Liverpool Street to Southend and waving from the window to people I didn't even know as we left – I just wanted to wave to anyone really, I was so excited. You can't lean out the window and wave today – the windows don't open any more and it wouldn't be allowed by Health and Safety!

Kids would be in the compartments jumping up and down and some families would have started on their food before they left the station – the noise and chatter was deafening, like the noise on the old hop specials that took the families down to Kent for six weeks picking in the summer. Like the seaside specials those hop trains were still going in the early 1960s – hard to believe it, but it's true!

When we got to Southend we'd all pour out of the station and down to the pier, where we got another little train out to the end of the pier – the pier was more than a mile long. The train actually ran back and forth all day just along the pier, but I think

British resorts
The main attractions of Blackpool in 1945 were the tower and the Pleasure Beach, already half a century old. Situated on the Thames estuary at the opposite end of the country, Southend was often nicknamed "East London by the Sea" because of its proximity to that part of the capital and the number of east end residents who had moved there. A short train ride away, Southend was an antidote to the slums.

Southend pier
Extending 2,158 m (1.341 miles) into the Thames estuarary Southend has the longest pleasure pier in the world, At peak times in the postwar years there would be four passenger trains in service along the pier.

it's long gone now. Then it was ice creams and What-the-Butler-Saw machines all day. We didn't really mind if it rained, it was all so different from all our other days. I think Butlin's really killed the day trippers' seaside special. But things change, don't they? You just have to accept it, and though the seaside specials were fun it was just one day, and when we could have a cheap one-week holiday instead, we did."

THE ONLY WAY TO TRAVEL

The commercial potential of seaside holidays had long been recognised by the railway companies and none more so than the Great Western Railway, as Tom Shackle recalls.

"I remember endless sunshine. All of it was exciting, from the journey down by train from London to the walks along the coast."

Visitor levels
The numbers of holidaymakers at Southend peaked at 5.75 million between 1949 and 1950, exceeding the pre-war numbers. More novelty attractions opened to satisfy the increasing numbers of visitors, including the Dolphin Café, Sun Deck Theatre and a Hall of Mirrors.

The GWR was always seen as the holiday railway because it served the West Country – land of wide beaches and glorious weather. Towns like Sidmouth, Swanage and Weymouth grew rapidly after the arrival of the railway – they became rich in fact – and when I was a boy we still went every year, as people had done in the late 19th century when the hotels and sea front houses were built to accommodate the summer arrivals.

We always went to Weymouth, which still has its lovely seafront houses. People like my family stayed in the same boarding house overlooking the sea year after year. I remember breakfast, which we all had in the dining room, and the long days in the sun on the beach. It's rubbish to say it always rains – I remember endless sunshine. All of it was exciting, from the journey down by train from London to the walks along the coast. The Great Western Railway even published books on the holiday towns they could take you to and they were best-sellers. One was called Holiday Heaven. And all their lovely posters – some designed by famous artists – showed happy beach scenes. It was the same on the Southern Railway – in the 1830s only a few thousand people a year went to Brighton, but by the 1840s more than 300,000 were going in the summer months alone. By the late 1950s it was probably in the millions."

Family motors

Britain's enduring love affair with the motor car began in the 1950s. Despite rationing and the fact that the UK was on the verge of bankruptcy the real price of cars did gradually come down during that decade, as Europe rebuilt its shattered industrial and commercial base and America surged forward as the new world power.

For those who could afford a car this was a time of enormous freedom. And the sense of freedom can be attributed not just to the car itself but also to the fact that the roads were virtually empty by the standards of more recent times, as Nat Budgen recalls.

Southern delights
Poster advertising promoted the benefits of holidays by rail.

Boarding houses
Women were particularly keen on a week free from household chores, which boarding houses could provide. Guests planned and bought the meals that the landlady then cooked. Once a nice boarding house was found, it would generally be visited again.

New freedom
Before the war there had been only two million private motor cars, but by the mid-1960s there were more than nine million. This had revolutionary consequences for the individual's freedom, providing much more choice on where they could spend their leisure time.

On the road
Car manufacturers were quick to promote the benefits of using their latest vehicles for the family holiday, as in this 1958 magazine advert from the British Motor Corporation. Note the famous British car names brought together under one banner.

"I saved for years, did masses of overtime and even got a second job for a while, and all because I was absolutely determined to get myself a car. Much later on cars were taken for granted – people got them with their jobs and could buy them really cheaply, but back in the 1950s they were incredibly expensive relative to pay. At last I was able to buy one. I bought a second-hand Morris Oxford Mark II and was the envy of the street. And the first thing we did when we got the car – apart from going out to admire it every five minutes – was to plan our driving holiday. My wife used to laugh at me and say that I only wanted to go on holiday because it meant I could drive the car farther and actually I have to admit that is true. She wanted to see the sea and visit the West Country and wasn't much interested in the vehicle that would enable us to do it. My main interest was the car, and I suppose even today it's still a bit like that. Cars and men just seem to go together.

Anyway when we set off for Devon in August for our two weeks we left at six in the morning and knew we wouldn't get there till very late. Without motorways we went through endless narrow lanes, through forgotten villages and got lost countless times. Road signs were all still those old metal finger posts and there were no motorways. Even trunk roads, which is what we used to call A roads, were few and far between and often they were just as narrow as the little village roads. But we had great fun and never fell out when we got lost. It felt like a real achievement, too, driving all that way and seeing the sea at the end of it. I felt like an explorer! Within 20 years, of course, the same journey was much quicker and all on a boring motorway."

Beach pleasures
The seaside holiday was as British as fish and chips. Resorts on the south and east coasts had been closed due to the defences put in place during the war, but with the end of hostilities the restrictions were lifted and people flocked to the beaches to enjoy themselves.

Party time
With the grim realities of war over, the British felt it was time to throw off uniforms and drabness and enjoy themselves. This beach scene at Margate in Kent was typical of the mood that gripped people across the country.

DAY TRIPPERS

Nat was one of a small if growing band of car owners. Most people still relied on trains for their holidays, which were still predominantly day excursions. The rail companies laid on special trains to get them there and back and, as Reg Coote recalls, the boom in excursion specials coincided with the arrival back on civvy street of tens of thousands of demobbed soldiers:

"...the war being over, everyone was absolutely determined to celebrate."

"Immediately after the war there was very little work in winter for us train drivers, so we spent a lot of time in the pub! But as the years went by it picked up. By the mid 1950s summer was incredibly busy – nonstop in fact, because millions of soldiers were back; they had money and more than anything else they wanted a good time. A big part of that was going on holiday. I can remember in August there would be a train out of Victoria bound for the south coast every ten minutes for holidaying soldiers. Some were day excursions too – it was as if, the war being over, everyone was absolutely determined to celebrate. Firms organised outings for their workers, too, because the old days when the management felt they could squeeze as much as they could from their workforce were now frowned on. Workers' rights were the big thing and on a works' outing everything would be paid for by the company owners – they'd even have a bar on the train and send up beer to us men on the footplate!"

Lido fun
In the late 1940s there were more than 300 open-air pools across Britain, used by families and children for picnics and days out.

Fashion accessories
Modern sunglasses were a prewar American invention, and much used by US pilots and soldiers during World War II. They then became popular and useful in Britain, as shown by this postwar Woolworth's advertisement.

For most people day trips were still all that could be afforded. Seaside towns had boarding houses it is true, but they were still largely patronised by the middle classes, simply because money was still very tight, as Lisa Edwards recalls.

"We used to listen in awe to the few people we knew who could afford to go on holiday and stay in a hotel or boarding house. We thought we were quite well off but that kind of holiday was just too expensive. We had lots of day trips though and loved them – no one felt that a day trip was second-best because it was what most of us had. I can remember going to look round a big old house that's now owned by the National Trust. We thought it might be boring but it was fascinating, and left me with a lifelong interest in old houses. Children had more educational trips too – they'd go up to London to the art galleries and museums. It was as if the whole country was on the move again!"

But for those who could afford a week in a seaside boarding house it wasn't all luxury, as Tom Shackle recalls.

"... on a works' outing everything would be paid for ..."

"Well, to tell the truth they could be bloody awful, with snooty or bad-tempered landladies trying to do everything on the cheap, damp rooms and terrible meals. We eventually found one we liked and went back for years. Mrs Middleton – we never got on first-name terms – would make us sandwiches for the beach and not charge for them, and she'd look after people's children if they wanted to go out at night. She was a real treasure but she was a rarity and I've never forgotten her."

Outward bound

With no paid holidays and a seven-day working week still common in the 19th century, the great outdoors was something few had time for. Country people it is true had always used ancient footpaths and bridleways to get about, but the idea of going for a long walk for the fun of it would have seemed absurd. But between the wars working people, particularly in the north of England, had realised that you didn't have to go thousands of miles for fresh air and spectacular scenery. The hills and fells of the Peak District and the Lakes were close to the major industrial centres of Manchester and the Midlands, Liverpool and Sheffield. From days out walking on the fells it must have seemed a natural progression to camping on them. Certainly for Bob Sharpe the uplands became a passion in the years after the war.

"We loved walking – or hiking, as people tended to call it back then. Weekends and holidays were spent in the Lakes mostly and we'd take our terrible little ex-Army tents and try to camp. At first we knew so little about it that the rain would come in and all our clothes would be soaked. We had no idea how to light fires or even use a compass or read a map. Gradually we got the hang of it and camping and hiking became a passion for my friends and me. I can remember that when we first started to go we'd hardly ever meet anyone, but by the end of the 1950s many of our favourite places had become quite crowded. Tents improved – they eventually even had groundsheets! – as did sleeping

Holidays by rail
The Lake District offered spectacular outdoor holidays in the postwar years, and railway companies made sure that they were forerunners for travel to the region. Promotional posters celebrated the famous poets linked to the region, including Shelley, Coleridge and Wordsworth, and the artist and writer John Ruskin.

Stepping out
The Lake District became England's largest national park in 1951, containing the country's highest mountain, Scafell Pike, and the deepest lake, Wastwater. By 1957 there were ten such parks in England and Wales, allowing valuable landscapes and ways of life to be protected as well as giving tourism industries in the areas a boost.

Paid holidays
Brathay Hall, near Ambleside, run by a charitable trust, was opened in 1946 to provide holiday accommodation and activities for young people in work. On holiday from jobs in factories and mines, young people would stay at the hall and explore the surrounding Lake District at the expense of the trust and their employees. The vision of the centre was to enable young people to realise their full potential.

bags, and then lightweight waterproof materials came in. The thing about walking is that it takes you so far from your everyday cares yet you don't have to get in a plane and cross half the world."

John Rogan recalled his walking holidays, which had become increasingly popular as working people realised that a day or two in the countryside was not only hugely enjoyable but also cheap.

"We used to go for a few days' camping each summer. Our tent was hopeless as ground sheets and waterproof materials weren't available then and there always seemed to be endless rain. We walked ten miles each day and stopped at country pubs for lunch. We went on the North Downs in Surrey, sometimes the South Downs in Sussex and just camped wherever we liked – I think you'd be arrested for that now! We hardly ever saw another walker. It just wasn't something many people did back then."

"Lots of cafes used to put up signs in their windows saying 'Cyclists Welcome'."

That sense of escape was keenly felt by Londoner Peter Eagan, who cycled hundreds of miles in the late 1940s and early 1950s.

"I had a terrible old bike that I gradually tinkered with until it was quite good. I remember reading that the Green Belt had been introduced around London so that the city wouldn't grow so big that a cyclist couldn't get out to the countryside in one day, so I thought, well, let's see if I can get out. First time I tried I went to Box Hill in Surrey, which was great fun. In those days even cycling down through the London suburbs, which is what we had to do to get to Box Hill, wasn't too bad, because there was less traffic. Future trips on that old bike took me to the South Downs – I remember leaving my bike in Eastbourne and climbing the Seven Sisters and then sleeping in my pup tent – don't ask me why it was called a pup tent – before cycling back the next day. I also cycled down to Brighton a few times, to Oxford and even to Norwich. Cycling was really big back then when cars were so expensive. There were lots of cafés that used to put up signs in their windows saying 'Cyclists Welcome'."

Butlin's and holiday camps

The seaside had always been the mainstay of the British holidaymaker, and it was to the British resorts that people returned when the barbed wire and landmines had been cleared. Naturally, Billy Butlin – the name most associated with holiday camps, those peculiarly British holiday centres – sited his camps at already popular destinations. Amy Capper remembers her holiday on the Somerset coast:

"We went to Butlin's at Minehead for a week in 1955. It was so exciting because we'd never been on holiday before – we'd had days at the seaside and days walking in the countryside, but that was all.

Butlin's offered all sorts of entertainment for children and adults – there was cabaret, dancing (ballroom dancing),

Pedal power
Bicycles were an intrinsic part of life in postwar Britain. Bicycle manufacturers, such as the James Cycle Company of Birmingham, worked hard to meet the demand. A survey in 1948 found that "as the social scale is descended the proportion of men using using bicycles increases and the proportion of women decreases". As a result, advertising was generally aimed at upper- or middle-class women or families. The tandem was hugely popular, and was marketed as a means to a cheap, family day out.

swimming pools for the kids and baby-sitters so parents could have some time on their own. Butlin's wasn't seen as a poor alternative to a holiday abroad as it later became. It was hugely popular and even the well off went!"

"Butlin's wasn't seen as a poor alternative to a holiday abroad as it later became."

The Butlin's holiday reached a peak of popularity in the late 1950s, but Butlin had opened his first camp as early as 1936. While staying in Skegness he had noticed that holidaying families were not allowed to stay in their boarding houses during the day and that as a result their children became bored and tired. He'd seen holiday camps while in Canada and decided to try the idea here. At its peak there were 15 different locations around the country where you could enjoy the Butlin's experience. The camps became hugely popular, as Rose Plummer recalls.

"We loved very minute of it and I'm only sad we couldn't afford to go more often. The little chalets they put you in were brand-new and very modern and clean, and we didn't mind a bit that you had to go to a big block nearby when you wanted to go to the loo or have a hot bath.

There was a Beaver Club for kids and every morning you were woken up to the sound of Butlin's Radio. Children were encouraged to think of the famous Redcoats as their aunts and uncles, and at night the idea was that the Redcoats walked around listening for children crying while their parents were out playing bingo, dancing or eating.

There were all sorts of competitions too, with really silly titles – Knobbliest Knees for the men, Best Head of Hair and Glamorous Granny for the women. There were swimming pools and organised games and various rides and playgrounds,

Family relaxation
The first two of his holiday camps were opened by Billy Butlin at Skegness and Clacton before World War II. Butlin's became popular in post-war Britain with family entertainment and activities available for the equivalent of a week's pay. Further camps had opened by the 1960s at Bognor Regis, Minehead and Barry Island.

so no one worried if it rained. There was always something to do, including tea dances for the adults. Food was definitely boring by today's standards – very plain, and you could only have porridge or bacon and eggs for breakfast and only at fixed times – but it was all a huge improvement on what we'd had before, which was pretty much nothing except day excursions. What put people off in the end, apart from cheaper foreign holidays, was the fact that you were in a camp with a high fence all the way round to keep everyone out, and it could feel a bit like a prison!"

Where Butlin's led others soon followed. Harry Warner put a camp on Hayling Island and then Fred Pontin opened a number of camps closely following the Butlin's model. By the early 1960s there were hundreds of camps all over the country, and they were hugely popular. The companies who ran them liked to call them villages by the sea, and there is no doubt their popularity would have continued if cheap flights to the Continent had not come along in the early 1960s. But once the southern coast of Spain became affordable the decline of the holiday camp was rapid, and within 20 years only a handful remained.

Brits abroad

For centuries working people in Britain had rarely travelled more than 30 or 40 miles from their home villages and towns in a lifetime. That distance was dictated largely by the distance a horse could travel in a day. But as the railway network spread in the 19th and early 20th centuries, as car ownership increased and travel became cheaper and faster, things began to change. Two World Wars finally broke the mould, and British people even began to explore the Continent.

Middle and upper-middle-class people would drive slowly to the south of France to stay in rented houses, but they were few in number

Knobbly knees
Butlin's camps always provided a huge range of organised entertainment for everyone, as in this competition for the knobbliest knees. The cheerful adults, known as Red Coats, started at the Skegness camp.

Come to Butlin's
Butlin's was keen to promote holidays for all the family. Brochures were regularly produced outlining the camps' numerous attractions, with "something for everyone".

Beauty contest
The American influence at Butlin's showed in some of the activities, but most notably the beauty contests – or "Miss Blighty" as they were known – which were *de rigeur.*

Feed the birds
Venice had always occupied an almost-mythical place in British culture, and visitors to the city began to grow in numbers after the war.

Party time
If the end of the war brought a holiday mood to Britain, the chance of joining a coach trip to the south of France was almost unheard of. Holidays abroad were an exciting and real possibility now for many, and enjoyment was obligatory.

and certainly too few to fuel a specific tourist industry, as Pam Tarlton recalls.

"One summer in 1954 we drove in our old Morris to a house at Roquebrune in the south of France. We took several days, nearly a week in fact, to get there but as we spoke French – almost all educated adults did then – we simply stopped at small hotels on the way, and we knew the farmer from whom we rented the house. There were no motorways and the only other English people I remember meeting were friends who rented houses nearby. There were no real tourists in the sense we know them today. We were very privileged I suppose."

By this time, less well-off people had also begun in growing numbers to cross the Channel, as Anne Scott remembers.

"We holidayed one year in the early 1950s in the Italian Lakes. We went by train of course and I remember that, once on the Continent, the trains seemed constantly to be changing engines, backing up and waiting, but when we went through that long pass under the Alps and then emerged into sunlight and Italy it really was heavenly. I remember that in the tunnels under the Alps all the windows were shut to stop the carriages filling with smoke, because of course all the trains then were steam-powered.

We stayed at Lake Como, where the atmosphere was totally different from anything you would experience today. Every English person in the hotel seemed terribly buttoned up and concerned not to mix with anyone who was not of the same class. You would see people looking each other up and down in the hotel dining room. People were terribly concerned not to be seen to be mixing with people who were of a lower social class, although as far as I could see we were all pretty much the same. It was like something out of Forster's Room With a View. And people were less confident about travel then – we were nervous and anxious in a way people weren't later on. People wanted foreign holidays desperately because they were such an adventure and a luxury, but they often hated the local food and were slightly afraid of the local people, who they clearly thought were addicted to garlic, too much oil and loose living!"

The idea of lying on a sunny beach for two weeks would have been anathema to these early holidaying pioneers, for these were the days when women tried desperately to avoid getting any sun on their faces and ruining their pale complexions. Going abroad for those lucky enough to be able to do it meant getting around, seeing and doing things.

Passport to the Continent
By the early 1960s foreign holidays were becoming more common, and British and French Railways promoted the advantages of taking a family car on one of their ferries.

Tom Shackle recalls walking trips to Switzerland.

> "No one went ski-ing from England in those days. If you went to Switzerland it was always in summer to walk in the mountains. My family still thought completely of holidays as educational – we stopped to identify plants, looked at the scenery and walked as much as ten or twelve miles every day. It was exhausting and I only realised how privileged we were much later. Very few of my friends had ever been abroad. What I mostly recall are small villages where no one spoke English, narrow roads, very polite local people and hoteliers who still saw visitors as interesting and unusual. It was all a far cry from more recent times, when English tourists with their reputation for rowdiness are sometimes viewed with horror by local people."

However, travel abroad remained a relatively rare thing until the 1960s, but that didn't stop the British Government worrying that money was leaking into another country's economy at a time when the UK could least afford it. Pam Tarlton remembers the annoying restrictions imposed on taking currency out of the country.

> "There were the silliest currency rules at that time too – you could only take £50 each abroad for one holiday. Mind you, £50 was rather a lot then: about four times a working man's weekly wage, but the idea was to stop wealth leaking out of the country. There was a perception that we were still nearly bankrupt after the war."

Alpine excursion
Walking tours of the Alps had been popular with the wealthy classes since Victorian times, but the postwar years saw more Britons begin to visit the mountains in summer for a holiday. It was especially popular as a romantic holiday destination.

ALL FOR YOUR DELIGHT

Butlin's holiday camps

Cheap foreign holidays have perhaps made us forget the sheer joy of a Butlin's camp holiday back in the 1950s. For a generation that had lived through the War, Butlin's was far more than exciting; it was a luxurious liberation from the drab world of austerity Britain. Children were catered for with swimming pools, rides and games and there were childminders who freed their parents for seemingly endless nights of bingo and dancing.

Butlin's badges

When arriving at Butlin's each camper was issued with an enamel badge to wear for the duration of their holiday. Badges were worn with pride and were issued every year from the first season in Skegness in 1936 up until 1967 when they were discontinued.

Cheap entertainment
The accessibility of the Butlin's resorts was undoubtedly a reason for their popularity. They offered family entertainment and activities for the equivalent of a week's pay.

Paid holidays
Opportunities for holidays and breaks were on the rise with increasing affluence and the growth of paid holidays. Tourism was now a big industry for Britain's seaside towns.

The Red Coats
Butlin camps provided a range of organised entertainment for both children and adults. Friendly rivalries were encouraged between the different dining rooms known as "houses" which resulted in various inter-house competitions which culminated in grand finals held at the end of each week.

Military use
The first Butlin's holiday camp was opened by Billy Butlin in 1936 in Skegness following his success in the development of amusement parks. A second camp soon followed in Clacton in 1938 and construction of a third began at Filey in 1939. With the outbreak of World War II, the Filey site was postponed and the camps at Skegness, Ayr, Pwllheli and Clacton were given over for military use. All had returned to holiday use by 1947.

Index

Picture credits

Advertising Archives 18, 20l, 31tl, 45l, 75tr, 75bl, 79r, 91r, 98r, 108l, 108r, 110l, 118tl, 131b, 143l, 149r, 156tl, 209br, 210bl, 211tl, 211tr, 213tl, 242l, 247t, 253r; Alan King / Alamy 11r; Amoret Tanner / Alamy 244l; Antiques & Collectables / Alamy 11t, 103bl, 103br, 249m; ClassicStock / Alamy 150, 151t; Corbis. All rights reserved 104bl, 175, 185br, 235b; The Francis Frith Collection 115, 116; Getty Images 4, 8, 10, 12, 13, 14, 15, 16, 17, 19t, 19b, 20tr, 21, 22, 23, 25, 27, 31br, 32, 34, 35, 36, 37t, 37b, 38, 39, 40tl, 40b, 42, 43, 44, 45tr, 48, 49, 50tl, 51br, 52, 53, 54bl, 55m, 56, 58, 60, 61, 62, 63, 64, 65, 66, 68, 69, 70bl, 71tl, 71br, 73, 74, 75tl, 75br, 76, 79r, 80, 81tr, 81r, 82, 83, 86, 87, 88, 90, 91tl, 92t, 92r, 93, 94, 95, 96, 97, 98l, 98br, 99br, 100, 102, 104t, 105t, 106, 108tl, 110br, 111tr, 113m, 117r, 117br, 118r, 119tr, 120, 122, 123tl, 123br, 125, 126, 127, 128, 129, 130, 131t, 132, 133, 134, 135, 136tr, 136b, 137, 138, 139br, 140, 142, 144tr, 144bl, 146, 147, 148tl, 149l, 151b, 152t, 152b, 153, 154b, 155t, 157, 158, 159, 161br, 162, 164, 165, 166, 167tr, 168bl, 169b, 170, 171tr, 171b, 172, 173tl, 174, 177tr, 177bl, 178, 179, 180, 182t, 183tr, 184bl, 185tr, 186, 188, 189, 190, 191, 192tl, 192tr, 193, 194, 196, 197, 198, 199tr, 199br, 201, 202, 203t, 204, 205, 206, 207, 208, 209tr, 210t, 212m, 213tr, 213bl, 216, 218, 219, 220tl, 220bl, 221, 222, 224, 225tr, 225br, 226, 227t, 228, 229tr, 230, 232, 233t, 233b, 234tl, 234bl, 235tr, 238, 239t, 240l, 241br, 242tr, 245l, 246, 247b, 248, 250tl, 251r, 252m, 253tl; Health Education Authority/SSPL 183r; IMAGEPAST / Alamy 105b; INTERFOTO / Alamy 155br; Lordprice Collection / Alamy 160tl; Mary Evans Picture Library 41, 46, 78, 103tr, 112, 113tr, 114tr, 114bl, 143r, 184br, 231, 240tr; Mary Evans Picture Library / Alamy 109b, 235r; Mira / Alamy 2; Mirrorpix 54r, 107, 181; Museum of London 185bl; The National Archives 167r, 169r; National Media Museum/SSPL 145r; National Railway Museum/SSPL 241t; Nearby / Alamy 234b; Nic Hamilton / Alamy 11; PA Photos 160bl, 161b, 161tr, 184r, 253br; Photoshot 31tr; Pictorial Press Ltd / Alamy 249br; The Robert Opie Collection 31m, 50m, 54br, 55bl, 93l, 99tl, 118bl, 119tl, 119br, 139l, 139tr, 145t, 154l, 156b, 212bl, 213r, 253tr; Roger Mayne / Museum of London 24, 28, 29; Science Museum/SSPL 173br, 182r, 239r, 245tr, 251t; TopFoto 26, 30, 51; Trevor Smith / Alamy 55tr; Trinity Mirror / Mirrorpix / Alamy 7, 84, 85, 89, 124, 139tl, 148br, 168t, 176, 195, 229br, 236, 243t, 243b, 244t, 249tr, 250b. Front Cover by English Heritage / NMR. Back Cover by Getty Images.

Acknowledgements

Thanks to all those whose memories are included in this book, but especially Ruth Wadham and Bob Baylis.

Thanks also to Verity Muir, Emily Pitcher, Neil Baber and James Loader and last, but by no means least, I'd like to thank Emma, Katy, James, Alex, Charlotte and Jo.